DATE DUE

OCT 1 2 2009			
MR 30 '10			

Demco, Inc. 38-293

Using Literature to Help
Troubled Teenagers
Cope with Family Issues

Using Literature to Help Troubled Teenagers Cope with Family Issues

Edited by
Joan F. Kaywell

The Greenwood Press "Using Literature
to Help Troubled Teenagers" Series

Greenwood Press
Westport, Connecticut • London

Library of Congress Cataloging-in-Publication Data

Using literature to help troubled teenagers cope with family issues /
   [edited by] Joan F. Kaywell.
       p.   cm.—(The Greenwood Press "using literature to help
   troubled teenagers" series)
   Includes bibliographical references and indexes.
   ISBN 0–313–30335–5 (alk. paper)
   1. Bibliotherapy for teenagers.   2. Teenagers—Family
relationships.   3. Young adult literature—Study and teaching
(Secondary)   I. Kaywell, Joan F.   II. Series.
RJ505.B5U84   1999
615.8'516'0835—dc21   98–28288

British Library Cataloguing in Publication Data is available.

Library of Congress Catalog Card Number: 98–28288
ISBN: 0–313–30335–5

First published in 1999

Greenwood Press, 88 Post Road West, Westport, CT 06881
An imprint of Greenwood Publishing Group, Inc.
www.greenwood.com

Printed in the United States of America

(∞)™

The paper used in this book complies with the
Permanent Paper Standard issued by the National
Information Standards Organization (Z39.48–1984).

10 9 8 7 6 5 4 3 2 1

This book is dedicated to my siblings

Carol Kelly Tompkins, John A. Kaywell, James W. Kaywell,
& Father Jerome P. Kaywell

Contents

Series Foreword

The idea for this six-volume series—addressing family issues, identity issues, social issues, abuse issues, health issues, and death and dying issues—came while I, myself, was going to a therapist to help me deal with the loss of a loved one. My therapy revealed that I was a "severe trauma survivor" and I had to process the emotions of a bad period of time during my childhood. I was amazed that a trauma of my youth could be triggered by an emotional upset in my adult life. After an amazing breakthrough that occurred after extensive reading, writing, and talking, I looked at my therapist and said, "My God! I'm like the gifted child with the best teacher. What about all of those children who survive situations worse than mine and do not choose education as their escape of choice?" I began to wonder about the huge number of troubled teenagers who were not getting the professional treatment they needed. I pondered about those adolescents who were fortunate enough to get psychological treatment but were illiterate. Finally, I began to question if there were ways to help them while also improving their literacy development.

My thinking generated two theories on which this series is based: (1) Being literate increases a person's chances of emotional health, and (2) Twenty-five percent of today's students are "unteachable." The first theory was generated by my pondering these two statistics: 80% of our prisoners are illiterate (Hodgkinson, 1991), and 80% of our prisoners have been sexually abused (Child Abuse Council, 1993). If a correlation actually exists between these two statistics, then it suggests a strong need for literacy skills in order for a person to be able to address emotional turmoil in healthy or constructive ways. The second theory came out of work I did for my book, *Adolescents at Risk: A Guide to Fiction and Nonfiction for Young Adults, Parents and Professionals* (Greenwood Press, 1993), and my involvement in working with teachers and students in middle and secondary schools. Some of the emotional baggage our youth bring to school is way too heavy for them to handle without help. These students simply cannot handle additional academic responsibilities when they are "not right" emotionally.

THEORY ONE: BEING LITERATE INCREASES A PERSON'S CHANCES OF EMOTIONAL HEALTH

Well-educated adults who experience intense emotional pain, whether it is from the loss of a loved one or from a traumatic event, have several options available for dealing with their feelings. Most will find comfort in talking with friends or family members, and some will resort to reading books to find the help they need. For example, reading Dr. Elizabeth Kübler-Ross's five stages for coping with death—denial, anger, bargaining, depression, and acceptance or growth—might help a person understand the various stages he or she is going through after the death of a friend or relative. Sometimes, however, additional help is needed when an individual is experiencing extreme emotions and is unable to handle them.

Consider a mother whose improper left-hand turn causes the death of her seven-year-old daughter and the injury of her four-year-old daughter. It is quite probable that the mother will need to seek additional help from a therapist who will help her deal with such a trauma. A psychologist or psychiatrist will, more than likely, get her to talk openly about her feelings, read some books written by others who have survived such a tragedy, and do regular journal writing. A psychiatrist may also prescribe some medication during this emotionally challenging time. This parent's literacy skills of talking, reading, and writing are essential to her getting through this difficult period of her life.

Now, consider her four-year-old daughter who is also experiencing extreme grief over the loss of her beloved older sister. If this child is taken to counseling, the therapist will probably get her to talk, role-play, and draw out her feelings. These are the literacy skills appropriate to the developmental level of a four-year-old child. Such a child, if not taken to a counselor when needed, will manifest her emotions in one of two ways—either by acting out or by withdrawing.

Lev Vygotsky, a well-respected learning theorist, suggests that without words there could be no thoughts and the more words a person has at his or her disposal, the bigger that person's world. If what Vygotsky suggests is true, then a person with a limited or no vocabulary is only capable of operating at an emotional level. *The Story of My Life* by Helen Keller adds credibility to that view. In the introduction to the biography, written by Robert Russell, he describes Helen Keller's frustration at not being able to communicate:

> Perhaps the main cause for her early tantrums was plain frustration at not being able to communicate. . . . Not being able to hear, Helen had nothing to imitate, so she had no language. This meant more than simply not being able to talk. It meant having nothing clear to talk about because for her things had no names. Without names, things have no distinctness or individuality. Without language, we could not describe the difference between an elephant and an egg. Without the words we would have no clear conception of either elephant or egg. The name of a thing confers identity upon it and makes it possible for us to think about it. Without names for love or sorrow, we do not know we are experiencing them. Without words, we could not say, "I love you," and human beings need to say this and much more. Helen had the need, too, but she had not the means. As she grew older and the need increased, no wonder her fits of anger and misery grew. (pp. 7–8)

Helen, herself, writes,

> [T]he desire to express myself grew. The few signs I used became less and less adequate, and my failures to make myself understood were invariably followed by outbursts of passion. I felt as if invisible hands were holding me, and I made frantic efforts to free myself. I struggled—not that struggling helped matters, but the spirit of resistance was strong within me; I generally broke down in tears and physical exhaustion. If my mother happened to be near I crept into her arms, too miserable even to remember the cause of the tempest. After awhile the need of some means of communication became so urgent that these outbursts occurred daily, sometimes hourly. (p. 28)

If Vygotsky's theory reflected by the illuminating words of a deaf, blind, and mute child is true, then it is no wonder that 80% of our prisoners are illiterate victims of abuse.

THEORY TWO: 25% OF TODAY'S TEENAGERS ARE "UNTEACHABLE" BY TODAY'S STANDARDS

Teachers are finding it increasingly difficult to teach their students, and I believe that 25% of teenagers are "unteachable" by today's standards. A small percentage of these troubled youth do choose academics as their escape of choice, and they are the overachievers to the "nth" degree. That is not to say that all overachievers are emotionally disturbed teenagers, but some of them are learning, not because of their teachers, but because their very survival depends upon it. I know. I was one of them. The other adolescents going through inordinately difficult times (beyond the difficulty inherent in adolescence itself) might not find the curriculum very relevant to their lives. Their escapes of choice include rampant sex, drug use, gang membership, and other self-destructive behaviors. Perhaps the violence permeating our schools is a direct result of the utter frustration of some of our youth.

Consider these data describing the modern teenage family. At any given time, 25% of American children live with one parent, usually a divorced or never-married mother (Edwards & Young, 1992). Fifty percent of America's youth will spend some school years being raised by a single parent, and almost four million school-age children are being reared by neither parent (Hodgkinson, 1991). In 1990, 20% of American children grew up in poverty, and it is probable that 25% will be raised in poverty by the year 2000 (Howe, 1991). Children in homeless families often experience developmental delays, severe depression, anxiety, and learning disorders (Bassuk & Rubin, 1987).

Between one-fourth and one-third of school-aged children are living in a family with one or more alcoholics (Gress, 1988). Fourteen percent of children between the ages of 3 and 17 experience some form of family violence (Craig, 1992). Approximately 27% of girls and 16% of boys are sexually abused before the age of 18 (Krueger, 1993), and experts believe that it is reasonable to say that 25% of children will be sexually abused before adulthood (Child Abuse Council, 1993). Remember to note that eight out of ten criminals in prison were abused when they were children (Child Abuse Council, 1993).

Consider these data describing the modern teenager. Approximately two out of ten school-aged youth are affected by anorexia nervosa and bulimia (Phelps & Bajorek, 1991) and between 14% to 23% have vomited to lose weight (National Centers for Disease Control, 1991). By the time students become high school seniors, 90% have experimented with alcohol use and nearly two-thirds have used drugs (National Institute on Drug Abuse, 1992). In 1987, 40% of seniors admitted they had used dangerous drugs and 60% had used marijuana (National Adolescent Student Health Survey). In 1974, the average age American high school students tried marijuana was 16; in 1984, the average age was twelve (Nowinski, 1990).

By the age of 15, a fourth of the girls and a third of the boys are sexually active (Gibbs, 1993), and three out of four teenagers have had sexual intercourse by their senior year (Males, 1993). Seventy-five percent of the mothers who gave birth between the ages of 15 and 17 are on welfare (Simkins, 1984). In 1989, AIDS was the sixth leading cause of death for 15- to 24-year-olds (Tonks, 1992–1993), and many AIDS experts see adolescents as the third wave of individuals affected by HIV (Kaywell, 1993). Thirty-nine percent of sexually active teenagers said they preferred not to use any method of contraception (Harris Planned Parenthood Poll, 1986).

Ten percent of our students are gay (Williams, 1993), and the suicide rate for gay and lesbian teenagers is two to six times higher than that of heterosexual teens (Krueger, 1993). Suicide is the second leading cause of teenage deaths; "accidents" rated first (National Centers for Disease Control, 1987). An adolescent commits suicide every one hour and 47 minutes (National Center for Health Statistics, 1987), and nine children die from gunshot wounds every day in America (Edelman, 1989). For those children growing up in poor, high crime neighborhoods, one in three has seen a homicide by the time they reach adolescence (Beck, 1992).

Consider these data describing the dropout problem. In 1988, the dropout rate among high school students was 28.9% (Monroe, Borzi, & Burrell, 1992). More than 80% of America's one million prisoners are high school dropouts (Hodgkinson, 1991). We spend more than $20,000 per year per prisoner (Hodgkinson, 1991) but spend less than $4,000 per year per student. Forty-five percent of special education students drop out of high school (Wagner, 1989).

Numbers and statistics such as these are often incomprehensible, but consider the data in light of a 12th grade classroom of 30 students. Eight to 15 are being raised by a single parent, six are in poverty, eight to ten are being raised in families with alcoholics, four have experienced some form of family violence, and eight of the female and five of the male students have been sexually violated. Six are anorectic or bulimic, 27 have used alcohol, 18 have used marijuana, and 12 have used dangerous drugs. Twenty-two have had sexual intercourse and 12 of them used no protection. Three students are gay. Eight will drop out of school, and six of those eight will become criminals. Everyday in our country, two adolescents commit suicide by lunchtime.

These are the students that our teachers must teach every day, and these are the students who need help beyond what schools are currently able to provide. Think about the young adults who are both illiterate and in pain! Is there anything that can be done to help these young people with their problems while increasing their literacy skills? Since most of our nation's prisoners are illiterate—the acting out side—and most homeless people are not exactly Rhodes scholars—the withdrawal side—it seems logical to try to help these adolescents while they are still within the educational system.

Perhaps this series, which actually pairs literacy experts with therapists, can help the caretakers of our nation's distraught youth—teachers, counselors, parents, clergy, and librarians—acquire understanding and knowledge on how to better help these troubled teenagers. The series provides a unique approach to guide these caretakers working with troubled teenagers. Experts discuss young adult literature, while therapists provide analysis and advice for protagonists in these novels. Annotated bibliographies provide the reader with similar sources that can be used to help teenagers discuss these issues while increasing their literacy skills.

Joan F. Kaywell

REFERENCES

Bassuk, E. L. & Rubin, L. (1987). Homeless children: A neglected population. *American Journal of Orthopsychiatry, 57* (2), p. 279 ff.

Beck, J. (1992, May 19). Inner-city kids beat the odds to survive. *The Tampa Tribune.*

Craig, S. E. (1992, September). The educational needs of children living with violence. *Phi Delta Kappan, 74* (1), p. 67 ff.

Edelman, M. W. (1989, May). Defending America's children. *Educational Leadership, 46* (8), p. 77 ff.

Edwards, P. A. & Young, L.S.J. (1992, September). Beyond parents: Family, community, and school involvement. *Phi Delta Kappan, 74* (1), p. 72 ff.

Gibbs, N. (1993, May 24). How should we teach our children about sex? *Time, 140* (21), p. 60 ff.

Gress, J. R. (1988, March). Alcoholism's hidden curriculum. *Educational Leadership, 45* (6), p. 18 ff.

Hodgkinson, H. (1991, September). Reform versus reality. *Phi Delta Kappan, 73* (1), p. 9 ff.

Howe II, H. (1991, November). America 2000: A bumpy ride on four trains. *Phi Delta Kappan, 73* (3), p. 192 ff.

Kaywell, J. F. (1993). *Adolescents at risk: A guide to fiction and nonfiction for young adults, parents and professionals.* Westport, CT: Greenwood Press.

Keller, H. (1967). *The story of my life.* New York: Scholastic.

Krueger, M. M. (1993, March). Everyone is an exception: Assumptions to avoid in the sex education classroom. *Phi Delta Kappan, 74* (7), p. 569 ff.

Males, M. (1993, March). Schools, society, and "teen" pregnancy. *Phi Delta Kappan, 74* (7), p. 566 ff.

Monroe, C., Borzi, M. G., & Burrell, R. D. (1992, January). Communication apprehension among high school dropouts. *The School Counselor, 39* (4), p. 273 ff.

Nowinski, J. (1990). *Substance abuse in adolescents and young adults.* New York: Norton.

Phelps, L. & Bajorek, E. (1991). Eating disorders of the adolescent: Current issues in etiology, assessment, and treatment. *School Psychology Review, 20* (1), p. 9 ff.

Simkins, L. (1984, spring). Consequences of teenage pregnancy and motherhood. *Adolescence, 19* (73), p. 39 ff.

Tonks, D. (1992–1993, December–January). Can you save your students' lives? Educating to prevent AIDS. *Educational Leadership, 50* (4), p. 48 ff.

Wagner, M. (1989). *Youth with disabilities during transition: An overview of descriptive findings from the national longitudinal transition study.* Stanford, CA: SRI International.

Williams, R. F. (1993, spring). Gay and lesbian teenagers: A reading ladder for students, media specialists, and parents. *The ALAN Review, 20* (3), p. 12 ff.

Preface

This volume—focusing on family issues—was written in hope that the caretakers of our nation's distraught youth can acquire understanding and new knowledge on how to better help troubled teenagers cope with various family problems in healthier and more constructive ways. By combining the expertise of literacy experts with psychologists, psychiatrists, or therapists, perhaps together we can provide a means to increase these adolescents' literacy while offering them the special help they need.

As mentioned in the Series Foreword, my escape and my salvation during my teenage years came from books—not drugs, alcohol, sex, food, gangs, or guns. Think about young people who are both illiterate and in pain! Not too long ago—after experiencing extensive therapy for being a "severe trauma survivor"—I asked myself, "Is there anything we can do to help unfortunate teenagers with their problems while increasing their literacy skills?" Since most of our nation's prisoners are illiterate—the acting-out side—and most homeless people are not exactly Rhodes scholars—the withdrawal side—it seems logical to try to help these adolescents while they are still within the educational system. I believe we can help, but all involved parties must learn how to communicate better; much can be learned by combining the expertise of different helping professionals.

Like education, psychology as a profession has become research based. Educators and parents, by and large, have not been exposed to various terms frequently used by counselors. I did not even know, for example, what a "severe trauma survivor" was, much less realize that I was one. With the exception of the opening chapter written by Chris Crutcher, who is a writer and therapist combined, each chapter has two authors: a literacy expert and a therapist. The literacy expert selected a representative work of fiction that best spoke to his or her co-author's area of expertise in relation to a family issue. Topics addressed in this volume include dealing with the death of a sibling, alcoholism, delinquency, divorce, abandonment, eating disorders, homosexuality, and suicide. For each chapter, a therapist read the novel and provided therapy to the young adult protagonist, using appropriate terminology wherever possible. Because the protagonists and families are all fictional characters, helping professionals may discuss each case without fear of libel.

The final chapter of this volume sets up the possibilities that exist if therapists choose to use young adult (YA) literature to help troubled teenagers discuss their problems. Using actual reader responses based on a literary selection that captures how family problems are passed on from generation to generation, a licensed psychologist treats both her co-author as well as the young adult protagonist. We all know what it's like to find the perfect card or song that expresses our feelings just right. Because it is much easier to talk about someone else's problems using words artistically conveyed by masterful writers, therapists might consider using young adult literature to offer their patients words, ideas, situations, and feelings.

CHAPTER 1

My Three Faces: The Writer, the Therapist, and the Man

Chris Crutcher

INTRODUCTION

Contributing to this project allows me to combine two areas of my life about which I am passionate. For 15 years I have been stealing the seeds for stories from the lives of the people with whom I work, careful, of course, to use only patterns and generalities, and to create the specifics in my imagination. I am in constant and thankful awe of the way in which my two lives inter-twine: how the exploration of human pain and courage contributes to the richness of stories, and how writing those stories helps me uncover new per-ceptions of humanity, which I take back into my therapeutic work and into my life. I can't tell a good story without first considering the real-life truths of my chosen characters and circumstances.

There are other similarities between doing therapy with adolescents and writing stories about them. Both exist in some strange Neverland. As a writer of literature about adolescents I am the redheaded stepbrother of real writers, my product the bastard child of *real* literature. There is no real place for it in bookstores, no true home of its own in many libraries. No matter how lyrical my prose, how laser-like my presentation of a situation, it still represents a time in most adults' lives that we seem to want to remember se-lectively, a time whose importance we discount and therefore tend not to read about or revisit.

I think we often treat teenagers in the same way we treat their literature, though that may be putting the horse before the cart. Adults encounter ado-lescent love and call it "puppy love," or some other throwaway cliché that allows us to discount its importance and intensity. We see adolescent depression as immature, adolescent angst as overdramatized. It is easy to identify certain behaviors as attention getting. We want teenagers to learn the lessons we have learned by listening to us, by *avoiding the mistakes we made* through listening to our lectures. We want *them* to learn from *our* experiences. In other words, we want to cheat them out of their own experiences because their pain causes our discomfort. It is interesting that we can celebrate discovery evident in newborns or toddlers, yet not have the same respect for development when it comes to teenagers.

It is my belief that experience is the only teacher. That doesn't mean nothing we say gets through, or that it won't be remembered or considered, but it does mean what we say needs to touch the imagination, because it is through the imagination that thought becomes experience. That's why stories are so much more powerful than lectures, and why allowing adolescents to re-live their own lives through those stories and through other forms of expression is far more useful than simple instruction. Teenagers don't need us to "fix it"; we can't anyway. Like most of us, they need a witness, someone who can hear their stories and connect with the emotions those stories elicit—and withhold judgment.

LEARNING LIFE'S LESSONS

I learned my lessons about the need for expression, the need for congruence between interior and exterior not from teenagers, but from children five and under. About ten years ago I met my publisher, Susan Hirschmann, in Boston following a two-person panel discussion/interview with Robert Cormier at Simmons College. I was feeling full of myself even to have my name mentioned in the same sentence with Mr. Cormier, much less having participated in a successful and well-received program with him. Susan and I walked in a park near the college, and she said she believed I could now make a living as a writer, if I so chose. Her publishing company was paying me substantial advances for my books and was willing to make two-book contracts. I immediately gave my six-month notice at the Spokane Community Mental Health Center where I worked as a child and family therapist, arrogant enough to believe I had achieved what many writers only hope for, and that I could walk away from the compelling power of the work I did.

At the time, the center was involved in a pilot program with Head Start, in which one Head Start classroom was composed of two- to five-year-old children with significant histories of abuse or neglect. There had been court action on each of these children: many resided in foster care, and all were dependents of the court. Their parents worked in group and individual therapy with adult counselors on site and spent at least one day each week in the classroom working with their kids. Head Start provided a teacher and teacher's aides, and the center provided child therapists to help the kids work through their traumas of abuse and loss. Because I was to be leaving the center in six months, my supervisor placed me there as one of the child therapists, believing that my leaving would have less negative impact if I were leaving groups rather than individuals.

ABOUT DAVID, MY TEACHER

Not long after I started in the summer, a boy—I'll call David—entered the program. David was nearly four, blond, with huge, vacant blue eyes, no speech, his most effective communication tool being a clicking sound made at the back of the throat, slower when things seemed relatively okay, faster when anxiety increased. During his first days with us he would place himself equidistant from each play group and watch. Efforts to get him to join in were met by increased clicking.

Toward the end of the first week, I looked up from a group of boys helping one of their friends keep his mother's boyfriend in a cardboard box jail that kept falling apart, to see Heidi, a parentified four-year-old, holding David's hand. Tears streamed down his face. "David's crying," she said, "Do something." So I gently moved him closer to us and let him watch. The tears dried, and his attention became riveted to the powerful action of these children gaining—through play—control over their abusers.

We had the best possible luck with David's circumstances. His foster parents realized that as David improved, his behavior would get worse. They were prepared for it: keeping him safe in his times of expressing fear and rage, and always coming for help when he got so out of hand it scared them. Relatives from a wing of his biological family appeared, seemingly untouched by the ravages of drug use and violence that were staples in his mother's and father's lives, ready and willing not only to give David a home, but to learn about his life and help him try to heal.

Over a period of months, David began developing language skills and each morning he would sit in the front seat of the mental health center van with me, naming everything we passed, the clicks giving way to real words. He began having relationships with other children, admittedly sometimes oppositional, but relationships just the same. In the end his foster parents drove him hundreds of miles to Montana on several consecutive weekends to visit his new adoptive family, so when they finally handed him over, it would be a transition between loving friends. We couldn't have scripted it better.

The day David was to leave, I picked him up early and we started our last trip together to Head Start. The other children and some of the parents had planned a going away party; it was to be David's day. He climbed into the van, buckled his seat belt, and began clicking like a telegraph operator warning of an impending train crash. No amount of my cajoling got a response; he stared straight ahead and clicked out his call for help. In the classroom the chairs were still upside down on the tabletops, the staff just arriving. David dropped his coat and moved directly to a table, sweeping the chairs onto the floor with his arm. He moved to the next table and repeated the action. The teaching staff watched in astonishment, waiting to see what the therapist would do. I watched in astonishment with them, waiting to see what I would do. I didn't know what I was seeing, only that it was important. David then moved to the area where we kept the smaller toys—the toy soldiers, Legos, and small He-Man and She-Ra figures—emptying them from their plastic storage baskets, tossing many across the room. Guttural, incomprehensible sounds escaped his throat as he trashed that play area, then moved to the mid-sized stuff—the play garage, Weeble People, cars and trucks—and did the same. The other children began to arrive, along with the second play therapist—a real-thing-true-play-therapist—who thought I knew what I was doing and assembled them by the door to take them away to the gym along with the rest of the staff so David and I could work our therapeutic magic. The only people remaining were me, David, and three practicum students from nearby Gonzaga University, who stood wide-eyed, I'm sure, considering a transfer to the School of Business.

Occasionally, as David continued his march to the Head Start Sea, I would almost make out a word, or a sentence, but not quite. Then, sometime during the casting of the wooden blocks against the slate wall, I heard him say, clearly, "I hate this place," and I understood. With that I began to help. David would throw a block and I would throw a block. One by one we emptied the wooden crate, raining the wall with blocks and epithets. When the last block was thrown, David looked around the wrecked room with satisfaction, took my hand and led me out. (I have to mention that, on our way, I noticed a shelf of books still standing and pointed it out. Together we made short work of it. I must admit, it was quite cathartic.) David led me to a storage room filled with empty cardboard boxes that once held desks or chairs or school appliances, at the far end of the building. At his direction we built a space ship from several of the boxes, and he gave me a magic marker—lifted from the wreckage of our classroom—directing me to write his name and my name all over our star ship. For the rest of the morning we flew through his universe, trying to put it in order. We flew over his foster home and saw his foster parents in the yard, waving goodbye to us. He waved back with tears in his eyes. We flew over Head Start, which he hated and which we bombed repeatedly. We flew over his new and scary home in Montana, one time a welcoming place, the next time forbidding. We flew over my house, and he wanted to land, only to take off again very quickly. Too scary, another thing he couldn't have.

At 11:30 I said, "David, they're having your party now. Wanna go back to the room?" He looked at me as if I'd hawked a loogie in his ice cream and continued piloting our ship. At five minutes before noon, I told him we had only a little bit of time, set the chronometer on my watch for five minutes and gave it to him, telling him when it beeped we were outta there.

At the sound of the alarm, he handed the watch back, took my hand and we marched back down the hall. As we passed the classroom David glanced in at the children eating his cake and ice cream, opening his presents, and having his party without him among the ruins. Bless her heart, the other therapist had not picked up one toy. David smiled and we continued toward the exit to the parking lot. His foster parents were there, ready to take him to Montana. David hugged me, we both cried, and he got in the car and headed for his new life.

Two sensations rolled over me as I turned to go back inside. One was immense relief in the knowledge that I had to drive several of the other kids home and couldn't stay to clean up our mess, and the other was a sense of wonder at what had just happened that I would only come to understand with time and assistance from the other therapist.

That day with David sealed my fate as a part-time writer for at least another ten years. Think about it. How could I leave the source of so many stories, and so many truly gifted storytellers? How could I leave the place that would bring me to know the importance, for me, of my own stories? David, and every kid like him, is a master storyteller. He knows why stories have to be told. Head Start was the only place in the world that had ever been safe for him, the only place apart from his foster home where he was cared for and loved unconditionally. There, he was allowed to express his feelings of fear and hopelessness and loss. There, those expressions were celebrated. How could he leave a place like that? He couldn't. So he had to trash it. He did what most of us do when we have to go away from someplace or somebody we love. He filled it with sour grapes. A four-year-old with lessons for every age.

As with so many clients, I don't know how David's life turned out. His adoptive parents have sent pictures once in awhile of David standing with the rest of the family, growing tall and strong. I've been in the business too long to think that's a fair representation of his life, but seeing him smiling with his Mickey Mouse ears and Disney World T-shirt gives me a sense of hope.

What brings me back to earth, and causes me great concern, is the fact that we have very little—if anything—for adolescents that encourages or celebrates the kind of expression of fear and pain and loss that I unwittingly allowed for David (mostly because I didn't know how to stop it). We don't create safe places for them to tell their stories, nor do we respect that they have stories to tell, and we pay far more attention to their behavior than to their interiors. When they grow to full physical height, we tend to think they have arrived at their emotional and psychological height as well. In doing that, we disrespect nature. We disrespect human development.

ABOUT ME

David's story is one of dozens that keeps me paying attention to the connection between healing and expression. Each time I tether myself to something solid and allow myself to be lowered into someone's private hell in order that together we might find a way through, I am offered a greater understanding of my own life as well as the challenge to help that person discover the tools that will make for a better managed life. What happens is reciprocal, and if I deny my own discovery and learning, I will cheat my client out of the richness of perspectives that will be offered us both. And my stories will suffer.

I have a theory for why it is so difficult for many of us to work with teenagers—we focus our attention in the wrong direction. Many years ago, about the same time I was thinking of putting patches on my sports jacket and buying a pipe and horn-rimmed glasses so I could be a real writer, I was fortunate to cross paths with a truly inspired and world renowned child psychiatrist, who is also a Buddhist monk. The nature of working in the Child and Family division of the mental health center often required ten-hour days with no lunch, bouncing between group therapy, individual therapy, parenting classes and meetings. Dr. Milner was aware of the crisis nature of the business, and at one point said, "No matter how many appointments you have in a day, always be sure to make one for yourself." At the time I assumed he meant to go home, draw a hot bath, put on soothing music and let yourself drift. Upon reconsideration, I know he meant to look at your responses and reactions to your clients, struggle to make sense of them for yourself, discover which incidents or disclosures had profound effects on you and why. That way, you know who *you* are in the therapeutic process. The value in that is as true for the teacher or the case manager or the counselor—and the storyteller.

GETTING ON THE SAME SIDE WITH ADOLESCENTS

A few summers ago I was speaking at a symposium on adolescent literature and children at risk at Boise State University. The audience was composed largely of teachers from around the state gathering continuing education credits. I talked about certain characters from my books, who they were in real life, where they came from, and how I might treat them in therapy, focusing on the theme of *relationship*. During the question and answer period, a teacher said, "I teach six classes a day and there are up to 30 students in each of those classes. I don't have *time* to have a relationship with every one of them." Normally when someone makes a statement or asks a question for which I have no answer, my heartbeat quickens, my stomach dances a little and my sweat glands creak open. All of that happened. I knew she was absolutely right on one level. She was expressing what many educators believe: that they are being asked on a daily basis to do the impossible, and they are being asked to do it in most cases with few resources in high stress situations. I share that belief. I also knew she was absolutely wrong.

What came out of my mouth was, "You don't have a choice."

By virtue of the fact that each of those students comes into your room, into your presence, you have a relationship with her or him. The physical, psychological, emotional and spiritual atmosphere of that room is part of the relationship. The way you express yourself—your willingness or unwillingness to share intimacies—is part of that relationship. Whether you believe you have a relationship or not, each student has one with you. They come to your class for a period a day. You have an effect. They have a response. It is safe or it isn't. It is nurturing or it isn't. And you as teacher are the author of that.

Herein lies at least a portion of the problem. What the teacher was really saying at the Boise State Symposium is that she doesn't have time to know enough about each student to have the kind of relationship she needs to perform the task at hand. That information isn't in the records, and most students would rather have unanesthetized root canal work than give it to you. So how can the teacher take advantage of the tenuous, misunderstood relationship rather than be victim to it? My belief is that as teachers, counselors, therapists, helpers of any kind, we have to find a way to get *on the same side* as the kid. That's easier said than done, because developmentally adolescents are pulling away. They're supposed to be pulling away. And one of our jobs is to give them something to pull away from. However, by identifying the situation as clearly as we possibly can, by addressing our own frustrations with it, by identifying the conflict, we can help both them and ourselves get a clearer perspective.

My B.A. degree out of college was in psychology and sociology. That meant, with my teaching credential, I was considered most qualified to teach social studies. There were psychology and sociology classes in the curriculum, but I wasn't allowed to teach them because they were considered "plums" due to the caliber of student enrolled. Those classes were taught by teachers who had put in their time, whether they had credits in those disciplines or not. My teaching load consisted of U.S. History, U.S. Government, and Geography. I *hated* Geography. I knew nothing about it, had no passion to learn more than that, and was bored out of my mind from the moment I stepped into the classroom each day until the bell mercifully rang 50 or 60 mind-numbing minutes later. My only incentive to do a good job was the embarrassment of incompetence, so each day I went in armed to the teeth with recently acquired geographic information. It was hell.

Out of desperation, I finally fessed up to the kids. I identified the boat we were in, what creek we were up without a paddle. I talked about what it felt like to struggle with it each day, my empathy for them having to put up with it. At the same time I told them we were stuck with it. I needed a certain amount of discipline in the classroom to do my job, and I had to get through a certain amount of information. Any ideas they had, I told them, would be appreciated and as long as they moved us toward our goal, they would be considered.

I won't even begin to say that we had a "successful" geography class. In fact, I should probably issue a class-action apology to anyone who ever took geography from me. At least I don't have to worry about them hunting me down; they'd never find me—they took geography from me. But what we did have was a successful experience finding our way through a difficult situation and finding ways to learn what none of us knew very well. When it was all finished, we each had a relationship. Of course, some were stronger than others, but we were all better because of our joint experience.

I could only get to that point by identifying my own responses to the negative situation. In the beginning I was angry with the kids because they wouldn't sit there and accept the information I had spent the previous night dredging up. I blamed them for not being willing to learn the simplest of concepts. I lied to myself about my own intent. Only when I was able to say "I hate this" out loud was I able to free myself to find a way to teach.

Any teacher who reads this will already have a thousand teaching strategies better than I possessed at the time, and most will have far greater passion than I had for the subject material. That isn't the point. The point is that working with kids in any fashion is a *human* experience, and if we treat it as such we have a greater chance of getting through. We have to be able to view a situation through the eyes of the kids we work with. That doesn't mean we have to solve our problems the way the kids would solve them, but it does mean that walking a mile in their shoes, or even across the street, can give us perspectives and strategies we could never come to by power-struggling with them.

Were I better read, I could offer more insights and information gathered from the wealth of good stories out there presented as young adult (YA) literature. Books by Terry Davis, Will Weaver, Rob Thomas, Lois Lowry, Richard Peck, Rich Wallace, Christopher Curtis, Norma Fox Mazer, Robert Cormier, Anne LeMieux, Chris Lynch, and Walter Dean Myers, to name only a few, eloquently and humorously chronicle the voices of young people trying to find their way. Because I am not better read, I am stuck with being an expert only on my own work and my own life; hence, my examples come from there.

Bo Brewster

In my book *Ironman*, Bo Brewster is a 17-year-old boy who has been in a power struggle with his father for all of his memory. Both his father and his football coach are men who believe that you have to tighten the screws on kids, create tough situations and never back down for *their own good*. Neither man is flexible in that regard, and Bo, following in his father's stubborn footsteps, is not willing to let anyone step in and run his life. So, with the best of intentions, these men—who could be important teachers of life for Bo—become locked in a struggle against him, a struggle he won't give in to. Bo's father was raised on rigid discipline and, forgetting the rancor he feels toward his own father, has turned that same discipline on Bo. Never mind that it is not needed. Never mind that Bo is tough enough on himself and truly needs someone to help him find acceptance, to help him find the truth of his mistakes. What Bo's father does instead is to take himself off that short list of people his son can turn to. He also takes himself off the list of people worthy of respect, for he has confused respect with fear. Once Bo gets out from under his thumb—once he is physically big enough to stand up for himself and lives in a separate house due to his parents' divorce—his father has very little influence on him other than as an opponent. Bo is forced to turn to a teacher/coach who believes the best help is to listen, and to join him by telling stories about his own youth that mirror Bo's. That teacher doesn't tell him what to do but rather talks of what worked and didn't work for *him*—magic, just a short walk along the same path.

I didn't give Bo's father many unusual characteristics, other than maybe better than average tenacity. Bo's father is a classic example of an adult who believes a child should look through the eyes of an adult, rather than the other way around. He does not consider even the most rudimentary truths about human development.

I think a reason we have such a hard time dealing with adolescents is that we don't see them as *us.* I am always amazed and amused when a 40-year-old man going through what we call "mid-life crisis" says, "I'm acting just like an adolescent," as if that meant he were acting like someone *else.* As any adolescent would say, DUH! Maybe if that 40-year-old man had been encouraged to work through the developmental challenges that presented themselves back then—the sexual challenges, the challenges of rebellion and separation, the *Who Am I?* challenges—he wouldn't be so confused by them at forty. Adolescents embarrass us and so we tend to turn away from them in embarrassment. That does not put us on their side.

Mr. Nak

A favorite character of mine is Mr. Nak from *Ironman*. Mr. Nak has my childhood friend and college roommate's name, and is a five-foot-six-inch Japanese cowboy from El Paso, Texas, who teaches high school shop classes. Mr. Nak runs the before-school anger management group to which Bo Brewster has been relegated because he can't seem to stop himself from calling his football coach/English teacher an asshole in the heat of their arguments. The anger management group is filled with what Bo calls "the future freeway snipers and serial killers of my generation," and he is terrified to have to walk among them. Mr. Nak is a smart, quiet guy with Zen-like perceptions and limitless patience. I imbued him with wisdom and kindness worthy of a saint, and for much of the book we don't really get a picture of him as a human being, but rather as the voice of reason for kids who have been raised without reason.

But in the end, Mr. Nak comes clean. He has decided to go back to Texas and get on the senior rodeo circuit. He calls the members of his raggedy group together to give them a gift. He tells them he knows he sometimes comes off as some kind of Ghandi in a cowboy hat with all the answers who may seem above it all, but he doesn't want them to remember him that way. He wants them to know what they got from him came from a human being. Then Mr. Nak proceeds to tell how on a winter night in his young adulthood he was driving drunk with his kids in his car in what turned out to be a sudden west-Texas ice storm. An eighteen-wheeler came around the corner, "them headlights bearin' down on me like the devil's eyes," and he couldn't react. His car hit the truck, his children were killed, and he was left unscratched. His marriage quickly fell apart, and he was left alone to try to fix something the universe wouldn't let him fix. He tells the anger management kids how grateful he is that they let him into their lives, and he returns the gift by letting them into his.

I didn't know about this incident in Mr. Nak's life in the early chapters of the book. I knew I would have to make him human if he were to be a character to be believed. What I ended up giving him was something the kids could relate to, something I believe all of us can relate to—an incident he would sell his very soul to be able to wipe out, and the wisdom and power to buy his way back into grace. All Mr. Nak did in the end was stand up for himself, stand up and say who he was, and his lessons for the kids became instantly more valuable because they came out of experience. He worked his way into their imaginations—into their essences—with his story.

Angus Bethune

A favorite scene of mine comes from a short story in *Athletic Shorts* called "A Brief Moment in the Life of Angus Bethune." Angus is a senior in high school who is not all that physically attractive and is packing about 50 extra pounds. Both his parents are married gay people, so when he is with his father he is also with his stepfather and when he is with his mother he is also with his stepmother. He has learned to cope fairly well when held up for public ridicule, sometimes with flashes of rage but more often with self-deprecating humor. Someone in his class has played a cruel joke and engineered his election as Winter Ball King, and Angus knows he has to go out on the dance floor alone with a girl he has watched from a distance since grade school. Angus is clever and humorous right up until the moment of truth, when, terrified, he sits on his bed beside a purple tuxedo that, once on, will "undoubtedly cast me as a giant plum." His stepfather comes into the room, sees his desperation and says, "Superman's not brave." Angus isn't particularly interested in Superman's predicament, as his own is at the moment, dire. He is a fat kid with two sets of gay parents—facts he has lived with all of his life—but the pressing problem now is *he can't dance.* "I'll send him a card," he says of Superman.

"You don't understand," his stepfather says. "He's indestructible. You can't be brave when you're indestructible. It's guys like you and me, Angus, guys who can be crushed, and know it, but go out there anyway." It is the moment that gives Angus what he needs to go ahead because *it changes his perception.* He sees what he is about to do as an act of bravery rather than an act of humiliation. It will still be tough, but he is now armed with information that could get him through.

I said before that I believe experience is the only teacher. A change of perception is experience. It isn't cause-and-effect thinking by the numbers. It's an *Aha!* It's a shift, a psychological and spiritual experience. And it's worth its weight in therapy sessions.

I believe there is no true act of heroism that does not include standing up for oneself. Though we don't often articulate it this way, we have to take stock of ourselves before committing any heroic act, whether it be running into a burning building to pull out trapped children, or stepping up to verbally defend the downtrodden, serving meals at a soup kitchen on Thanksgiving, or simply standing up to ridicule. In our moment of decision, we have to ask ourselves who we are, and whether we can do this. That may be a decision made in a split second, or over a period of weeks, but without an answer, we don't proceed. The process of helping adolescents find the power to take control of their own lives in some responsible way very often includes helping them become heroes—finding a way to stand up, a way to be proud of who they are. Given that so many of our messages to them—the same ones we received—are messages of incompetence or of caution, help requires finding a way to change perception. An oft-used term behind the closed doors of many therapists' offices, is this: "You can change the way you feel by changing the way you think." Changing the way you think requires that change of perception.

Stacy

I grew up in a small Idaho lumber town of fewer than a thousand people in the mountains of west central Idaho. In 1952, when I was six, a man-and-wife pair of doctors moved to our town and stayed until their retirement. In their time there, no one, no matter how poor, went without needed medicine or medical care. They contributed to every charity and financially baled out any number of people and institutions when the need arose. They contributed to scholarships for any number of kids who couldn't have afforded college without their help. In the summer after my freshman year in college, Dr. John called me to his house (he had long been a family friend) and told me his niece was coming to live for the summer, that she was pregnant and was to deliver her baby there, then go back home somewhere in the South. The rest of the townspeople, apart from my parents and me, would be told that she was married to a serviceman off in Vietnam and had simply come to relax for the summer. He asked that I be kind to her and take her places, etc.

Dr. John was a man I respected, who had done a lot for me, and I was more than ready to return the favor. Yes, of course I would squire his niece around. I don't remember whether she knew I had been told the truth or not, whether there was any chance for her to talk about what was happening in her life; I only remember that she didn't. What I also remember is an immense sadness in her. What must she have thought of herself to have this elaborate lie created "for her own good"? What must she have said about herself to have committed an act no one could talk about? She may well have welcomed it on the surface, but what about inside? When the summer was over and she delivered the baby, it was put up for adoption, and she returned home to finish her senior year in high school. I remember thinking that I didn't believe she would ever be very happy.

I put a variation of that into *Chinese Handcuffs* some 25 years later. I had written myself into something of a corner, given a character, Stacy, a baby that her mother and father claimed they adopted from some vagrant, shoestring member of the family. Stacy did the same thing the doctor's niece did, went away to have it beneath the umbrella of some elaborate lie, and then came back about the same time as the supposed adoption. But the lie got too heavy for her, and she realized it was toxic to her life. So, in a scene where Stacy changes perceptions for herself, she gets on the school intercom during morning announcements and tells the entire truth. Again, it was the act of a character with more guts than her creator has, and I didn't know it was going to happen. But I felt immense relief when it did, and it instantly turned me into a better therapist, focusing me to help look for any way a given client could find grace in the simplicity of truth.

In the murky world of sexual abuse, we often find victims blaming themselves for what has happened. In the beginning there is sometimes the question, "What is wrong with me, that I was chosen?" If the abuse is long-term, very often the victim has become what appears to be a willing participant in order to defend herself or himself from more traumatic or painful forms of abuse. The self-loathing that results is suffocating. Often an early treatment goal is to get the victim to consider the possibility that he or she is a hero, that surviving the secrecy and the shame and the acts themselves is nothing less than heroic, and hooray that they're still standing among us. It is not only a changed perception; it is a true perception.

While that is easy to see in situations as traumatic as sexual abuse, we tend to overlook that same process in lesser, more common situations. If we can ever get young people to consider the possibility that all hard times are challenges, then there is the chance with each to come out on higher ground; in other words, to reframe for them what seems like a conspiracy of life against them, we have helped them empower themselves. Of course, that's far more easily said than done, because so often the past experiences of kids are so damaging that we have to start with the most basic of their perceptions, celebrate every baby-step we take toward our goal, and be willing to say that we are very limited in our ability to help. Again, when we come to that point as teachers or counselors or anyone working with young adults, we have to look at ourselves and consider who we are in the process. We may even have to change our perceptions of what help really is. So, as we're working toward helping adolescents change their perceptions, we may very well have to change our own.

CONCLUSION

There is a tendency for us to say that life is harder for teenagers than it was for us at that age and that might be true in some ways. Certainly the level of drug availability is a wild card that many of us didn't have to deal with until we were much older, and the potency and variety of those drugs is reportedly far greater. But the *range* of emotion, the *extremes* we feel are the same now as they have always been. We can't use the excuse that we don't understand them, or throw up our hands and say, "What's the matter with kids today?" If we are to help guide them, and thereby guide ourselves, we have to find ways to be intimate with them. And a good deal of intimacy is the ability to tell the truth about yourself out loud.

So it is an interesting dilemma in which we find ourselves. Do we hold the line and demand certain behaviors of adolescents, maintaining our distance and honing our communication skills to precision in hopes that our experience and rational thought will lead to understanding, or do we roll up our sleeves and get close, thereby exposing our own insecurities and doubts to partially developed human beings who may not treat those insecurities delicately?

So there it is. As I write this I have no idea how the other writers and therapists will attack this project. I do know it has marvelous, unlimited possibility and magnificent scope because of the interconnectedness of the disciplines. Good therapy with adolescents demands relationship between therapist and client. Good writing demands relationship between author and character. Both demand intimacy, and each is done at tremendous emotional risk. Writing magnifies that intimacy, I believe, in that to tell a good story an author must do what the good therapist does: tell all about her or his character, and suspend judgment so that each character can be seen in the full, rich light in which all human beings need to be seen if we are to be understood.

REFERENCES

Crutcher, Chris. (1991). A brief moment in the life of Angus Bethune. In *Athletic Shorts*. New York: Dell Laurel-Leaf.
Crutcher, Chris. (1991). *Chinese handcuffs*. New York: Dell Laurel-Leaf.
Crutcher, Chris. (1995). *Ironman*. New York: Greenwillow Books.

CHAPTER 2

Coping with Parental Illness: Family Discord in *Ordinary People*

Pam B. Cole & Augustus Y. Napier

INTRODUCTION

When emotional or physical illness strikes a family member, the effects on children and other family members can be catastrophic. Families are unsettled; they are torn, and sometimes, when members are unable to cope, the family disintegrates. Though husbands and wives struggle in the wake of a spouse's illness or that of a child, children can suffer more since they have limited experiences dealing with pain and loss. Additionally, healthy spouses consumed by the demands of an ill family member and by their own disparate feelings can, without meaning to do so, lose sight of children's needs, leaving them feeling isolated, afraid, despondent, sometimes even depressed.

In an effort to cope, children sometimes turn to peers or to trusted adults. More often than not, however, they try to cope with the situation alone, and because their experiences are limited, they often make harmful or unwise choices. Well-written children's and young adult (YA) literature which features characters who experience similar losses, pain, et cetera can provide support for troubled children looking for answers. Such literature can aid children in understanding that they are not alone, that many individuals their own age experience similar tragedies and develop good coping skills to deal with difficult family situations. Judith Guest's *Ordinary People* is one such novel.

WHY *ORDINARY PEOPLE*?

Though a respectable body of literature exists that deals with family tragedies, specifically parental illnesses, *Ordinary People* ranks among the finest in quality and in realism. Not only is it superbly written, but it is also an excellent glimpse into the realities of both parental and child illness. It beautifully and pragmatically reveals the impact that the death of a family member can have on the entire family structure, and it effectively illustrates how family members sometimes cope in a tragic aftermath. Furthermore, unlike most YA novels written today, *Ordinary People* deals with a "traditional" family coming apart at the seams. One need only examine the covers of YA novels to discover that most novels dealing with parental illness or other family tragedies focus on only one parent and the relationship of that individual to his or her child or children. Though these novels are real and appropriate, we wanted a novel that illustrated, even in "perfect" or seemingly "ordinary" worlds, things are not really all that perfect or ideal. Bad things can and do happen to "ordinary people."

ORDINARY PEOPLE BY JUDITH GUEST (245 pp.)

Synopsis

Ordinary People begins after the death of Buck Jarrett, the older son in the Jarrett family, who died in a boating accident. Buck's only brother, Conrad (Con), has just returned from a lengthy stay in a mental hospital, where he has received intensive care for depression, including shock treatment. Unable to cope with his brother's death, Con had attempted suicide. The story opens with Con's return home where he, his mother (Beth), and father (Calvin) are attempting a return to normalcy. From the onset of the novel, Calvin exhibits excessive concern for Con; he constantly questions Con about his day, about his feelings, and he searches for suicidal warning signs in Con's behavior. Beth, on the other hand, avoids questioning Con but moves through her day as if nothing has happened, living in her own world of illusion. Con returns to school and begins, at his father's request, making routine trips to Dr. Berger, a therapist who helps Con sort through his feelings. Tensions within the family heighten. Beth and Calvin begin arguing, and a chasm swells between them. Con has his own problems. He feels isolated from his friends, feels smothered by his father, and senses resentment from his mother which heightens his own guilty feelings about his brother's death.

By the end of the story, Calvin and Con have grown in the grief process; both have accepted Buck's death and are ready to move on with their lives. Beth, on the other hand, is still in a state of denial, claiming Con's attempted suicide was an act of vengeance against her. Despite attempts on both Calvin's and Con's part to reconcile their relationships with Beth, she is unable to absolve her depression; thus, she moves out, leaving Calvin and Con behind.

A Psychological Perspective

In this compelling novel, we follow a family's descent from the "ordinary" world (which is equated with being "normal") into the nether region of grief, alienation, and despair—a realm from which only the father and son emerge. Before the accidental death of their older son, the Jarretts tried very hard to do things right, and by external measures, they succeeded. The father, Calvin, is a prosperous tax attorney who seems to have overcome a difficult childhood spent in an orphanage and is a well-liked and respected figure; he even plays a decent game of golf. His wife, Beth, is admired by her friends as a model of attractiveness and efficiency; she seems to do everything perfectly. Bold and something of a risk-taker, Jordan (Buck) was a successful athlete, had good friends, and made good grades. He was the idol of his more introspective, high achieving younger brother, Con. Buck's accidental death, however, becomes the broken thread that slowly, but surely, unravels the family unit.

Conrad

Con tries hard to be like Buck, to live Buck's life, and his effort takes its toll—Con attempts suicide. Though he grieves, Calvin focuses his energies on Con's life after Con's suicide attempt. It is he who looks after Con, questions him in an effort to understand how he is feeling, and sees that he visits a therapist. He is the dutiful father who tries hard to pull the family together after the tragedy. Beth, on the other hand, withdraws from Con and Calvin. She loses herself in her outside interests and draws slowly, but surely, away from her son and her husband, leaving both Calvin and Con to question their relationships.

Con, having been involved in the boating accident, feels partially responsible for his brother's death. He is what clinicians call the "symptom-bearer" or the person in the family who is unconsciously elected to bear the family's pain and grief. He is burdened with guilt over his brother's death and his own narrow escape. While everyone in the family feels guilt and grief about Buck's death, Con seems to take these feelings on as his personal burden, as if he were somehow responsible for this tragedy. He is, after all, a perfectionist like his mother, a maker of lists, and a self-control expert. How could someone who tries so hard to do everything right have let his brother die? This poignant excess of responsibility which children often assume in the face of family distress finally overcomes Con, and it ulti-mately leads to his suicide attempt.

After Buck's death, the family rallies, goes back to their routines, and tries to live *as if nothing has happened*. Their dedication to "normalcy" and their denial of their feelings leads to increasing isolation from each other. They essentially find themselves trapped in their individual coping mecha-nisms. With less well-practiced defenses, Con becomes clinically de-pressed. He does not eat well, begins to fail his courses, does poorly at swimming, and finally is unable to sleep at all. He eventually tells his thera-pist that he tried to kill himself in order to get some sleep; but his situation is, of course, much more complex than that.

At the beginning of the book, we meet Con as he has returned home from months of psychiatric hospitalization. He seems to have had a good relationship with the psychiatrist there; he received shock treatment; and he met a number of memorable characters. As he moves back into the "normal" environment, we realize that Con is far from well. His teachers are watching him for signs of depression that they now realize he had evi-denced before the suicide attempt; his friends too are wary. Isolated now by his status as "psychiatric patient," Con feels that he is the problem in his family.

Family therapists see many more problems in Con's family than his de-pression; in fact, some of the family's problems preceded Buck's death and made it difficult for them to cope with this tragedy. The foremost of these problems is the family's inability to express their feelings and to talk hon-estly about them. The scene at the beach at Christmas before Con's suicide attempt typifies the family's denial of feeling and reveals their escape into frantic activity. In this unreal atmosphere, Con feels deeply depressed, and he senses that his pain is invisible. His parents do not want to see his pain be-cause they do not want to see their own. While the mother, Beth, believes that Con aimed the suicide attempt at her and distances herself from Con (Con's new psychiatrist, Dr. Berger, makes the same suggestion), one won-ders if Con's suicide attempt were not targeted at the family's inability to talk about the emotional reality of their situation.

Con is affected deeply by her withdrawal and in a silent plea for under-standing and acceptance, Con comes downstairs, upon his parents' return from a short trip visiting relatives, and awkwardly hugs his mother. This move by Con, though a gesture of affection, is also a cry for acceptance and forgiveness. Beth does not hug him back or speak, but rather, buries her head in her book, distancing both Con and Calvin from her even more.

Calvin

As we witness Beth's relationship with Con, we see her as a perfectionist. She is dedicated to appearances, and her retreat into silence and into busyness make us question her love for her son and doubt her ability to cope honestly with life. These are certainly thoughts that occur to her husband, who is drawn deeper into supporting Con emotionally. Perhaps as Calvin sees Beth's rejection of Con, he sees an image of himself as a child, being rejected by a mother who placed him in an orphanage. And as Beth sees Calvin's dedication to Con, she herself feels rejected. Why can her husband not take her side in conflicts with Con? Why does he always support Con? Why is Calvin not worried about *her*? As Beth focuses on her own illusions of reality, she loses sight of Con's needs, forcing Con not only to deal with his own guilt at Buck's death, but also with his mother's rejection of him as well, a rejection which deepens Con's sense of worthlessness and guilt.

After Con's suicide attempt and hospitalization, Calvin seems to "get it." Perhaps his difficult life in an orphanage has made him more open to pain and tragedy. As Con struggles to reassemble his life, Calvin realizes that something is terribly wrong. He watches Con intently, asks him constantly about his experiences, and worries over him. He knows what it is like not to have a "sponsor" in life, and, perhaps for the first time, he feels the terrible weight of emotional responsibility for his son. Without any help from his own father in growing up, and with little support from a mother who placed him in an orphanage at age four and who died when he was eleven, this earnest man tries anxiously to support his son. It is he who pushes Con toward Dr. Berger, he who buys him a car, he who goes to Con's room after the disastrous fight between mother and son, and, ultimately, he who finally reaches Con.

This emotional triangle among Calvin, Beth, and Con is a common occurrence in families. Rather than the deepest bond in the family being between the parents, the closest relationship develops *across the generations—* in this instance between Calvin and Con. Some therapists would see this triangle as a "perpetrator-victim-rescuer" pattern, with Beth of course being the perpetrator, Con the victim, and Calvin the rescuer.

Yet Calvin does seem to love his wife. When she comes into a room, he is moved by her beauty. He enjoys their lovemaking and is disappointed when she turns away afterward; he really does seem concerned about her dilemmas. As the husband-wife relationship deteriorates, Calvin is confused and distraught about the loss of their former closeness. In the face of terrible loss and pain, Calvin gradually engages with what life has dealt the family, but Beth does not seem able to do so. The deepest schism between them is created by Calvin's willingness to grow in the face of tragedy, while Beth hangs on desperately to her yearning for safety and perfection.

We see some of these differences between Calvin and Beth in Chapter 11 when he runs into Carole Lazenby and they talk about Beth. Calvin recalls the years when they had two young boys, and how frantic Beth was in the face of all the turmoil and mess of young children. He remembers how she would burst into tears because of a toy left out of place and how, when Calvin tried to confront her about her perfectionism, she flew into a rage, railing at him. Regardless of the hardship on her or the family, everything had to be perfect. Certain things drove Beth to the brink of madness: dirt tracked in on a freshly scrubbed floor, water-spotted shower stalls, articles of clothing left out of place. Calvin admits depending on the order Beth brought to their lives and to being something of a perfectionist himself: "(until) the summer before last and an unexpected July storm on Lake Michigan. He had left off being a perfectionist then, when he discovered that not promptly kept appointments, not a house circumspectly clean, not membership in Onwentsia, or the Lake Forest Club, not power, or knowledge, or goodness—not *anything*—cleared you through the terrifying office of chance; that it is chance and not perfection that rules the world" (pp. 83–84).

These differences in perception of the world and in what each values are what finally separate the couple. Calvin begins to look beneath the surface of his life; and as his son is drawn into self-examination and self-reflection in therapy, Calvin moves that way, too. Finally, he asks to see Dr. Berger himself, an indication of his move toward self-inquiry and growth.

Beth

And what can we make of the enigmatic and troubled Beth? As Calvin and Con struggle with her, both try to understand her difficulties; and indeed, her relationship with them (and with her parents) reveal much about her underlying conflicts. Family therapists would look carefully at Beth's parents for clues to her personality and to her orientation toward others; for it is these pivotal parent-child relationships that shaped her.

Beth's parents are highly conventional people, strongly focused on the socially acceptable. From his constant position of forced cheerfulness, Beth's father, Harold, speaks in stereotypes; in fact, Buck and Con have a game called "Grandfather Trivia" which consists of answering questions with Howard's predictable remarks. As Con anticipates his stay with his grandparents when his parents go to Texas to visit his aunt and uncle, he thinks about the house on Green Bay Road that reeks of his grandmother's too-sweet perfume (the analogy being artificial cheerfulness). He says that he loves his grandmother, but talking to her is like being on a quiz show—her questions are difficult to answer, difficult because they often contain accusations. Con sees her use remarks to keep Harold in line. She is gentler with Con, but the technique is the same.

When Con arrives at the grandparents' house, the reader is treated to an illustration of the grandmother's style as she grills Con about his long hair, forces him to eat so that he will put on weight, and critically reviews his grades. When she wonders how he once managed a plethora of lessons and activities and still got all A's, Con quips that he might have been over-programmed. His grandmother does not understand that possibility. She sniffs, " 'Overprogrammed. What's that? Keeping busy is not being overpro-grammed, Con. What are you doing with all your time?' " (p. 181). She then launches into a lecture about how over-protected he is and how he leads the "easy life." The grandfather tries ineffectually to intervene but is pushed aside. Only Con's defensive wit finally coaxes a smile from his grandmother.

We can easily imagine Beth as a child in Con's position. As the persistent target of her mother's insistent prying, controlling criticism, and judgment, readers can see that Beth must have dedicated herself to trying to please this very demanding mother. Beth's mantra must have become, "If you are go-ing to be loved, you have to keep busy, do everything right—be perfect." Beth must have also learned to withdraw and to keep her own counsel in the face of such interrogation. It is interesting to note that Harold, who is also the target of his wife's judgment and who takes Con's side in the harangue at the dinner table, may have done the same when criticism was directed at his daughter. That is, he may have formed a coalition with Beth in much the same way that Calvin does when he feels that Con is being victimized by Beth. As the one who judges and blames, Beth is now in *her own mother's position in the family*, and Calvin is in the position of Beth's father. As we often see in families, history repeats itself.

When her son dies accidentally, Beth is totally unprepared for this inex-plicable event. Her perfectionism does not allow her to grieve (only Con and Beth were stony and silent at the funeral) or to admit her very human dilem-mas. Her "script" insists that she keep busy and keep trying to be perfect. There is simply no room in her life for her own feelings. Further, if she can-not admit to her own sadness and grief, how can she see these emotions in her son? In a world in which virtue and hard work are supposed to be re-warded, how does she explain this terrible event? Beth's mother's constant recourse to judgment implies that *someone or something must be at fault*. And who is to blame for Buck's drowning? Eventually we guess that Beth must blame herself, but this attribution is so devastating that she must evade it through projecting blame onto her son and husband, whom she sees as blaming her. (Projection is a "defense mechanism" first labeled by Freud in which someone sees in another a denied or disliked aspect of the self.)

Clearly, Beth is depressed, though it is a silent and largely invisible depression, camouflaged by her busyness. We see evidence of this depression repeatedly when she comes home, speaks briefly to Con, and goes to her room. Instead of staying awake like Con, she retreats into sleep, silence, and self-absorbed isolation. Even in moments of extreme distress, she insists on keeping her own counsel, maintaining that no one can help her.

As we learn more about her, we also see that Beth's thought processes are distorted. Her blatant misperception of others' motives is most obvious in Beth's confrontations with Calvin and Con. When Beth finds out from Carole Lazenby that Con had quit the swimming team a month prior, she is embarrassed and humiliated; and she sets out to shame Con by forcing him to reveal the secret to Calvin. Cornered, Con lashes out: " 'I'm sure I would have told you . . . if I thought you gave a damn!' " (p. 101). His father takes this statement personally: " 'What the hell does that mean?' 'Never mind,' (Beth) says, 'It's meant for me. Isn't it? I wish I knew, Con, why you try to hurt me!' " (p. 101). When Con protests that it is she who is trying to hurt him, Beth retaliates, citing her humiliation in a roomful of her friends when she learns that he has been lying to her and Calvin. She then attacks further, accusing Con of deliberately lying, disappearing, covering up.

At this point it is helpful to recall Beth's mother, who frames everything in terms of judgment, which is what Beth is doing to Con. In fact, she may be doing to others what was done to her. Feeling unfairly accused, Con accuses his mother of not caring about him, citing painfully her refusal to visit him in the hospital. When Con walks out in tears, Beth remains intransigent, not allowing herself to be comforted by Calvin. Instead, she rails at him, " 'Go ahead, that's the pattern, isn't it? Let him walk all over us, then go up there and apologize to him!' " (p. 102). Calvin tries to get Beth to lay off, and she then accuses him of talking to her the way Con talks to him.

Torn between son and wife, Calvin again tries to comfort Beth, and she allows him to do so for a moment. When Calvin wants the two of them to go to Con's room, she refuses, saying that Con wants his father, who will accept everything he does without criticism. Calvin chides Beth, saying that the conflict tonight could have been handled better. Beth again lashes out, " 'You see! Everything he does is all right! Perfectly understandable! And everything I do is mixed up, and wrong, and could have been handled a better way' " (p. 103). Again, Calvin tries to get Beth to go upstairs to Con, and she resists strongly, " 'I will not be pushed' " (p. 103). Then she says calmly,

" 'I will not be *manipulated*' " (p. 103). Again, Beth grew up in a highly manipulative and judgmental household, and she transfers these perceptions to her husband and son.

While Calvin is perhaps not the ideal husband at this moment, he is trying to be compassionate and fair. He attempts to comfort Beth, yet he does have difficulty acknowledging her pain verbally. And there is good reason for him to question Beth's primitive emotional reactions—her blaming, and her attribution of hostility to her son, who clearly feels unloved and hurt by his mother. In her despair, Beth sees Con as a figure of threat and judgment, *as if he were her judgmental, manipulative and dominating parent*. She thus parentifies Con—a process in which the child is perceived as having the power of a parent. She may also project onto Con some of the negative feelings she has about herself.

When Calvin walks away from Beth to comfort Con and to reassure him that his mother does not hate him, one wonders if this is not a symbolic turning point in the marriage. Calvin chooses his son's vulnerability over his wife's, leaving Beth caught in the drama of her own perceptions. As we think about Calvin's life, we may wonder if he unconsciously scripts Beth into rejecting him, especially since he was rejected by his mother and probably unconsciously anticipates that he will be rejected by the woman he cares about.

The separation between the couple is even more painfully portrayed later in the public fight at Beth's brother's home in Texas, a conflict that begins when they discuss a vacation trip and Calvin assumes that they would take Con. Soon they are into the old fight in which she accuses Calvin of overprotecting Con and he gets defensive, then they become mutually blaming. Finally Calvin asks her calmly, " 'I am asking you to tell me . . . what I've done that's made you so angry with me' " (p. 219). Beth replies, " 'It's not what you've done; it's what you think I've done' " (p. 219). Calvin seems genuinely confused. He does not think she has done anything. She calls him a liar: " 'You do, and you know it. You blame me for the whole thing' " (p. 219). Calvin wonders *what* whole thing, and Beth replies, " 'That whole vicious thing! He [Con] made it as vicious, as sickening as he could! The blood—all that blood! Oh, I will never forgive him for it. He wanted to kill me, too!' " (p. 219).

Here one recalls that when she had young children, Beth could be driven mad by an out of place toy, by the mess of parenthood. Here she does seem nearly mad: blaming Con for his attempted suicide, seeing it as an attack on her, blaming Calvin for blaming her for causing it. Yet there are tangled threads here, all around.

When Buck dies, Beth is depressed and unable to grieve, and she deals with her pain by withdrawing into herself and into her activities. Did she wish that Con had died instead of her favorite child, the sunny Buck? Though the film of this book made something of that theory, we can only speculate about such; certainly thoughts like these would have been abhorrent to Beth, and she might have needed to see hostility as emanating from Con. Did Beth avoid the increasingly depressed Con because he reminded her of her own hidden depression? Did she not know how to express love toward him? Was she afraid to love him for fear that she would lose him too? Did she feel abandoned when Calvin began to focus on Con and pay less attention to her dilemmas? Did Con, hurt by his mother's distance and full of guilt, begin to blame her? Did he in fact strike out at her and her unrelenting perfectionism in his suicide attempt? "All that bloody mess" certainly did attack her image of perfect order. Was Con responding to a life-long sense that his mother blamed her children for ruining her pursuit of perfect order? Was there a deep coalition between Beth and Buck, and one between Calvin and Con, that pre-dated Buck's death and that masked the hidden divisions between these marital partners?

Like all good works of fiction, *Ordinary People* raises questions that it does not answer. We can be certain, however, that Beth is not a pure villain; that we are simply not able to see deeply enough beneath her cool, polished exterior. After Buck's death, she is the family's true casualty, pursuing in her lonely way a world without change.

Dr. Berger

Con's story is the center of this drama, and his relationship with Dr. Berger is refreshingly alive and appealing. Of course the family plays its part here, too. If we look closely at Karen—Con's friend in the mental hospital who finally succeeds in taking her own life—we can see an example of a father who encourages Karen to rely on herself and on God (but not on therapy), and a cold mother who discourages outsiders from contacting her daughter. Con, on the other hand, is pushed by a loving father to see this talented and engaging therapist; and Calvin's support for Con never wavers.

Much of what Dr. Berger does is skillful. He joins with Con's cynicism, humor, and verbal jousting; he is honest and real. Dr. Berger both cajoles Con into questioning his self-condemnation and entices him into considering more positive interpretations of himself and of others. Over time, he comes to genuinely care about Con, tracking him carefully as Con gains confidence in confronting his past and its ghosts. Events like Karen's death, that might have been devastating had Con dealt with them alone, become instead catalysts for growth. As Con develops more and more support in his relationship with Dr. Berger, he dares to recall, and finally to feel, the traumas of his past. In this cathartic, shared feeling, Con finds release from his demons.

Perhaps Dr. Berger could have brought both of Con's parents into the therapy in order to help them with their own difficulties. He could still have helped Con in the compassionate way that he did, but he might also have helped him improve his relationship with both parents. Maybe Calvin would not have needed to be such a rescuer if someone had helped Beth with her self-doubts, her depression, and her distortion of others' motives. Calvin tried to do this, but like most spouses, she resists being treated by her partner. Perhaps Dr. Berger could have saved this marriage from being that other statistic: the 80% of couples who lose a child who later divorce. But then, some things are not perfect; they just are.

CONCLUDING THOUGHTS

Masterfully written, *Ordinary People* is an in-depth, realistic look at one family unit trying desperately to cope with a tragic family loss. Though Calvin, Beth, and Con must individually deal with Buck's death, they each manage their grief differently, for their coping skills are highly influenced by their own prior experiences. In Calvin's and Beth's cases, their former family structures heavily influence their behaviors.

The story is an appealing choice for individuals dealing with similar struggles because it lacks a neatly packaged or contrived ending. Calvin and Con struggle through and learn that some things just happen; some things are just out of human control. Though Beth does not appear to grow in her understanding or acceptance of Buck's death, her failure to reconcile her feelings is realistic. As painful as her character may be, Beth is a practical look at how parents can, and often do, deny their feelings of grief, and place blame for tragedies on others and, in doing so, inflict further pain on their own children and other loved ones.

RECOMMENDED READINGS

Numerous other books are available for adolescents and families dealing with parental illnesses. Listed below are several fiction and nonfiction works which deal with parental illnesses and which are appropriate for both middle school and secondary students. Some of the books end with parents recovering, and healthy relationships being formed within the family unit;

others are less optimistic, but offer hope and reassurance for troubled children. In these latter cases, we tried to include works in which the human spirit triumphs and prevails.

Fiction

2.01.   Arrick, Fran. (1984). *Nice girl from a good home*. New York: Bradbury. 199 pp. (ISBN: 0–02–705840–9). High School (HS).

Dory, a sophomore, lives a seemingly normal life; however, when her father loses his job, the entire family must adjust. His job loss becomes a catastrophe, and Dory's mother cannot face reality and commits suicide. Parallels can be found between Dory's mother and Con's. How will Dory cope?

2.02.   Avi. (1994). *The barn*. New York: Avon. 106 pp. (ISBN: 0–380–72562–2). Middle School (MS).

Nine-year-old Benjamin's teacher says Benjamin is the best student he has ever taught. Benjamin can do more than farming when he grows up. Unfortunately, Benjamin's father becomes seriously ill, and Benjamin must return home to help out. Returning home, Benjamin desires to do something great while his father is still alive.

2.03.   Blume, Judy. (1981). *Tiger eyes*. New York: Dell. 222 pp. (ISBN: 0–440–80115–X). MS, HS.

When Davey Wexler's father is shot to death in a grocery store holdup, Davey, her mother, and brother move to New Mexico to live with relatives to try to recover from their loss. Davey not only must deal with her own personal loss but with her mother's own depression as well. This is a beautifully written story about grieving, learning to let go, and picking up the pieces and moving forward. It offers an insightful look at how a mother deals with the loss of her husband and how her grief affects her child.

2.04.   Boyd, Candy. (1988). *Charlie Pippin*. New York: Puffin. 192 pp. (ISBN: 0–14–032587–5). MS.

Charlie's father serves in the Vietnam War. When he returns home, however, he is severely traumatized by the experience; he is bitter, and Charlie has difficulty understanding his changed personality. Wanting to understand what has happened to his father, Charlie decides to research the

African American contribution to the war. In doing so, he learns that his father, and other African Americans, contributed more than their fair share to the Vietnam War effort.

2.05.   Bridgers, Sue Ellen. (1981). *Notes for another life*. New York: Alfred A. Knopf. 250 pp. (ISBN: 0–394–94889–0). HS.

Wren's mother is focused on a career and Wren's father, a victim of depression, lives in a mental hospital. Thirteen-year-old Wren and her older brother, Kevin, live with their grandparents. Wren has the potential to be a concert pianist; however, she feels torn between two lifestyles. Should she become a concert pianist and model her mother's selfish lifestyle, or should she choose an alternative path—a path like her grandmother's, in which she lives for her family?

2.06.   Brooks, Bruce. (1984). *The moves make the man*. New York: HarperCollins. 252 pp. (ISBN: 0–06–447022–9). HS.

Using basketball as a metaphor for life, Brooks weaves a masterful tale of mental illness. Jerome meets Bix, an emotionally disturbed white boy who is grappling with his mother's insanity. Together they form a bizarre relationship.

2.07.   Brooks, Bruce. (1989). *No kidding*. New York: Harper & Row. 207 pp. (ISBN: 0–06–020722–1). MS, HS.

Fourteen-year-old Sam lives in the 21st century, a society plagued with alcoholics. Sam's mother is among those plagued, and Sam must take responsibility for his family. Sam concocts an elaborate scheme to save his family. Brooks has written a story of austere devotion. Though the setting seems a bit bizarre, the responsibility imposed upon Sam is realistic. Many of today's youth find themselves in situations in which they have to make important decisions about their siblings.

2.08.   Brooks, Martha. (1994). *Traveling on into the light and other stories*. New York: Orchard. 146 pp. (ISBN: 0–531–06863–3). MS, HS.

This collection of short stories focuses on teens and their relationships with friends and family. Brooks addresses a number of issues common to dysfunctional families, among them alcoholism, abuse, and suicide. Written mostly from first-person perspective, these stories are sure to appeal to both middle school and secondary students.

2.09.   Cannon, A. E. (1991). *Amazing Gracie*. New York: Dell. 224 pp. (ISBN: 0–440–21570–6). MS.

Gracie actually sews her mother's wedding dress and even wears a horrible dress that her stepfather picked out to her mother's wedding to protect her mother's feelings. Gracie does everything she can to adjust to living with a new stepfather. Despite Gracie's efforts, her mother slips into depression and attempts suicide.

2.10.   Carter, Alden R. (1990). *Dancing on dark water*. New York: Scholastic. 144 pp. (ISBN: 0–590–45600–8). MS, HS.

Shar has always been close to her father; however, when her father suffers from a brain hemorrhage, he loses his sense of emotions and moves about the house like a robot. Shar, her brothers, and their mother struggle to maintain the family unit. While Shar's mother and Shar's brothers give up hope, Shar maintains optimism that her father will regain his normal state.

2.11.   Carter, Alden R. (1991). *Up country*. New York: Scholastic. 256 pp. (ISBN: 0–590–43638–4). HS.

Carl lives in poverty with his alcoholic mother who parties too hard. Dreaming of a better life, Carl repairs stolen car stereos and saves the money, hoping one day to leave the rundown apartment building and the aggravation of dealing with an alcoholic mother. This is a memorable and believable novel about one lone youth's struggles to understand, accept, and deal with family alcoholism.

2.12.   Caseley, Judith. (1992). *My father, the nut-case*. New York: Alfred A. Knopf. 185 pp. (ISBN: 0–679–83394–3). MS, HS.

In this hopeful novel, 15-year-old Zoe, her mother, and sisters are dramatically affected by Zoe's clinically depressed father. Zoe is struggling with her own identity. She blames her father for being ill and for all the problems his illness has caused the family. Zoe eventually works through her anger and learns to accept her father and his illness. Depression is presented realistically in this novel.

2.13.   Clark, Clara. (1993). *Annie's choice*. New York: Boyds Mill Press. 196 pp. (ISBN: 0–56397–053–8). MS.

Secondary education was not a given for children growing up in our country in the 1920s. This novel reveals the hopes, dreams, and struggles of one young girl who wishes to attend high school. Fourteen-year-old Clara lives in a rural community in upstate New York. Though she yearns to receive a secondary education, she must make a painful choice: abandon her family and her ill mother who is weakened from childbirth or follow her dreams. This work, with well-developed characters, is a gentle reminder to teens of obstacles some have faced to receive a higher education.

2.14. Con, Pam. (1988). *Taking the ferry home*. 224 pp. New York: HarperCollins. (ISBN: 0–06–021318–3). HS.

Ali spends the summer on an island with her father, a writer and recovering alcoholic. Though Ali spends the summer looking for romance, she also tries to understand her father and worries over her mother, who is also a chronic alcoholic and a drug user.

2.15. Conley, Jane Leslie. (1993). *Crazy lady*. New York: HarperTrophy. 180 pp. (ISBN: 0–06–440517–0). MS.

Vernon makes fun of Maxine, the neighborhood alcoholic whom everyone calls the "crazy lady." Vernon and his friends tease and harass Maxine and her mentally handicapped son. Once Vernon gets to know Maxine and begins to understand her and her son's life, he realizes the powerful love between a mother and son. It is then that Vernon begins dealing with his own loss, the death of his mother.

2.16. Cormier, Robert. (1988). *Now and at the hour*. New York: Dell. 165 pp. (ISBN: 0–440–20882–3). HS.

A devoted husband and father, Alph LeBlanc gets lung cancer and becomes an invalid in his own home. While Alph struggles with his own death and helplessness, his children and wife search for strength, courage, and reassurance in this dark time. Though Alph's feelings and thoughts are central to the book, an adolescent struggling with a terminally ill parent may gain insight into the thoughts and feelings of a parent inflicted with a fatal illness.

2.17. Deaver, Julie Reece. (1995). *Chicago blues*. New York: HarperCollins. 170 pp. (ISBN: 0–06–024675–8). HS.

At her alcoholic mother's request, 17-year-old Lissa takes her 11-year-old sister Marnie to her art school in Chicago. Lissa and Marnie live on a meager income supplied by their father, who is a musician. Lissa handles the responsibility of her little sister pretty well until her father decides to take Marnie on the road as part of his act, and their recovering alcoholic mother shows up and wants to reenter their lives.

2.18.   de Jenkins, Lyll. (1989). *The honorable prison*. New York: Puffin. 208 pp. (ISBN: 0–14–032952–8). HS.

Because Marta's father opposes governmental rule in an unnamed South American country, he and his family are exiled. Food and money are scarce, and the cold, damp weather wreaks havoc on her father's already weakened health. To survive, Marta must become independent.

2.19.   Delffs, Dudley. (1993). *Forgiving August*. New York: Pinion Press. 254 pp. (ISBN: 0–89109–747–3). HS.

The summer preceding the first year of college is a time of excitement for most teens, a time of building dreams and setting goals. Bounty has dreams and visions of his own—he longs to attend the University of Tennessee, but he must obtain a student loan or he will have to attend the local community college and stay home. Bounty's summer is complicated further as his father resorts to alcohol and his mother submits to his father's authoritarian behavior.

2.20.   Ferris, Jean. (1995). *Signs of life*. New York: Farrar, Straus, & Giroux. 160 pp. (ISBN: 0–374–36909–7). MS.

Hannah loses her twin sister in an accident and struggles to accept her loss. Likewise, her father puts up a facade, and her mother drops into deep depression. The family takes a trip to France where they begin the healing process.

2.21.   Fox, Paula. (1995). *The eagle kite*. New York: Dell. 127 pp. (ISBN: 0–440–21972–8). MS, HS.

 Liam's father is dying of AIDS, and his mother claims he got it from a blood transfusion. But Liam knows the truth. Once, a few years back, Liam saw his father embrace a young man on the beach. Liam wants to confront his father but feels betrayed.

2.22.   Fox, Paula. (1986). *Moonlight man*. New York: Dell. 179 pp. (ISBN: 0–440–20079–2). MS, HS.

Catherine spends one unforgettable and puzzling summer with her alcoholic father, Harry Ames. Harry is unreliable, unpredictable, and sometimes drinks himself into oblivion; at other times, he and Catherine spend tender, unforgettable moments together. Catherine questions whether she will ever understand her father.

2.23.   Friedman, Carl. (1994). *Nightfather*. New York: Persea. 133 pp. (ISBN: 0–89255–193–3). HS.

Written by the daughter of a Holocaust survivor, this novel illustrates the impact the Holocaust has had on the children of Holocaust survivors. Everything the children do leads to a story by the father about the Holocaust, and the children fall victims to the horrifying details. The narrator and her siblings feel consumed by the events.

2.24.   Gibbons, Kaye. (1988). *Ellen Foster*. New York: Random House. 126 pp. (ISBN: 0–394–75757–2). MS.

Eleven-year-old Ellen hates her father. He beats her ill mother and would even abuse Ellen if she would let him. Ellen's mother dies, and Ellen is left to deal with her drunken father on her own. Ellen's spunk and determination make her a strong role model for young teens.

2.25.   Green, Connie Jordan. (1992). *Emmy*. New York: Macmillan. 152 pp. (ISBN: 0–689–50556–6). MS.

When Emmy Mourfield's father is permanently injured in a mining accident in an Eastern Kentucky mining town, Emmy and her five brothers and sisters must help their mother manage the house, earn money to support the family, and deal with their embittered father. Though Emmy's family works hard to prepare meals for the hungry coal miners, they face possible eviction from their home.

2.26.   Hartnett, Sonya. (1995). *Sleeping dogs*. New York: Viking. 130 pp. (ISBN: 0–670–86503–6). HS.

Griffin Willow is an insane, cruel, volatile man who lives with his wife and children. Together, they run a trailer park and a rundown farm where he makes one of his children, Jordan, his scapegoat. Jordan develops an incestuous relationship with his sister which the two try keeping secret. Oliver, the youngest, discovers the secret and tragedy follows. For mature readers, this novel is a riveting account of madness within the family structure.

2.27.   Hassler, Jon. (1989). *Jemmy*. New York: Fawcett. 160 pp. (ISBN: 0–449–70302–9). MS.

Jemmy is multiracial and has a difficult time in school because of her mixed heritage. When her mother dies and leaves her with two younger siblings and an alcoholic father, the father insists that Jemmy quit school to take care of her brother and sister. Jemmy is relieved at first, but then she finds herself struggling with problems too mature for her years. Jemmy is taken in by the Chapman family, who help her find a place for herself and her siblings.

2.28.   Hobbs, Will. (1988). *Changes in latitudes*. New York: Atheneum. 126 pp. (ISBN: 0–689–31385–3). MS, HS.

Travis's mother is angry at his father for not joining the family on a vacation in Mexico. Despite his mother's anger, Travis is determined to enjoy his vacation. His dreams are shattered, however, when he learns that his mother is having an affair and is emotionally distancing herself from the family.

2.29.   Hosie-Bounar, Jane. (1993). *Life belts*. New York: Dell. 165 pp. (ISBN: 0–440–21931–0). MS.

Nita appears to have it all—she is popular and pretty, but her mother is dying. She spends her time at the beach, swimming and sailing with her friends, Molly and Eddie. Nita tests fate by seeing how far she can distance herself from the shore.

2.30.   Jensen, Kathryn. (1989). *Pocket change*. New York: Macmillan. 171 pp. (ISBN: 0–02–747731–2). HS.

Josie's dad has begun to behave strangely. He is moody, violent, makes unusual demands, leaves the house for extended amounts of time, and works infrequently. Josie's stepmother denies there is anything wrong with him, but Josie knows there is. Josie contacts a professional and learns that her father is experiencing post-traumatic stress as a result of his years spent in the Vietnam War.

2.31.   Klass, David. (1994). *California blue*. New York: Scholastic. 200 pp. (ISBN: 0–590–46688–7). HS.

Seventeen-year-old John Rodgers and his father do not get along. John is a distance runner who lives in his father's shadow. When his father, a former athletic star, is stricken with leukemia, John must sort out his feelings for his dad.

2.32.   Klause, Annette. (1990). *The silver kiss*. New York: Delacorte. 208 pp. (ISBN: 0–385–30160–X). MS, HS.

Zoe's mother is dying of cancer, her best friend is moving, and Zoe feels alone. When Zoe meets Simon, a vampire, he seems to be the only one who understands her loneliness. Though a supernatural story, Zoe's feelings are realistic and accurate.

2.33.   Lasky, Kathryn. (1996). *Memoirs of a book bat*. San Diego: Harcourt Brace. 224 pp. (ISBN: 0–15–201259–1). MS.

Harper's family is torn by her father's alcoholism. When her father and mother join Family Action for Christian Education, he stops drinking and his wife resumes domestic work around the house. Harper's parents become fanatics about censorship and set out in a motor home to educate people about the evils of certain books. Harper loves to read and starts hiding books for fear her parents will disapprove. This novel is sure to provoke discussion about parental rights and authority.

2.34.   Lynch, Chris. (1994). *Gypsy Davey*. New York: HarperCollins. 179 pp. (ISBN: 0–06–023586–1). MS, HS.

Though she loves her children, Davey's mother is an emotional basket-case and just cannot handle life anymore. Two-year-old Davey is left in the care of his seven-year-old sister as his mother goes out—anywhere. Life could be easier if their indifferent father cared.

2.35.   Lynch, Chris. (1994). *Iceman*. New York: HarperTrophy. 181 pp. (ISBN: 0–06–447114–4). MS, HS.

Eric lives with parents who are consumed with inner rage. His father's only joy is in watching Eric brutally abuse other hockey players, and his mother sees no good in him; everything he does is wrong. Eric wonders if he can find a way out of his predicament.

2.36.   Martinez, Victor. (1996). *Parrot in the oven*. New York: HarperCollins. 216 pp. (ISBN: 0–06–026704–6). MS.

In this coming-of-age story, Mandy wants to be respected; but his father is always telling him that he is worthless—just a penny compared to million-, thousand-, and hundred-dollar people. Central to the novel is the father's alcoholism and the effects that this illness has upon the family. This National Book Award novel depicts the life of a poor Mexican-American boy and his family's struggles.

2.37.   McAfee, Carol. (1992). *Who's the kid around here, anyway?* New York: Ballantine Books. 153 pp. (ISBN: 0–449–70411–4). MS, HS.

On the surface, Maddy Winchurch has it made; she is both popular and smart. Underneath, however, this junior harbors a secret—Maddy's mother is an alcoholic and her father is contemplating divorce. Maddy turns to O'Keefe, a boy who introduces her to drugs and alcohol. In the end Maddy learns to cope with the aid of the school guidance counselor.

2.38.   McDonald, Megan. (1993). *The bridge to nowhere.* New York: Orchard. 160 pp. (ISBN: 0–531–05478–0). MS.

Hallie's father is an unemployed steel worker who has not worked in years. He is withdrawn, emotionally unstable, and explodes with anger over the smallest of things. Hallie fights hard to understand his erratic behavior.

2.39.   Myers, Walter Dean. (1992). *Somewhere in the darkness.* New York: Scholastic. 168 pp. (ISBN: 0–590–42411–4). MS, HS.

Jimmy's father, Crab, is serving prison time for murder. Unannounced, he returns from prison and takes Jimmy on a journey with him to Chicago and Arkansas; he is very ill. Crab maintains his innocence, and Jimmy must choose whether to remain with him or to return to live with his grandmother.

2.40.   Nelson, Theresa. (1994). *The beggar's ride.* New York: Dell. 256 pp. (ISBN: 0–440–21887–X). HS.

Clare's mother lives in bars as a nightclub singer who spends a great deal of time with men. Clare cannot accept her mother's lifestyle and runs away. She joins a gang of homeless teens who steal for survival.

2.41.   Nelson, Theresa. (1996). *Earthshine.* New York: Dell. 182 pp. (ISBN: 0–440–21989–2). MS.

Slim's father is dying of AIDS. In an effort to save her father's life, Slim joins a support group for families of AIDS victims. There she meets Isaiah, who convinces Slim that a Miracle Man in the "Hungry Valley" has a cure for the deadly virus. Slim and her family travel with Isaiah's family to find this Miracle Man.

2.42.   Nelson, Vaunda. (1985). *Possibles*. New York: Putnam. 192 pp. (ISBN: 0–399–22823–3). MS.

Sheppy is very close to her father and is devastated when he dies of cancer. Sheppy feels she has no possibilities in life after her father's death and takes a job tending Miss Montgomery, an ill woman who harbors her own secrets and pain. Together, Sheppy and Miss Montgomery begin seeing other directions, other possibilities for their lives.

2.43.   Rodowsky, Colby. (1994). *Hannah in between*. New York: Farrar, Straus, & Giroux. 152 pp. (ISBN: 0–374–32837–4). MS, HS.

Hannah's mother is an alcoholic, but no one seems to notice except Hannah. Hannah is embarrassed by her mother's public drunken display and wants help.

2.44.   Rodowsky, Colby. (1992). *Lucy Peale*. New York: Farrar, Straus, & Giroux. 167 pp. (ISBN: 0–374–44659–8). HS.

Seventeen-year-old Lucy is pregnant and must face the wrath of her overbearing, evangelic father. Unable to stand his abuse, Lucy takes off with no money and no place to go. She feels lost and alone until she meets Jake.

2.45.   Rosenberg, Liz. (1996). *Heart and soul*. New York: Harcourt Brace. 213 pp. (ISBN: 0–15–201270–2). HS.

Seventeen-year-old Willie struggles to understand her passive mother and her father who is seldom home. Unable to cope with her mother's passiveness and her father's neglect, Willie lapses into depression until she finally takes control of her life and her emotions.

2.46.   Soto, Gary. (1994). *Jesse*. San Diego: Harcourt Brace. 166 pp. (ISBN: 0–15–240239–X). MS, HS.

Jesse is a young Mexican-American boy struggling with poverty, prejudice, neighborhood violence, and a drunken stepfather. Growing up amid the confusion of the Vietnam War, Jesse is determined to receive an education. Laboring hard to pay for his schooling, Jesse represents hope, faith, and determination.

2.47.   Voigt, Cynthia. (1985). *The runner*. New York: Scholastic. 281 pp. (ISBN: 0–590–48380–3). HS.

Bullet is the best runner on the school team. Consumed by rage toward his insanely domineering father and his submissive mother, Bullet refuses to be a team player and has become accustomed to closing himself off from people. If given a choice, Bullet would rather be cut from the team.

2.48.   Voigt, Cynthia. (1988). *Tree by leaf*. New York: Ballantine. 167 pp. (ISBN: 0–449–70334–7). HS.

Clothilde's father enlists in World War I, and Clothilde, close to her beloved father, anxiously awaits his return. When he returns, his face is badly scarred and so is his heart. He withdraws from everyone around him and moves to the boathouse to live. Clothilde struggles with her father's dark personality and her mother's depression and feels she must take charge of the farm.

2.49.   Voigt, Cynthia. (1994). *When she hollers*. New York: Scholastic. 177 pp. (ISBN: 0–590–46714–X). HS.

Tish's mother lives in a world of denial, oblivious to her husband's nighttime trips to her daughter's room. Tish's stepfather sexually abuses Tish, and her mother refuses to acknowledge the truth. Tish lives in her own agonizing world until she decides one morning to confront her stepfather. She does so in front of her mother, only to learn that her mother doesn't believe her. Tish searches for a solution.

Nonfiction

2.50.   Bode, Janet. (Ed.). (1993). *Death is hard to live with: Teenagers and how they cope with death*. New York: Delacorte. 192 pp. (ISBN: 0–385–31041–2). MS, HS.

Bode interviews teenagers who have had to adjust to the death of loved ones or have family members who are terminally ill. Medical doctors and a therapist offer suggestions for dealing with death.

2.51.   Donnan, Geoffrey & Burton, Carol. (1992). *After a stroke: A support book for patients, caregivers, families, and friends.* Berkeley, California: North Atlantic Books. 160 pp. (ISBN: 1–55643–130–9). HS.

This easy-to-read guide can aid adolescents in understanding the causes and consequences as well as the limitations and effects of a stroke. Ways in which a family can gradually return to normalcy are included.

2.52.   Fassler, David. (1990). *What's a virus anyway? The kid's book about AIDS.* New York: Talman. 67 pp. (ISBN: 0–914525–17–4). MS.

This book addresses the most frequently asked questions about the AIDS virus and is most recommended for those who may have reading difficulties.

2.53.   Greist, John & Jefferson, James. (1992). *Depression and its treatment.* New York: Warner. 164 pp. (ISBN: 0–446–60029–6). HS.

This guide defines depression and suggests possible treatments. Written in layman's terms, the book can aid teenagers in understanding the nature of this illness.

2.54.   Hayden, Torey L. (1980). *One child.* New York: Avon. 221 pp. (ISBN: 0–380–54262–5). HS.

Abused by her mother and neglected by her alcoholic father, a six-year-old girl displays deviant behavior at school. Fortunately, one teacher sees her genius, has her removed from the class, and helps her begin the healing process.

2.55.   Hein, Karen & DiGeronimo, Theresa. (1993). *AIDS: Trading fear for facts.* Yonkers, New York: Consumer Reports Books. 232 pp. (ISBN: 0–89043–721–1). MS, HS.

In simple, straightforward language, this work answers frequently asked questions about AIDS. Information about how the virus is transmitted, how one is tested, and where one can go for help are provided.

2.56.   Middlebrook, Christina. (1996). *Seeing the crab.* New York: HarperCollins. 212 pp. (ISBN: 0–465–07493–6). HS.

Middlebrook gives an honest and personal account about living and struggling with advanced cancer. Though realistic, and often painful, this book offers a clear account of what a terminally ill person needs from family members and other loved ones.

2.57.   Pomeroy, DanaRae. (1996). *When someone you love has cancer.* New York: Berkley. 162 pp. (ISBN: 0–425–15129–8). MS, HS.

Those reading this book will learn ways of coping with stress and find answers to concerns they may have about loved ones who have cancer. The work explains emotions associated with the dreaded disease—anger, anxiety, denial, fear, guilt, etc.—and can help adolescents understand the erratic behavior individuals exhibit when they discover they are terminally ill.

2.58.   Shemiberg, Elaine. (1990). *Strokes: What families should know.* New York: Ballantine. 235 pp. (ISBN: 0–345–36209–8). HS.

The author of this book has survived a stroke and describes life after the trauma. Shemiberg suggests ways to care for stroke victims and offers insights to readers in regard to feeling less overwhelmed, worried, and confused through such an ordeal.

REFERENCE

Guest, Judith. (1976). *Ordinary people.* New York: Ballantine.

CHAPTER 3

Paul Zindel's *My Darling, My Hamburger:* A Study in School and Family Conflicts

Jeffrey S. Kaplan & William A. Long, Jr.

INTRODUCTION

> Sean rarely thought of suicide anymore, although he used to think about it often. He had ruled out an overdose of sleeping pills because he knew all they did was relax the diaphragm, and to him that was the same as suffocating to death. He decided the best way would be a .357 magnum pistol. (p. 14)

Teenagers and suicide. Not a healthy combination. But the adolescent years are a time of great pain and agony, and anything is possible. Even suicide. For the most part, none of us would want to relive adolescence—at least, not for a long period of time. In a moment of folly, perhaps we might entertain the thought of going back for a day, maybe a week, or perhaps for an idyllic summer month at favorite resort or camp. But no one, in his or her right mind, would go back for the entire duration. No one wants to repeat the pain of growing up—from the ages of 12 to 17 or 18—when life's uncertainty and hormones are in full swing. Nothing is as trying. Nothing is as complex.

Young people are incomprehensible forces. Although they might beg for saving, there is no known technique to mold one human being into an image prescribed by some adult's knowing mind's eye. Simply, these irreconcilable people are whirlwinds of imagination and strength who are determined to step to the beat of their own inner drummers. Time and time again, teenagers stand in complete defiance to their protective parents and guardians. No matter how much their adoring providers and caregivers try to help or change them, nothing happens. These defiant young souls do not bend. They merely follow their own inner directions, seeking solace in their own wisdom and direction. Sometimes their paths lead to productive lives and sometimes they falter. But their choices are entirely their own.

MY DARLING, MY HAMBURGER BY PAUL ZINDEL (128 pp.)

Paul Zindel's gritty, slice-of-life, young adult (YA) novel *My Darling, My Hamburger* portrays four young adults—Elizabeth, Maggie, Sean, and Dennis—in the grips of adolescence where each is coming to terms with "Who am I?" and "What do I represent?" issues. The book is not only perfectly suited for young adults, but is most appropriate for an in-depth discussion about the myriad of problems which confront young people coming into their own. It is a good read of an all too common story of young people caught in very adult problems. Liz, the quintessential teenage rebel is angry at the world, and at her mother and stepfather specifically, as she lashes out at everyone who stands in her way to get what she wants. Liz's sometime boyfriend, Sean, knows what he wants—Liz, in particular—but is willing to give up everything (including the girl he loves) to get on with his life. Maggie, Elizabeth's best friend, feels deeply committed to justice and truth and won't allow anyone to stand in her way, even when it means stepping on the toes of her best friends. Last is Dennis, a quiet, shy, diffident young man who is just coming to understand the cruelties of growing up and facing life's inevitable defeats.

Synopsis

During their senior year, Liz, the ringleader and central figure in this short novella, wants to strike out on her own. Unhappy at home and frustrated at school, she tries to form a lasting and loving relationship with Sean, but he is not ready to commit. Sean likes Liz and desperately wants to be intimate with her, but he certainly does not want to start a lifetime affair. Yet, as fate and young adult experimentation tend to go, Liz and Sean share a night of passion. As a result of a series of mix-ups, Liz ends up at the school dance with a boy who mistreats her. Sean comes to her rescue but his car breaks down. (I know what you're thinking—not that excuse! But it is true.) As Sean curses at the wind, Liz dutifully calls home. She relays the news to her parents, only to experience a stinging rebuke from her stepfather.

> "We had a flat," Liz said. "It's a bit complicated, but I had a fight with the boy that took me to the dance." . . . Liz slowed her voice, then stopped. She felt she was saying all the wrong things.

"Get home here!"
The tone of his voice made her sink.
"Do you hear me, you little tramp?" (p. 67)

And with that, Liz freezes. She removes the receiver from her ear and stares in disbelief. Her own stepfather has called her a tramp. "Go to hell," she says under her breath (p. 67). With her self-esteem crushed and in the wake of the blow from her stepfather, Liz sinks slowly into Sean's arms and nestles into his embrace. And the result—an inevitable, unwanted pregnancy. The repercussions, as one might suspect, start a chain of events, which reveal the true makeup their lives, and inevitably, the development of the novel's four distinct personalities.

Meanwhile, Liz's best friend, Maggie Tipton, wrestles with her own inner demons; she wants to be cool like Liz. Maggie seeks the affection of Dennis, a geeky kid with a "face like an undernourished zucchini" who is always "wearing the same baggy sweater" (p. 5). Maggie grows in her love of this vision of teenage pubescent angst, admiring his gentle demeanor and goodness.

While shopping for prom dresses, Liz tells Maggie that she is pregnant and wants an abortion. Maggie nearly has a nervous breakdown as she struggles to absorb Liz's startling news—A baby? An abortion? How? When?—while Liz rattles off, almost matter-of-factly, that Sean is the father and that he doesn't know. Liz wants to know if Maggie will lend her money for the abortion and then all will be well. For Maggie's help, Liz will be eternally grateful, or at least until they graduate. Of course, Liz adds quickly that no one must know.

Maggie finds all of this difficult to grasp and tries to convince Liz to do otherwise, but Liz is obstinate and determined to live her own life. Things abruptly change when Liz speaks to Sean, and he asks her to marry him. Now, suddenly all will be well. Liz informs Maggie that she and Sean will graduate, move to California where one of them will go to school, and they will eventually come back to New York a few years later with baby in tow. And no one will be the wiser! Liz, however, is only elated for a short while. Soon, her plans fold.

Sean, worried and reluctant to be a young father, has a heart-to-heart with his own father. In a roundabout way, Sean tells his dad about "a friend" who got his girlfriend pregnant, and what, if anything, should his friend do. Sean's father replies that his son's friend should pay for the girl's abortion and get on with his life. He bellows, "He thinks he loves her now, but if he's thinking of marrying her—forget it! Is he planning on going to college, or is he some kind of dummy?" (p. 90).

Without ever admitting that he is the father in question, Sean heeds his father's advice and tells Liz that he cannot marry her; instead, he will pay for her abortion. Hurt and defiled, Liz grabs the money and storms out on Sean. Devastated, Liz rants and raves that Sean won't marry her, or even take responsibility for his child, except paying for the abortion. "You son of a bitch," she fumes (p. 99). With Maggie's help and without her parents' knowledge, Liz sneaks out of the house on prom night and drives to a doctor in a nearby town who will perform the abortion without parental permission. The procedure appears to be fine until Liz begins bleeding during the drive home.

> Maggie was momentarily paralyzed with fear. Then suddenly it was as if she could see only one way out of the nightmare. She opened the car door and started to run toward the house.
>
> "Don't tell them. Don't let them know," Liz spit out, raising her head in spite of the pain. Maggie ran toward the front door. She saw a light on in an upstairs bedroom. Again and again she rang the bell. Someone had to be home.
>
> "Let me die!" Liz screamed from the car. "Let me die, you lousy traitor!" (p. 108)

Maggie, being the good person that she is, tells Liz's parents the whole story. While unraveling Liz's world and liberating her own, Maggie—the aggressive do-gooder—rescues Liz—the aggressive rebel—from her own self-destruction.

During all of this, Sean stays out of the fray while Dennis wallows in his own self-pity. Maggie ditched Dennis' invitation to the high school prom at the last minute because she felt compelled to help Liz with the abortion. Dennis feels Maggie's rejection and has always felt generally estranged from Liz and Sean. He is the grand outsider who's never privy to the goings-on of the inner circle. Dennis is lost in a whirlwind of confusion and adult talk while pining for his soul mate, Maggie. Maggie graduates from high school, leaving her feelings of insecurity and awkwardness behind. As for Liz, she must delay her graduation as she clashes with her angry and bewildered parents; her hysteria has finally caught up with her.

LONG'S THEORY: FOUR PERSONALITY TYPES

Dr. William A. Long Jr., a practicing pediatric physician who specializes in adolescent medicine, has made it his business to decipher how "teenagers tick." He enjoys working with "adults in the making" and associating with young folk who are still wrestling with life's larger questions. Dr. Long tries, of course, to help the parents and guardians deal with their inevitable inconsistencies and vagaries. He knows full well that there is no known cure for the disease we call benignly "adolescence," but that parents, of all persuasions, still valiantly try to control and manipulate their young charges into perfect and adoring teenagers. His numerous years of work and scholarship have allowed him to underline what he considers the essential psyche of young people, especially those caught in the throes of adolescence.

Teenagers will become who they are destined to become, and Dr. Long believes their destiny is evident at birth. As we peer through the nursery window, he contends, we can often see "wee young folk" exhibiting very strong and highly identifiable personalities. In fact, Dr. Long identifies four distinct types of individuals: the rebel, the follower, the loner, and the clinger. According to Dr. Long, these personalities are present at birth and their cause is most likely a genetic predisposition. Although Dr. Long has no pure scientific evidence to attest to a defined genetic link between personality and DNA, he believes—based on his years of training as a physician and pediatrician for young adults—that these qualities are innate and immutable. These four personality types manifest themselves in adolescence and can be found to be the underlying cause for so much teenage stress and parental anxiety. What is so fascinating, though, is that these personality traits travel with us throughout our lives, manifesting themselves most prominently during the height of adolescence. During the mid-teenage years, the most pronounced qualities of a human being's biological and psychological makeup are self-evident. It is during this time that young people exhibit who they really are in a full blaze of personal glory.

The Rebel

The rebel is the baby who, no matter what you do, is restless and listless. For these rebels, their "blankies" are never on, their legs are always kicking, and their mouths are always screaming; quiet is not known. They know what they want and will stop at nothing to satisfy their desires. Kicking and screaming in their nursery cribs, they are the first to be known. Teenage rebels are full-blown rebels, knocking down windmills, both imaginary and real, at every step of their way.

The Follower

The follower is the child who moves in perfect rhythm according to what babies should do. These are the babies we often see in delicate hues on peaceful and idyllic television commercials. These infants cry only when necessary, and otherwise, seem content as lambs nestled by their mother sheep. They coo, they gurgle, and they smile on cue. They make no immediate demands, other than to be fed and cuddled, and are better known as the "perfect babies." Teenage followers are the ones reveling in whatever prescribed activity that they enjoy. They are doing what they should be doing—whether at school or home—and are enjoying the rewards that follow in their suit.

The Loner

The languid child, or the loner, is the infant who is in his or her own world. These babies may or may not respond to hugging and cooing; but no matter what, they are not dependent on your undying affection. They are content to simply just be. They do not crave affection but take pleasure in the moment with no hidden agenda. They stare listlessly into space, lost in their own quiet and self-absorbing world. They are alone and happy in their aloneness. Teenage loners are content to sit idly by as the world rushes on, quietly doing what they enjoy without expecting reward or favor.

The Clinger

The clinger is the baby who must cling to someone for love and affection. Not content to stay by themselves, these infants are always looking for someone or something to hold. Whether it is their "blankie" or their mother's touch, these needy babies are in search of security, an elusive but highly tangible quality that is most often found in another human being. These babies are shaky, nervous, and are unsure of themselves and their new surroundings. They need the constant comfort of a reassuring voice or a soothing hand and are considered difficult infants because they are so demanding. Teenage clingers move with complete caution, anxious to please and bend. They live to fill a need, preferably yours, and are reluctant to strike out on their own for fear of retribution and failure.

FOUR BASIC REACTIVE BEHAVIOR TYPES

If one accepts the premise that young adults are full-blown versions of their adult selves, then one can safely assume that teenagers can be categorized into types, classifying them according to temperament and interests. Once they are divided into types, adults can begin to examine how we can handle, or at least understand, each distinct personality. In his medical practice, Dr. Long divides his many teenage patients into types; the same can be done in teachers' classrooms. A typical high school class is filled with all kinds of different students. According to Dr. Long (1975, 1985, & 1989), laden beneath all those types are four distinct personality traits based on what he calls reactive behavior patterns. Adolescents, ranging in age from the onset of puberty to well into their 20s (and in some cases even further), are often characterized by one word—ambivalence. They are progressing developmentally from a state of dependence to independence, and their ability to adjust to changes is reflected in the effects of environmental stimulation, obstacle formation, and stress. Midpoint in this development is the peak of ambiguity and unpredictability. Long argues that the major role of parents, guardians, and teachers is to remove—or at least realize—obstacles that inhibit normal progression. Young adults can exhibit a wide variety of behavior patterns often accompanied by unpredictable and severe mood swings. Like babies in the nursery, teenagers are susceptible to blatant personality changes, and often, predictable behavior patterns.

Long's theory is based on some important determinants of behavior. First, he believes that intellect plays a major role in determining behavior patterns and expressing ambivalence. Second, Long's personality model is dependent upon the sophistication of the young adult. Students with a considerably high level of intellect and sophistication express their ambivalence quite differently from those who are less sophisticated and intelligent. Furthermore, education and character impact the manner in which students cope with situations and people. And finally, rate of maturation defines the time frame through which all development takes place.

Long's reactive types are divided along two distinct dimensions: aggressive/passive and dependent/independent. Aggressive people have very high energy levels and tend to apply that force to life's situations; whereas, passive individuals do not bring nearly as much energy to the table. They are low-energy people who rarely exhibit the passion and energy that their counterpart, the aggressives, do. Dependent and independent people are marked by their relationship with others. Dependent individuals have a high need for approval from authority figures such as parents, guardians, and teachers; whereas, independent individuals require little or no approval from outside sources. Independents define their own paths, trailblazing venues that are often in direct contradiction to the authoritarian line. They are independent thinkers, not dependent upon the thinking of others. With these two distinct dimensions defined, Long characterizes four basic reactive behavior types: Aggressive-Independent (AI), Aggressive-Dependent (AD), Passive-Independent (PI), and Passive-Dependent (PD).

Aggressive-Independent (AI)

Imaging Exercise

Imagine you are a 16-year-old who is self-confident and self-assured. You know what you want and are not afraid to ask for it. You are willing to go anywhere, do anything, and defy anyone to get what you want. Now, imagine that you are an angry 16-year-old and someone has asked you to do something you don't want to do like go to school and do your homework.

Defined

Aggressive-Independent teenagers (AIs), or the rebels, are the kids who have the most difficulty adjusting to authority. They know what they want and are not likely to kowtow to authority when asked to conform. Not concerned with others' approval, they act on their own accord and often break rules just to get their own way. In short, they are a teacher's worst nightmare. Teachers do not long for AIs in their classrooms. These are the young adults who refuse to follow teachers' rules, complete teachers' assignments, and have no trouble voicing their displeasure. Acting on their own accord, they see beyond rules and regulations to their own Promised Land of freedom and rebellion. They are hell-bent on proving you wrong and them right. They are aggressive, impulsive, and action-oriented. They want results and they want them now.

They are known for their honesty. Their honesty coupled with their confrontational style can, in future years, either work for or against them. Aggressive-Independents have little tolerance for passive and agreeable people; they see weaknesses there. They tend to be highly ambitious in whatever their chosen field, good or bad. If they find enjoyment in productive adventures, they can become future world leaders and personalities. For example, many political, entertainment, and sports figures are prominent AI people. They have risked all, often against the sage advice of other more conventional thinkers, to become who they are, and have defied every conventional path to get there.

Aggressive-Independents who select the bad become just the reverse, future notorious bad people who steamroll everyone in their paths to achieve their goals and desires. This is ultimately the path to self-destruction, and at 15 or 16, the seeds for such destruction are often laid. Of all the personality types, AIs are the most difficult to nurture and teach. Their independent "act now–consequences later" attitude is, at best, a challenge to the most experienced caregiver and professional. (And they are the ones most likely not to do their homework!)

Aggressive-Dependent (AD)

Imaging Exercise

Imagine again that you are 16 but are the exact opposite of the teenager described above. You are not rebellious, impulsive, or a risk-taker. Instead, you are just you—quiet, responsible, dependable, reliable you.

Defined

Of the four personality types, Aggressive-Dependents (ADs), or the followers, are considered to be the most normal. They possess the same energy as the AIs, but ADs channel their drive in positive directions. These followers seek approval from authority figures and revel in the positive acceptance by others. They are the true leaders in any given climate. At school, they are the student scholars and office holders; and at home, they are the obedient youngsters and conscientious adults to be. In short, they are everyone's dream child.

Aggressive-Dependent young adults travel the straight and narrow path, bowing to authority and following conventional protocol. Their futures, as one might suspect, are bright as they become, if all goes well, the future leaders in conventional arenas such as politics, education, religion, etc. Unfortunately, their desire to be safe often precludes their becoming the mogul or boss. Because they possess an innate desire to always please, ADs rarely confront authority. They are uncomfortable in challenging people for fear of rejection. Aggressive-Dependents' hunger for approval and love from all audiences inhibits their ability to make hard choices. In groups, for example, their people-pleasing nature causes them to spend most of their energy maintaining harmony. To avoid conflict, they will often buckle and apologize even if they are not guilty of anything. Hence, ADs make excellent vice-presidents but rarely very competent presidents.

Aggressive-Dependents thrive in supportive and nurturing environments and need help asserting their independence. They will do well in their chosen endeavors, often driving themselves to exhaustion in an effort to please themselves and others. They usually fall apart when they feel that their efforts are going unrewarded or in the face of rejection. Aggressive-Dependents who have worked hard all of their lives only to be laid off or are underpaid for reasons beyond their control often feel hurt and lonely and will crash very quickly in their sudden and rash defeat. As ADs mature though, their energy and vitality accomplish much of the world's work and they are usually happy and productive individuals.

Passive-Independent (PI)

Imaging Exercise

You're 16 and your mother has asked you to clean your room. You have given her a half-hearted response like, "Sure, Mom, whatever" and then, the minute she leaves the room, you go back to whatever you were doing, ignoring her pliant command. You are not worried that your mother is worried. You have your own internal clock that tells you, "Don't sweat it. It's no big deal." Because you are not dependent upon the approval of others, it really doesn't matter to you when you clean your room or that your mother is upset that your room is such a mess. You figure, "Hey. I'll clean it when I'm good and ready, and if she gets mad, she gets mad." And sure enough, when your mother repeatedly returns to your room and finally pleads with you to clean it up, you still won't budge. What is more, you never get angry. You just let your mother rant and rave, while you sit idly by waiting for her temper tantrum to subside.

Defined

Passive-Independents (PIs), or loners, are the individuals with low-energy levels and little need for authoritarian approval. Listening to only themselves, they do what they want with little or no fuss. They are quiet, amiable, stubborn souls who defy authority silently and deliberately. They are not swayed by public opinion, not impressed by conventional approval methods, and unmoved by pleas for their participation in societal conventions. In short, they are like the New England transcendental philosopher, Henry David Thoreau; they prefer to do their own thing in a quiet and unobtrusive manner.

Parents and teachers are frustrated by PIs because they do not fight back. Instead, the more you push—do your homework, clean your room, eat your broccoli—the more they pull back. Passive-Independents do not like to be told what to do and prefer to do their own thing, even if it means starting something and not finishing it. Generally, they see advice as nagging, questions as ponderous, and deadlines as starting points. They deliberately frustrate their parents, knowing full well they are being annoying and it tickles them.

Their stubbornness in youth—refusing to engage in class with students and teachers, aloofness from all but a few friends, and monosyllabic responses to adults and authority figures—often results in steadfastness in adulthood. If they truly settle in on something that they really enjoy doing, they often become very productive, content, and perceptive adults. With little need to sway in the face of strong external pressures, PIs often become stable, responsible society members and defenders of the status quo without ever having to vocalize their concerns or dissents. Simply, they lead by example. They love what they do, and they relish in the quiet joy of their corner of the universe.

Passive-Dependent (PD)

Imaging Exercise

Finally, imagine yourself as a 16-year-old who is afraid to speak unless spoken to. You are 16 and afraid to venture outside of yourself for fear that you'll be ridiculed, belittled, and destroyed. You monitor your every move and are wary that your next move will be your last. You desperately seek advice—the right advice, the true advice, the holier-than-thou advice—so that, in the face of others, you will not fail. Instead, you will live to see another day.

Defined

Passive-Dependents (PDs), or the clingers, are young people who are basically afraid of their own shadow. As teenagers, they are reluctant to make a move or venture beyond the safe confines of their immediate universe without seeking the approval of some sovereign figure. These nervous wrecks are encumbered by all of society's pressures and then some. Their reluctance to assert their independence on their own, fiercely and unequivocally, is the cause for their downfall, and ultimately, depression.

Passive-Dependents are treated with kid gloves by teachers and parents. They are generally low-energy individuals who thrive on affection and approval. Passive-Dependents are slow to mature because, generally speaking, they are unable to express resentment or anger. They retreat into their protective shells at the slightest suggestion of disapproval. For fear of offending, they just do what they are told and rarely ask questions to clarify. Passive-Dependents will do their share but rarely more. They do not want to be perceived as failures, and they will cower if anyone intimates that they are. They would prefer to be labeled "anonymous" than "loser" and will take all precautions to avoid the perception. If PDs are to succeed, they must have a caring and nurturing environment.

Nevertheless, PDs also have many strong qualities. Although they are not assertive go-getters, they do make productive workers in later life. Like the PIs, once they find their life's work, they make loyal and sensitive laborers. They are kind, gentle people who need to be treated similarly. They will work long and hard and make excellent caregivers. If a person is ill, for example, call a PD because anyone's need is his or her need. They have no hidden agenda but live to please. Passive-Dependents mature more slowly than the other three types.

WHO ARE ZINDEL'S FOUR TEENAGERS?

To look at *My Darling, My Hamburger* from a clinical viewpoint is to take a snapshot of four troubled but typical teenagers. Maggie, Sean, Elizabeth, and Dennis are classic young adults who exemplify the problems faced by many young adults at home and at school. These particular teenagers' pronounced characteristics embody some of the more revealing traits of young adulthood. They are smart, energetic, resourceful, and always inventive. They are not afraid to stress their fears in very different ways, and their differences are what make them unique and fascinating study.

The Rebel (Liz)

As an Aggressive-Independent (AI), Liz Palladino is a determined young woman. During her senior year of high school, she barrels her way into everyone's life. She is angry at her mother and new stepfather, at her teachers for all general purposes, and her friends for an array of hidden slights and misdeeds. Liz is not a happy person, and she is determined to let everyone know it. Her anger boils over into many confrontations, verbal and otherwise, with her parents, teachers, and friends, until finally, she must come to terms with her own resentment and bitterness.

Liz is not the kind of teenager who will take no for an answer. As the typical rebel, she has her own agenda and is reluctant to comply with anyone's rules. Formal conventions are not for her. Instead, she prefers fast makeup, cars, and boys—and on her terms. When her mother objects to her choice of clothes, she retaliates with one-liners designed to wither her mother and repulse her stepfather who she repeatedly refers to as "my stepfather." When her parents try to monitor her comings and goings, she declares her independence and asserts her need to associate with whom she pleases. When

Sean wants to heat up the intimacy in their relationship, she pushes him aside by claiming she is not ready to fulfill his desires. She says and does outlandish things, often on whim and without any real cause, when she wants to draw attention to herself.

The Follower (Maggie)

As an Aggressive-Dependent (AD), Maggie Tobin is Liz's best friend and opposite. While Liz is outlandish, Maggie is calm and subdued. Unlike Liz, who enjoys undermining the status quo, Maggie enjoys pleasing and appeasing authority. Maggie is not one to rock the boat and as much as Liz tries, she cannot convince Maggie to join the other side and become a rebel like her. Instead, Maggie is intent on being true to her character—a good person out to help others.

Maggie is a youngster with a mission to please and be accepted. She is not like Liz, in that she does not defy authority or act on her impulses. Instead, she thinks twice before speaking and is always considerate of others. Maggie is a do-gooder in the truest sense of the word, and her prim and proper behavior drives Liz crazy. Maggie will follow Liz on her missions to stir up mischief and mayhem, but she will stop short of actually committing any dirty deed. Maggie is someone who sincerely wants to help Liz.

The Loner (Sean)

As a Passive-Independent (PI), Sean Collins is a bright, underachiever who excels in moodiness. He is a typical teenager in the sense that he drifts aimlessly through school, never really causing trouble or harm but purposefully not exerting himself either. A typical example comes in his pointed response to an assignment for English honors. When asked to write a poem, which reflects a social problem of our time, Sean writes,

> There was a young maid from Brazil,
> who depended each time on the pill.
> It all went just right
> Except Mardis Gras night
> And now there's one more mouth to fill. (p. 40)

Clearly, Sean is out to impress no one with his response to the assignment.

Sean wants Liz to give in to his sexual desires and also to stop her wacky and flighty behavior. He does not really care for her goofiness and annoying hysteria but cannot get her to relax, no matter how hard he tries. Sean sees a hyperactive and confused young woman and knows, deep inside, that Liz's zaniness cannot be abated. Although Sean loves Liz, he recognizes that his love must be kept in check for quieter and safer havens. Sean is not flamboyant or rebellious like Liz; instead, he is a thinker. His thoughts constantly tell him to play it cool, safe, and comfortable. Do not rock the boat, he believes, or at least don't let anyone see you.

The Clinger (Dennis)

As a Passive-Dependent (PD), Dennis Holowitz is the kid that Liz wants Maggie to date. Maggie isn't interested, but upon Liz's intense persistence and Dennis' cloying insistence, Maggie eventually agrees. Soon, Maggie and Dennis are an item. It isn't a match made in heaven, but they eventually learn to enjoy each other's company and grow up a little bit too. Through their relationship, Maggie learns to assert her independence and Dennis learns to build his self-confidence.

Dennis also figures in Sean's life but only tangentially. Dennis and Sean are casual friends. They do not really hang out together, but they respect each other's aloneness and solitude. Sean is more sexually active and aware, but Dennis is more sensitive to a woman's needs. Dennis thinks he is in love with Maggie, and he earnestly tries to win her affection. Unlike Sean, who directs his affection for Liz in a straightforward and abrupt manner, Dennis hints at his feelings and is careful to do nothing to hurt or offend Maggie. In fact, when Maggie does not return his affection, he blames himself. Dennis is not one to point the finger at others.

IS MY KID NORMAL?

Parents invariably get at their wits' end with teenagers who are either too lazy, or too sloppy, or too slow, or too rebellious, or too . . . , and they literally do not know what to do to change their child. These harried parents want earnestly to transform their indolent teenagers into productive adults. No matter what they have tried, they are usually unsuccessful. Why? Their teenager just does not want to change. Simply put, "kids are kids" and are susceptible to the same whims and fancies that adults are except more so. Caught in that nether land between childhood and adulthood, these "pubescent, hormone-raging aliens" inhabit their own world, emboldened with their own rules and passions. The kid who hates the universe collides with the kid who loves to please. Similarly, the kid who wants to hide in his own corner must live with the kid who hides in the corner out of desperate fear. Each has his or her own human dimension.

The intent to characterize human personalities, is not, as Long emphasizes, an attempt to label some teenagers inherently good, and others, inherently bad. To the contrary, Long believes, as I do, that although these labels may sound pathological, the intent is to view people in a purely clinical sense, recognizing that all human beings, and hence, all human types, have qualities which are both positive and negative. No one type is considered better than another, nor does one type predict later success in life. Instead, each personality type is unique, significant, and "normal."

THE FOUR ANCILLARY TRAITS

Long attaches his four defined personality types with four ancillary traits: phobic, impulsive, obsessive-compulsive, and hysterical. These four ancillary traits may attach themselves to the four personality types—Aggressive-Independent (AI), Aggressive-Dependent (AD), Passive-Independent (PI), and Passive-Dependent (PD)—in any singular or multiple combination. As a result, a person can be AI and phobic, AI and phobic and hysterical, or AD and obsessive-compulsive, etc. Long asserts that these four ancillary traits are normal, and most of us function quite well with them in moderation. If, however, they become extreme or exaggerated, then therapy and modification are often required.

Phobic

To be phobic means to have an irrational fear that something will go horribly wrong. Thus, phobic young adults think the worst will happen to them even if circumstances do not warrant such fears. Decision-making becomes difficult because they wrestle with every single possible outcome. Being phobic can be a desirable trait if a person is impulsive but debilitating if the person is indecisive.

Impulsive

To be impulsive means to act in an unpredictable and irrational manner. Impulsive individuals are quick to do things without forethought and planning. Again, impulsive behavior can be both a positive and negative force. Attached to responsible individuals, impulsiveness can result in good-natured fun but attached to irresponsible ones, it can lead to risky and questionable behavior.

Obsessive-Compulsive

To be obsessive-compulsive means to be highly methodical, organized, and fully planned. Obsessive-compulsives enjoy ritualistic behavior and live comfortably in a regimented existence. For quick-thinking, impulsive people, this trait can be calming and soothing; it slows down erratic behavior. Taken to the extreme, however, obsessive-compulsive behavior can result in driven individuals with little outside interests or balance.

Hysteric

To be hysteric is to treat all problems with the same degree of high intensity; everything becomes an excuse for a histrionic moment. Because they are happiest when in turmoil, people with the hysteric trait are born dramatists with little use for the quiet and mundane. They are highly creative and artistic and can become an asset when the situation calls for enthusiasm and color or obnoxious and dangerous when the event calls for calm and level-headed thinking.

THE FOUR PERSONALITY TYPES AND FOUR ANCILLARY TRAITS

All four ancillary traits are present, to a degree, in all human beings. Yet, when attached in large doses to individuals with innate problems, trouble can ensue. Imagine living with, working with, or teaching a teenager who is not only rebellious but hysterical as well. When they got mad, would they throw chairs? Think about a youngster who was both obedient and compulsive. Would they annoy you to death with their constant need to be perfect? Consider a young adult who was so intimidated by adult authority that he or she assumed that all adults were out to get them. How to properly deal with these youngsters is anybody's guess, but by looking at a work of fiction—particularly a YA novel like Zindel's *My Darling, My Hamburger* where these four personality types are neatly drawn—we can begin to find a workable solution towards understanding the human condition.

THE FOUR ANCILLARY TRAITS AS SEEN IN LIZ, MAGGIE, SEAN, AND DENNIS

The four ancillary traits—phobic, impulsive, obsessive-compulsive, and hysteric—are certainly present in Zindel's four literary figures. Liz is both impulsive and hysteric. She vents her anger dramatically and whenever the spirit moves her. Maggie has many obsessive-compulsive tendencies. In her desire to please, she asks what is expected of her and then goes the extra step. Maggie pleases her parents and teachers, making sure that she has accomplished her tasks to the nth degree. Sean, on the other hand, does not obsess. His mood swings are quiet and reserved, but he is given to acting impulsively when confused. Not knowing how to handle Liz, he acts on his passionate desires instead of backing off. When faced with her unintended pregnancy, he ruminates possible courses of action, and then, decides, hastily and without real parental approval, to pay for her abortion. Sean acts quickly to put his troubles behind him. And finally, Dennis demonstrates phobic tendencies. When Maggie rejects him, he assumes that he is to blame for her last minute refusal. Similarly, when reprimanded by his parents, he does not lash back in anger but looks inwardly to see how he can improve himself and his daily habits. He wants to please, and thinks and rethinks how he can improve his meticulous behavior.

Zindel's characters are well drawn, the situation is believable, and the dialogue is smart and sensitive. The work is neither contrived nor didactic. The lessons learned—that growing up requires painful choices—is presented in typical Zindel fashion, with great wit and style. Like Zindel's other works—*The Pigman*; *The Undertaker Has Gone Bananas*; *Pardon Me, You're Stepping on My Eyeball*—there is a clear line of street smartness and funny knowingness which teenagers find readily accessible and enjoyable. Paul Zindel writes with a keen sense of how young people think and feel, and these four young people in particular are most inviting. And a perfect example of what Long believes.

SO WHAT ARE ADULTS TO DO?

In his medical practice, Dr. Long sees many parents and guardians of children of all types and traits who invariably call with desperate questions: "How can I change my child, who is tearing out my heart with his rebellious ways, into a polite and adoring young person? How can I take my perfectionist, driven young daughter and change her into a pliant and easy going adult? How can I take my weak and defensive youngster and make him a strong and aggressive person, like me? How can I save my child?" And to each and every one, Long replies, "You can't." Except for the usual love, patience, and common sense, all any of us can do is try to listen to them and help them to help themselves.

Dr. Long believes that the best way to treat young adults in transition from the teenage years into adulthood is to assume the personality of the young adult in question. If the child is angry and blunt, you return the favor. If the child is dutiful, you be the same. If the child is diffident, you state your demands and then leave. If the child is neurotic, you be nervous and smart. You do not succumb to your nervousness; just acknowledge the young child's right to be nervous and then show them how to handle their uncertainty. In short, you play the wise fool. You will live longer, and so will your teenager.

One Example

Invariably, Dr. Long sees the parents first, not the teenagers, who are frustrated with their children. In one such example, the parents came to Dr. Long because they were upset that their son was not performing well academically. After all, they were always high academic achievers and could not understand what his problem was; they did not know what to do about it. When the father held weekly sessions in their family library on the research topic of the week, his son would typically ignore his father's request, and instead, sit idly reading comic books. Low grades and inattentiveness marked the son's schoolwork. The parents decided to send their "lazy son" to a private boarding school, hoping that the intellectual atmosphere would motivate him to perform. When the parents informed Dr. Long that they were sending their son away, Dr. Long cautioned them not to expect miracles. "More than likely," Dr. Long remarked, "your son is just exhibiting what comes naturally to him—Passive-Independent behavior—and will not suddenly transform into a model student at your request. Instead, he might retreat deeper into his shell."

The parents went ahead and sent their son to boarding school and were delighted to report to Dr. Long that his first semester resulted in a marked improvement in grades. Dr. Long was ready to eat crow, but then the young man in question showed up at his office to announce that he did not want to return to the boarding school; he was lonely, bored, and generally out of sorts. He really wanted to go home, but his parents were committed to having him stay and excel. Against Dr. Long's and the young man's wishes, he returned to the private academy only to turn his passive anger into poor grades and recalcitrant behavior. "In fact," recalls Dr. Long, "the father got a letter from the Spanish professor at the prep school who said he taught for 28 years and had met with so much frustration with the boy that he was taking an early retirement." The young man went home, attended public school (which he wanted to do all along), and began doing good work. Eventually, he grew into a healthy, productive adult, and now works as medical administrator at Dr. Long's university. The moral of the tale: Listen to adolescents; they know what is best for themselves.

Simple advice? Yes. Significant lesson? Absolutely. Teenagers innately know themselves, and, more importantly, their whims and fancies cannot be changed by outside forces. We can provide healthy, suitable, and affectionate environments, but we cannot dramatically alter mood and preference. Long contends that young people, especially teenagers at the height of their hormonal and intellectual powers, are apt to do what they want to do. As parents, as guardians, as clinical social workers, we can only make sure that their actions are safe, legal, and moral. But don't expect to change them! The young man who did not want to go to boarding school is a PI who just wanted to move at his own pace. As much as we would like our children to be in our own image—aggressive, go-getting, studious, straight-A students—the less likely they will be unless it is in their nature. Instead, they will be who they are.

Treating Liz

In *My Darling, My Hamburger*, the four high school seniors are all estranged from themselves and their adult worlds; Liz, Maggie, Sean, and Dennis are coming into their own. As much as we would like to set them on the straight and narrow, we can't. Liz is going to be rebellious because she sees authority figures as obstacles in her way. Listen to what she says: "How dare they say that to me? I'll show them!" Nothing we can do or say will prevent Liz from paving her own way in life, and she will speak openly to those who stand in her way.

When Dr. Long meets young adults like Liz, he enjoys their feistiness and combativeness; he has learned to speak their language. Aggressive-Independent teenagers are usually the first people he sees in his clinical practice because their defiance manifests itself in practically everything they do. Their outward behavior is deliberately troublesome, and their acts of violence and abuse will land them quicker in a doctor's office than any of the remaining three personality types. Dr. Long meets his rebellious young clients head-on. He fights fire with fire. When these angry AIs say they don't want to be with him, he tells them the feeling is mutual but they might as well make the best of it. When AIs say that they think he is old and out-of-touch, he retorts, "You're no beauty either, and I was not the one who invited you to my office. But, since we are together and have a problem to solve, let us do the best we can so we can get it over with and go our separate ways." Dr. Long uses open, direct, and frank language with AIs because he knows that AIs hate wimps. Aggressive-Independents admire strength, and Dr. Long has learned to embody boldness and immediacy. Aggressive-

Independents want to know the bottom line, and Dr. Long says the best advice is to give it to them.

Talking to Liz

Because Liz is an AI, it is best to let her talk until her aggressive tendencies come out. Dr. Long will not chastise or scold her; instead, he will simply talk to her in straightforward and frank terms about her outlandish behavior and the resulting repercussions. He will assume Liz's blunt and aggressive demeanor, showing her, essentially, her mirror image. Consider Dr. Long's approach:

Dr. Long. "Yes, you are angry at your mother and your insensitive stepfather. And yes, you are 'ballistic' because your boyfriend won't marry you even though he knows you were carrying his child. And yes, you are 'outraged' that your best friend told your parents that you had an abortion behind their back. So, what are you going to do to resolve this anger? If you had come to me first, I might not have recommended that you proceed with the abortion, especially by a disreputable doctor. But you didn't, and besides, that is not a decision for me to make. But the point is, you made it, you did it, and your best friend decided to save your life. Perhaps, you should be grateful that she was there, and that she cared enough to defy you. But then again, I can't tell you what to feel or how to act, so you better decide now just what it is you want me to help you do."

Treating Sean

Like Liz, Sean Collins is no mealy mouth. Although as a PI he is not one to defy authority, he is a master at skirting the edges. When Liz confronts him about her pregnancy, he recoils into himself and averts his anger inward in hopes of finding solace in contemplating the issue; he does. Turning to his father for advice, Sean speaks in the third person to further isolate himself from the real victims. Sean does not show anger or resentment, just moodiness and awkwardness in solving the problem. Sean's passive-independent nature defines his actions, leading him to take the path of least resistance. Paying for the abortion allows him to take enough responsibility without having to tell anyone. Sean can continue living in his protective shell relatively pain-free. Passive-Independents avoid confrontations; they prefer, instead, to do their own thing with the least amount of conflict. Sean, in effect, disassociates himself with Liz, so he can continue his life. He does not tell his friends, his parents, or his teachers but cleans up his own mess and moves on.

Talking to Sean

If Sean were to approach Dr. Long, he will be met with the same passive resistance. Dr. Long will not develop an elaborate plan to get Sean to share his range of feelings about Liz, about her abortion, about his not telling his parents, etc. Instead, Dr. Long believes that such needed therapy will come in Sean's own time. No one can force Sean to confront feelings that he has neatly compacted away; instead, it is best to let them surface on their own accord. Passive-Independents do not like to be pushed.

Dr. Long. "Although I do not approve of your hasty actions, like paying for Liz's abortion without parental notification or consent, I cannot condemn your actions. I can only tell you what I feel, and I will only tell you once. Life is complicated; it demands choices. You have made yours, and you will have to live with it. I am saddened by your pain and hope you have the emotional support you need. I am always available to listen whenever you are ready to talk."

Treating Maggie

As an Aggressive-Dependent do-gooder, Maggie Tobin has her own baggage, and Dr. Long is quite aware of her strengths and potential limitations. Maggie is a hard worker and is the kind of person who, as Dr. Long often says, "will not only mow, but trim." Dr. Long believes that the Maggies of the world are to be treasured because ADs are the "people who get the world's work done from day one" but their polite exteriors must be toughened. Throughout the novel, Maggie strives to do the right thing, pushing Liz to do the same. She, of course, fails since Liz has her own agenda and will not be swayed by a vision of righteousness. Inwardly, Maggie knows that too. In an effort to please all, ADs sometimes please none. Maggie's saving grace is that she learned, as a result of her association with Liz, to assert herself.

Talking to Maggie

If Dr. Long were to meet Maggie, he would acknowledge her growing maturity, and would applaud her with all the praise she so richly deserves. Aggressive-Dependents thrive on recognition and reward.

Dr. Long. "Maggie, you should be very proud of yourself for getting Liz the true help she needed when she hemorrhaged after her abortion. It must have been difficult for you to defy Liz in order to do the right thing and tell her parents. And it must have taken a lot of courage for you to rebuke Sean for his sheepish and irresponsible behavior. I hope you realize your strength of character for breaking up with Dennis as soon as you realized that he was not the boy for you. I know you know that it hurt him, but he must learn to deal with his own feelings; you are not responsible for his feelings—only yours. Is there anything that you want to ask?"

Treating Dennis

Sweet, insecure Dennis epitomizes the Passive-Dependent teenager. When Maggie calls to say she will not be going to the prom with him, Dennis does not become incensed or angry; instead, he immediately assumes that it is his fault for some reason. A million thoughts race through his head: "Was it something I said? Is it my face? My hair? My clothes?" Never once does he assume that Maggie is the one who is being a rat, and never once does he consider telling her off. Instead, he sulks. Their first encounter afterwards causes him to retreat deeper into himself. Dennis does not even bother to look her directly in the eye for fear she will hurt him even more. Can you imagine Liz doing that? Liz, by contrast, would tear him apart for daring to turn her down at the last minute. Maggie, on the other hand, would be all over him asking, "Why did you call at the last minute? What did I ever do to you?" Unlike Dennis, Liz and Maggie would not just let something happen. They both would demand reasons immediately—Liz, because she is defiant; and Maggie, because she is goal-oriented. They would not, as Dennis does, sweep their problems under the rug out of fear of retribution.

Dr. Long worries about the Dennises of the world because these goodie-goodies are often too perfect. Dennis never defies authority and is portrayed as having a perfectly idyllic and non-confrontational relationship with his parents. Dennis moves in a bubble that he is afraid will burst. He has such a strong dependency on doing the right thing that he does not confront any true anger or upheaval, except inwardly, and that is not healthy. Usually, PDs are terribly ambivalent and immature. They refuse to grow up because they are unable to make a decision.

Talking to Dennis

Dr. Long rarely sees PDs. More often than not it is their parents who come to his office to express frustration. For Dennis, Dr. Long would recommend that his parents help him, gently and carefully, to make mature decisions. A PD can be easily intimidated so one's speech must be honest, direct, and caring. It is important to convey to Dennis that it is time to make his own decisions or else it is possible that he will never leave home. Dr. Long would tell Dennis, or more likely Dennis's parents, that it is time to move on, to transfer his dependency onto someone else, and to know, that in time, Dennis will find his way.

Dr. Long. "Tell me what you were thinking when Maggie broke your prom date at the last minute. Would you have ever done that to her? How did her actions make you feel? Are there times when there are legitimate reasons for canceling on a person at the last minute? If so, how would you handle the situation? I understand that Maggie has decided to break up with you. Is there anyone else you've ever thought about dating? Let's think of some ways to ask a girl out on a date."

CONCLUSION

The four personality and ancillary traits are all normal. When seen in developing young people, they are just the resultant manifestations of who they are and eventually will become. Teenagers are at the peak of their emotional immaturity. They are full blown versions of what, in later years, will be modified versions of themselves. Thus, a 15-year-old is not the same person she or he will be at 21; instead, that person is a heightened version of the truth and should be treated as such. Patience is the key, urges Dr. Long. Most adolescents, contrary to what parents think, cannot stay moody or hysterical forever. Those with arrested development will require therapy in their adult lives.

Dr. Long's personality theory not only holds deep significance for understanding young people, but also can help teachers better serve young people by designing their classroom lessons accordingly. Dr. Long has defined many of the causes for teacher frustration: their seemingly endless struggle to teach and reach a wide variety of young people. The key is understanding who these young adults are.

So What's with the Title?

By now, you are probably wondering why Paul Zindel entitled his work *My Darling, My Hamburger.* The answer is simple, and it comes in the first chapter. Maggie is busy telling Liz that tomorrow, in school, Ms Fanuzzi is going to discuss sex education. Arousing Liz's curiosity, Liz asks for the advice her teacher gives for stopping guys who want to go too far. "Well," Maggie lowered her voice, "Miss Fanuzzi's advice was that you're supposed to suggest going to get a hamburger" (p. 6).

Ah, the wonderful world of adolescence. Would you want to do it again?

RECOMMENDED READINGS

Fiction

3.01.   Bennett, Cherie. (1994). *Surviving sixteen, number 3: Did you hear about Amber?* New York: Puffin High Flyer. 224 pp. (ISBN: 0–140–36318–1). Middle School (MS).

Amber lives on the wrong side of town but still manages to make everything work for her. She wins a scholarship to a private school, dates the richest and cutest boy, and forms her own dance trio. Yet, life doesn't appear to be as idyllic as it should be. Her falling apart is a touching and amusing account of how young people struggle to discover their values.

3.02.   Blume, Judy. (1987). *Just as long as we're together.* New York: Orchard. 304 pp. (ISBN: 0–531–05729–1). Elementary (E), MS.

In this coming-of-age novel, Stephanie and two of her friends adjust to typical adolescent problems and feelings. Young children will appreciate the reluctance of these 7th graders to express their true feelings about themselves and their emerging sexuality.

3.03.   Blume, Judy. (1986). *Otherwise known as Sheila the Great.* New York: Dell. 119 pp. (ISBN: 0–440–46701–2). E, MS.

A summer in Tarrytown, New York, is a lot of fun for ten-year-old Sheila even though her friends make her face up to some self-truths she doesn't want to admit.

3.04.   Bridgers, Sue Ellen. (1993). *Keeping Christina.* New York: HarperCollins. 288 pp. (ISBN: 0–060–21505–4). High School (HS).

Annie befriends a new girl in school, Christina, who slyly nestles her way into all aspects of Annie's life, including relationships with her best friend and boyfriend.

3.05.   Bunting, Eve. (1986). *Sixth-grade sleep over.* San Diego: Harcourt Brace Jovanovich. 96 pp. (ISBN: 0–152–75350–8). E, MS.

Janey is going on a sleep over in the school cafeteria, but she has one problem—she is afraid of the dark. Other fears expressed by her sleep mates are typical of sixth graders.

3.06.   Cardillo, Joe. (1996). *Pulse*. New York: E. P. Dutton. 200 pp. (ISBN: 0–525-45396–2). HS.

Two senior lovers are at war with a local construction group, which threatens to destroy their favorite nature preserve. As they clash, readers see how personalities can mold opinion.

3.07.   Cleary, Beverly. (1990). *Beezus and Ramona*. New York: Avon. 159 pp. (ISBN: 0–380–70198–X). MS.

This moving and loving story about the trials and tribulations of sibling rivalry involve dueling sisters who eventually come to terms with themselves and their emerging personalities.

3.08.   Cleary, Beverly. (1984). *Dear Mr. Henshaw*. New York: Dell. 133 pp. (ISBN: 0–440–41794–5). E, M.

In his letters to his favorite author, ten-year-old Leigh reveals his problems coping with his parents' divorce, being the new boy in school, and generally finding his own place in the world.

3.09.   Cormier, Robert. (1986). *The chocolate war*. New York: Dell. 191 pp. (ISBN: 0-440–94459–7). HS.

Jerry Renault is forced into a psychological showdown with Trinity School's gang leader, Archie Costello, for refusing to be bullied into selling chocolate for the annual fund-raising event.

3.10.   Creech, Sharon. (1996). *Absolutely normal chaos*. New York: Harper Trophy. 230 pp. (ISBN: 0–064–40632–6). MS.

Thirteen-year-old Mary Lou keeps a journal one summer that chronicles her first experiences with romance, homesickness, and death.

3.11.   Hahn, Mary Downing. (1995). *The wind blows downward*. New York: Clarion. 256 pp. (ISBN: 0–395–62975–6). HS.

Spencer and Lauren were best friends when they were eighth-graders, but now that they're high schoolers, their friendship has cooled. Spencer is moody and self-destructive, and Lauren wants to know why. Their eventual reconciliation leads to a greater understanding of the pain and turmoil experienced by teenagers entering adulthood.

3.12.   Hinton, S. E. (1989). *The outsiders*. New York: Dell. 156 pp. (ISBN: 0–440–96769–4). MS, HS.

Two groups of teenagers, one from the right side of the track and one from the wrong side, take out their adolescent angst with each other.

3.13.   Hinton, S. E. (1989). *Rumble fish*. New York: Dell. 111 pp. (ISBN: 0–440–97534–4). MS, HS.

A junior high school boy idolizes his older brother, the coolest, toughest guy in the neighborhood, and wants to be just like him.

3.14.   Hinton, S. E. (1989). *That was then, this is now*. New York: Dell. 224 pp. (ISBN: 0–440–98652–4). MS, HS.

Sixteen-year-old Mark and Bryan have been like brothers since childhood, but now, as their involvement with girls, guys, and drugs increases, their relationship gradually disintegrates.

3.15.   Hobbs, Valerie. (1996). *Get it while it's hot, or not*. New York: Orchard Books. 182 pp. (ISBN: 0–531–08890–1). HS.

This book chronicles several months in the lives of four 16-year-old California girls who have vowed to be friends to the end. Naturally, things do not run smoothly as the girls confront their own views on sexuality and growing into young adulthood.

3.16.   Horwitz, Joshua. (1985). *Only birds and angels fly*. New York: HarperCollins. 192 pp. (ISBN: 0–060–22599–8). MS, HS.

Danny and Chris, two young teenagers, set down the road to drugs and self-destruction, only to split apart when they begin to see life differently. Danny realizes he must leave Chris's world in order to live; he must establish his own identity.

3.17.   Klein, Norma. (1984). *Angel face*. New York: Viking Press. 208 pp. (ISBN: 0–670–12517–2). HS.

After his father walks out on his slightly crazy mother, 16-year-old Jason, the last child at home, has difficulty adjusting to his mother's increasing desperation.

3.18.   Korman, Gordon. (1986). *Don't care high*. New York: Scholastic. 256 pp. (ISBN: 0–590–43129–3). MS, HS.

Paul Abrams and Sheldon Pryor, two students from "Don't Care High," manage to hatch a wild and farcical scheme to get the most apathetic person in the school elected student body president.

3.19.   LeMieux, A. C. (1996). *Do angels sing the blues?* New York: Avon Books. 215 pp. (ISBN: 0–380–72399–9). MS, HS.

Best friends Boog and Theo are content in making music together, until Carey comes along into Theo's life. Their ensuing relationship shows how personalities can conflict and lead to unexpected trouble and hardship.

3.20.   McFann, Jane. (1995). *Nothing more, nothing less*. New York: Avon Books. 126 pp. (ISBN: 0–380–76636–1). HS.

Mackenzie Paige Cameron believes that falling in love is the key to a successful senior year in high school, but she thinks again when her problems multiply.

3.21.   Myers, Walter Dean. (1988). *Scorpions*. New York: Harper & Row. 160 pp. (ISBN: 0–060–24365–1). MS, HS.

Jamal is 12 years old and fearful of many things: intimidating teachers, school bullies, the police, drug dealers, and his impoverished neighborhood. He must come to grips with whether he is a leader or a follower when his brother asks him to become the leader of the Scorpions, a local gang.

3.22.   Namowicz, Gene Inyart. (1987). *To talk in time*. New York: Four Winds. 156 pp. (ISBN: 0–027–68170–X). MS.

What happens when your shyness is so pervasive you cannot function? This book is a sensitive portrayal of one young man's disability, a shyness so severe it makes him a virtual mute.

3.23.   Naylor, Phyllis Reynolds. (1992). *All but Alice*. New York: Simon & Schuster. 160 pp. (ISBN: 0–689–31773–5). MS.

For Alice, becoming part of the in-crowd at her junior high is a full-time job, especially without a mother or sister to show her the ropes.

3.24.   Paterson, Katherine. (1990). *Jacob have I loved*. New York: HarperTrophy. 244 pp. (ISBN: 0–064–40368–8). MS, HS.

Feeling like a deprived and unloved second, Louise must figure out who she is if she will ever experience the kind of happiness that has always come so easily to her twin sister, Caroline.

3.25.   Rinaldi, Ann. (1996). *Keep smiling through*. San Diego: Harcourt Brace. 188 pp. (ISBN: 0–152–01072–6). MS, HS.

A ten-year-old girl living in middle-class America during World War II learns a painful lesson about growing up and becoming her own person. She learns the beautiful truth that doing what is right is not always easy.

3.26.   Sachar, Louis. (1997). *The boy who lost his face*. New York: Alfred A. Knopf. 198 pp. (ISBN: 0–679–88622–2). MS.

David receives a curse from an elderly woman he has helped his schoolmates attack, and he learns to regret his weakness in pandering to others for the sake of popularity. A new girlfriend helps David become a stronger and more assertive individual.

3.27.   Thomas, Karen. (1986). *Changing of the guard*. New York: HarperCollins. 192 pp. (ISBN: 0–06–026164–1). MS, HS.

Maddy is buoyant, self-confident, and vivacious; whereas, Caroline is the exact opposite. They are drawn to each other and learn that, together, they have much in common.

Nonfiction

3.28.   Ames, Louise Bates, Ilg, Francis L. & Baker, Sidney M. (1989). *Your ten- to fourteen-year-old*. New York: Dell. 346 pp. (ISBN: 0–440–50678–0). HS, Adult (A).

Renowned child-care experts from the Gesell Institute of Child Development take a comprehensive look at peer pressure, sibling rivalry, and sexual awareness.

3.29.   Bauman, Lawrence & Riche, Robert. (1987). *The nine most troublesome teenage problems*. New York: Ballantine Books. 289 pp. (ISBN: 0–345–34290–9). HS.

In a straightforward, easy-to-follow format, the authors explore the nine most common problems that parents encounter with teenagers: sex, loneliness, lying, boredom, bad school performance, no communication, anger, hanging out with a bad crowd, and irresponsibility.

3.30.   Dreikurs, Rudolf & Soltz, Vicki. (1990). *Children: The challenge.* New York: Penguin Books. 335 pp. (ISBN: 0–452–26655–6). HS.

This guide is designed to meet the needs of parents in helping them to develop a consistent approach to raising children in a warm and nurturing environment.

3.31.   Eyre, Richard & Eyre, Linda. (1994). *Three steps to a strong family.* New York: Simon & Schuster. 235 pp. (ISBN: 0–671–88728–9). HS.

Packed with common-sense ideas, practical advice, and hands-on exercises, the Eyres present a helping guide for raising responsible children and making families flourish.

3.32.   Faber, Adele & Mazlish, Elaine. (1982). *How to talk so kids will listen and listen so kids will talk.* New York: Avon Books. 242 pp. (ISBN: 0–380–57000–9). HS.

Based on the work of Dr. Haim Ginott, the authors offer innovative ways to listen and understand children's concerns, to promote cooperation within the family, and to help children obtain a positive self-image.

3.33.   Fenwick, Elizabeth & Smith, Tony. (1996). *Adolescence: The survival guide for parents and teenagers.* New York: D. K. Publishing. 285 pp. (ISBN: 0–7894–0635–7). HS.

Every aspect of adolescence—from the anxiety teenagers feel about making friends and fitting into family crises such as divorce, drug use, or attempted suicide—is sympathetically addressed.

3.34.   Goleman, Daniel. (1997). *Emotional intelligence: Why it can matter more than IQ.* New York: Bantam Books. 352 pp. (ISBN: 0–553–37506–7). HS.

Drawing on groundbreaking brain and behavioral research, Goleman shows the factors at work when people of high IQ flounder and those of modest IQ do surprisingly well. These factors—which include self-awareness, self-discipline, and empathy—add up to one's smartness or emotional intelligence.

3.35.   Hoose, Phillip. (1993). *It's our world, too! Stories of young people who are making a difference*. New York: Little, Brown. 166 pp. (ISBN: 0–316–37241–2). HS.

Profiled here are 14 groups of young people who go against convention and take a stand for what they believe. This is an excellent resource that illustrates young people on a mission who will stop at nothing to accomplish their goals.

3.36.   Joslin, Karen Renshaw. (1994). *Positive parenting from A–Z*. New York: Fawcett. 425 pp. (ISBN: 0–449–90780–5). HS.

This comprehensive guide, arranged alphabetically, is filled with practical solutions to more than 140 child misbehaviors.

3.37.   Miller, Alice. (1997). *The drama of the gifted child: The search for the true self*. Translated by Ruth Ward. New York: Basic Books. 136 pp. (ISBN: 0–465–01690). HS.

Miller takes a fascinating look at how children, particularly those who have suffered at the hands of abusive relationships, manage to adapt and function in a normal world.

3.38.   Rimm, Sylvia. (1995). *Why bright kids get poor grades. And what you can do about it*. New York: Crown Trade Paperbacks. 425 pp. (ISBN: 0–517–88687–1). HS.

Drawing on both clinical research and years of counseling families, Dr. Rimm has developed a six-step program she calls the "Trifocal Model" to help parents and teachers work together to get bright children back on the right track.

3.39.   Rosemond, John K. (1996). *Parent power: A common-sense approach to parenting in the 90s and beyond*. Kansas City: Universal Press Syndicate. 331 pp. (ISBN: 0–8362–2808–1). HS.

This third book in Rosemond's parenting series explains the significance of each stage of a child's development and helps parents anticipate the problems, both typical and not-so-typical, to each stage. Practical advice for solving these problems is also included.

3.40.   Sulloway, Frank J. (1996). *Born to rebel: Birth order, family dynamics, and creative lives*. New York: Pantheon Books. 653 pp. (ISBN: 0–679–44232–4). HS.

Using the work of Darwin and the new science of evolutionary psychology, Sulloway maintains that the primary engine of history is really the nuclear family and its resultant interdynamics. This social historian demonstrates how birth order, genetics, and family influences play a significant role in forming personalities and establishing long-lasting relationships.

REFERENCES

Long, W. A., Jr. (1975). Adolescent maturation: A clinical overview. *Postgraduate Medicine, 57* (3), 54.

Long, W. A., Jr. (1985). The practitioner and adolescent medicine. In *Seminars in Adolescent Medicine*. New York: Thieme-Stratton Publishers, 85–90.

Long, W. A., Jr. (1989). Personality and learning: 1988 John Wilson memorial address. *Focus on Learning: Problems in Mathematics, 11* (4), 1.

Zindel, Paul. (1971). *My darling, my hamburger*. New York: Bantam.

Zindel, Paul. (1983). *Pardon me, you're stepping on my eyeball*. New York: Bantam.

Zindel, Paul. (1983). *The pigman*. New York: Bantam.

Zindel, Paul. (1989). *The undertaker has gone bananas*. New York: Bantam.

CHAPTER 4

Children of Alcoholics in Shelley Stoehr's *Crosses:* Teens + Alcoholic Parents = Problems

Diana Mitchell & Pat Zipper

INTRODUCTION

The National Association for Children of Alcoholics states that "76 million Americans, about 43% of the U.S. adult population have been exposed to alcoholism in the family. Almost one in five adult Americans (18%) lived with an alcoholic while growing up" (p. 3). Children of alcoholics (COAs) "are more likely to be truant, drop out of school, repeat grades, or be referred to a school counselor or psychologist" (p. 3). According to the American Academy of Child and Adolescent Psychiatry (1995, Facts for Families), children in alcoholic families are affected in a variety of ways: They are often unable to have close relationships and are apt to have a variety of problems associated with guilt, anxiety, confusion, anger, depression, and embarrassment. Children know that there is a terrible secret at home.

There are many variables that will play a part in determining how the alcoholism will affect each child: birth order, ethnicity, age of child when alcoholism is at its worst and age of child when treatment is provided, economic status of the family, gender of the child, which parent—mother or father—is the alcoholic or whether both parents are, interactional style of parents, whether or not there are other siblings, whether or not there is abuse, and whether or not there are other supportive adults in the child's life. Despite the many variables, the kids get very destructive messages. The most predominant ones received by children in alcoholic families are, "Don't talk! Don't feel." Children are not invited to discuss the drinking or the problems that result from it and perceive, early on, that no one wants to hear about how they feel. Feelings about the alcoholism are not talked about or acknowledged; they are denied or suppressed. The everyday life of the family is so chaotic and troubled that there is no energy to deal with the problems and concerns that the children may have. As a result, it is impossible for children to develop a clear, stable sense of self. Helplessness and despair usually pervade the family.

ALCOHOLIC PARENTS

Frequently alcoholic parents have come from alcoholic families themselves. They haven't learned the necessary skills for helping their children, and most aren't effective even if they recognize that problems exist. Instead of blaming alcoholic parents in a "what they are doing to their kids" fashion, it is important to remember to focus on what the alcoholism is doing to the family as a unit. These parents are not "choosing" to be alcoholics. In fact, alcoholism is an addiction or disease. Alcoholism, as defined by the National Council on Alcoholism and Drug Dependence, is "a primary, chronic disease with genetic, psychosocial, and environmental factors influencing its development and manifestations. The disease is often progressive and fatal" (p. 1). According to Ostrower (Kaywell, 1993, p. 124), children whose parents are alcoholics have a 50–50 chance of becoming alcoholics themselves. As the disease progresses, there is less choice; the alcoholic begins to *need* a drink. Eventually, the need for alcohol is central to the alcoholic's life and everything else becomes secondary—even the children. Again, it is important to remember that this dysfunction is not a conscious choice by the person or persons involved; it is the nature of the disease.

Effects on Children

Dealing with two parents in a nonalcoholic family is complicated for any child. In an alcoholic family, the child is dealing with two physical parents but emotionally many more. Active alcoholics are very different depending on the relationship to alcohol at any given time. An alcoholic isn't either drunk or sober; it's much more complicated than that. An alcoholic can be hung over and needing alcohol; just beginning to drink and be warm, funny, happy, and caring; or very drunk and irritable, angry, and sometimes violent. Small children cannot be expected to have any understanding of what is going on, and in an effort to avoid feelings of helplessness will determine that the change in the parents is related to something that they have done. The response, then, is that of trying always to do the right thing in order to get a comfortable response from the parents. This strategy, of course, doesn't work and the child becomes hurt, full of despair, frustrated, frightened, and finally full of rage.

Having one alcoholic parent is almost as bad as having two. If one alcoholic parent is in the household, the other parent may be more or less available. Unfortunately, the nonalcoholic parent is usually focused on and reacting to the alcoholic rather than the children. There is the worry about whether or not the alcoholic is drinking, how to stop him or her, and why she or he is drinking in the first place. The preoccupation changes the availability of that parent, and the child cannot depend on either of them. One of the aspects of this situation that is so hurtful to children is that they can never predict how either of the parents will be. Children cannot learn to feel safe when there is no predictable emotional safety and consistency in a family.

CROSSES BY SHELLEY STOEHR (153 pp.)

Synopsis

Fifteen-year-old Nancy deals with her alcoholic parents by participating in the very lifestyle that is driving her crazy; she drinks and takes drugs. Nancy's self-destructive behavior intensifies when she begins deriving pleasure from purging her food and actually cutting herself. Nancy befriends another troubled teen, Katie, and together they spiral downward into an existence dominated by the drive to alter their moods to get away from the emotional pain they don't know how to deal with. Both girls are sexually involved with their boyfriends, who don't approve of the girls' involvement with drugs and cutting. It is obvious that Nancy's inner agony is what forces her to continually hurt herself, but the adults in her life cannot see that Nancy is in need of professional help. Nancy's alcoholic parents can't deal with her because they are so involved in their own problems, and her teachers at school still want to see Nancy as a "good kid" who just needs one more chance. Nancy hears a clear message—no one cares enough to help her. As a result, Nancy's behavior becomes increasingly more outrageous and dangerous until she is hospitalized for repeatedly puncturing her wrists with nails. Nancy's story could be the story of countless teens across the country who cry out for help through their inappropriate behavior.

Nancy's Alcoholic Parents

One of the aspects of alcoholism that is so "crazy making" for kids is when a troubled family looks all right to the school and community. Nancy lives in a household where people on the outside see a two-parent family, both of whom work and apparently love their daughter. Both can operate at a superficial level, and neither is a falling-down drunk. In reality, though, Nancy's father is not available emotionally and her mother is rejecting, judgmental, and shaming. Both parents focus on their own problems and their drinking rather than on Nancy. When Nancy is "good"—a good student and behaving well—everything is okay with them. They are able to ignore her and any needs she might have; they do not have to acknowledge her existence.

Nancy subconsciously tries to get the attention she needs by getting angry and acting out. A lot of outside observers might think that Nancy is overreacting because they don't understand the emotional pain she is experiencing. People who think that way are not aware of the whole picture and might say, "So what's her problem? So what if Nancy's parents drink too much once in a while?" Of course, that really is not the case at all. Nancy has grown up in a situation that has become progressively worse since she was very small. Nancy's parents do not assume their parental responsibilities and probably never have. Because her parents are not emotionally available and have broken their promises, Nancy cannot trust anybody. In effect, Nancy knows that no one is available to help her get through a very difficult time for any kid—adolescence—and she is terrified.

In Nancy's case, neither of her parents is able to validate her pain; in fact, just the opposite happens. Her parents collude by creating a climate that denies the seriousness of their drinking. This denial leaves Nancy with only two alternatives: either join in the denial or try to clarify the confusion and pain that she is experiencing. The process of trying to clarify the confusion and cope with the anxiety goes on, for the most part, on an unconscious level. Hopefully, readers can see that Nancy does not know how to talk about her feelings and is pressured to deny them. This subtle process produces a child who blames herself for the problems while feeling helpless, confused, isolated, and alone.

When Nancy quits being "good," she acts out in progressively more dramatic ways but her parents don't see it. For example, Nancy comes home drunk on her birthday and her parents delude themselves into thinking that it is a one-time thing. In reality, she is drinking every day. Her parents don't see a problem because they are impaired and self-absorbed. As long as Nancy doesn't do anything too outrageous or offensive, they are able to ignore the situation and avoid conflict. As long as Nancy does not disturb them or have any emotional needs of her own, they are fine. The message Nancy gets is that it doesn't matter how she feels.

Nancy almost kills herself before her parents, especially her mother, hear the wake-up call. The situation is especially painful for her mother because she sees herself in Nancy. Nancy's mother also grew up in an alcoholic family and had a very difficult, painful, and stormy adolescence herself. This mother never processed what she experienced as a teenager. Nancy's mother tries to protect herself from the realization that she is doing to her daughter what was done to her by living in denial. No parent makes a conscious decision to be in denial. As a defense mechanism, people automatically protect themselves from what is too emotionally painful to see. When Nancy cried when she was little, her mother would slap her "to give [her] a good reason" (p. 6) to cry. This is a way of not dealing with how her daughter feels. There is a good likelihood that Nancy's mother grew up with those same words used to deny her feelings. In other words, the "Don't talk! Don't feel!" rules were learned by Nancy's mother before she taught them to Nancy. It took Nancy's suicide attempt to break through her mother's denial. It is so sad that most families must experience intense pain and anguish to reach a point that finally pushes them to get professional help.

Finally, Nancy initially does not respond to her mother's offer of help for two reasons. She is very angry and doesn't know how long her mother's support will last. Anger protects us from the more painful feelings of vulnerability, helplessness, abandonment, sadness, disappointment, and hurt. Even after attempting suicide, Nancy has no reason to believe that her mother will consistently be there for her since Nancy has never known what to expect in her life. In Nancy's case, both parents are alcoholic and neither parent is or has been available to any dependable degree. Trust is a major issue for Nancy.

Other Adults in Nancy's Life

Other adults who deal with and react to Nancy are unsure of what to do and are unable to see what Nancy needs. The biology teacher, Mr. Smith, apparently takes Nancy's coming to his class stoned as a personal affront and says, "How dare you come to my class drunk!" (p. 21). Nancy's art teacher, Mr. Lyme, also takes Nancy's behavior personally as reflected by this statement: "How dare you? How do you think I feel?" (p. 59). Like some parents, teachers sometimes see what goes on in their classes as a reflection of themselves and their teaching ability rather than a statement about the kids themselves. It is difficult for us to see another's pain, to see beyond our own issues and the limited information that we have, since our own histories and personal issues color what we see. Misbehavior by a student can feel like a slap in the face, like the student is being disrespectful of the teacher. Often, however, this is not the case at all. More times than not, a student is acting out because of personal reasons and can actually be complimenting the teacher. Ironically, students will sometimes act out in a class where they like and trust the teacher the most; sometimes, it is a cry for help.

By the time she reaches high school, Nancy is depressed, frustrated, angry, and desperate while dealing with the complex developmental tasks of adolescence. When Nancy was younger, her parents' alcoholism was not as severe as when she reaches adolescence. Adolescence is difficult to negotiate psychologically even in the best of circumstances. By high school, many kids are in so much pain that they are acting out all of the time. As her parents' disease progresses and Nancy's symptoms become increasingly visible, astute adults might have picked up that Nancy has serious problems that are not being addressed. Nancy initially was doing okay in school. When her behavior abruptly changes, no one questions why she is suddenly not doing okay. Excuses are made and nothing happens. Even when Nancy's art teacher calls her parents, nothing much really happens to address the source of her misbehavior. Her teachers only try to discipline her, and her parents aren't in any position to pick up on her problems because of their own. Up until then, her parents had simply refused to let her go out on school nights. They felt if they had that kind of outward control over Nancy that everything was okay. It's not until Nancy punctures her wrists with nails that she finally gets the help she has been asking for all along.

Why Teachers Overlook Deviant Behavior

Unfortunately, most teachers are unaware of the "hidden curriculum" or the students' emotional and social issues that are being acted out in school. School is the stage on which kids act out what is going on in other parts of their lives. When Nancy brings the beer to school, it is a loud cry for help, but a lot of teachers simply say, "This is a good kid" and that good kid syndrome is real. If Nancy gets good grades and doesn't act out, teachers tend to overlook other things because they don't see the severity of the problem. Adults who believe that everything is peachy in the world and that kids like Nancy are the exception, make some kids rebel. When kids don't think adults will tell them the truth, they become frightened and anxious, adding to the stress that is already being experienced. Teachers need more instruction on how to understand what they are seeing and what is getting in the way of that child learning. They need access to many more resources within the educational system to deal with these issues.

There isn't a teacher out there who hasn't had contact with a student who engaged in alcohol abuse in some way. Kids with problems can be so easily identified in schools long, long before high school. Some teachers know which kids are in trouble before they start showing it overtly but choose to ignore many problems because there are few—if any—avenues for them to take for action. Teachers can call parents, but if they get no reaction there is little else they can do. There are teachers who would like to help and some would even find ways, but the only channels in place in the system teachers are to deal with are reporting suicide threats and abuse. Nancy responded accordingly.

The controversy about whether a school is a social agency or not has been raging a long time. Many teachers truly believe they are there only to address intellectual and academic issues in school, not their students' personal ones. If these issues could be addressed at school, a lot of kids could be helped before their situations become life threatening. These tough issues often come out in English classes when students are discussing literature and life, but few teachers are trained beyond basic discipline procedures. Teachers can't do both—teach and treat kids' emotional problems—but it seems that the educational system must in some way be able to support these kids through some of it.

It would be nice if there were ways teachers and other students could get therapy for kids who needed it. Teenagers in schools are keenly aware of what is going on with their troubled friends. They know their friends need help, but they keep secrets because they don't think they are empowered to do anything. They could tell an adult, but they don't know *who* to tell. There is no systematic way to deal with drugs and alcohol abuse in school. If teens know an adult they trust, they will usually go to that person. If they don't know such an adult, they try to deal with it themselves. As a result, adolescents are often the only support available for their troubled friends but are not equipped to deal with serious problems. When adults refuse to talk about these issues in school, they seem to be saying, "These are tough issues—too bad. Figure it out on your own."

Some teachers and parents believe that reading controversial or disturbing books is harmful for kids because they might copy the deviant behavior. Actually, it might be beneficial for some kids to see that there are other troubled teenagers, including some who are in more emotional trouble than they are. First of all, there are not any behaviors in this book that troubled kids don't already know about. Second, adolescents whose lives are going along fine don't all of a sudden do something to end up in a juvenile facility. If that happens, something is usually very wrong. Residential treatment centers are full of kids like Nancy. People who do not think Nancy's story is realistic or believe that it doesn't happen very much are not in touch. These people are often the same ones who think that talking about birth control will encourage kids to have sex. Teens often know a lot more than adults think. Teenagers need to know what they want to know and they need to understand and be able to talk about what they see around them and what they experience. Protecting kids from truth is not helpful. Information needs to be carefully presented, with opportunities for discussion. Teachers can make an incredible difference and get to the root of students' misbehavior by being curious and open-minded about what they don't understand. If adults are able to ask what they want to know, teenagers will tell us. There must be an end to the silence.

Nancy's Relationship with Katie

Two dysfunctional people in a crowd seem to seek and find each other just as Nancy and Katie found each other. If Nancy hadn't befriended Katie, she would have found another friend just like her. Nancy needs somebody as dysfunctional as she is for understanding. No one likes to feel totally alone and different. Once she finds Katie, it is like the floodgates open. Katie accepts her for who she is and that is exactly what Nancy needs since she doesn't get that validation at home or from her boyfriend. There is a terrible sense of shame, of being seen as basically defective, that develops in alcoholic families. Nancy feels like a "bad person" and wants a friend who won't judge her no matter what.

Nancy's Relationship with Her Boyfriend Mike

Nancy chooses a boyfriend who has the same ambivalence that she does, a "preppy type" who acts out sexually with her. An astute adult might be curious to know why he chooses Nancy as a girlfriend. Perhaps he has issues of his own that he is expressing in the relationship. In other words, he is conflicted in some way that having Nancy as a girlfriend expresses. People choose friends, boyfriends, or girlfriends for their own psychological reasons. If people were able to understand why they, or in this case Nancy and Mike, make these choices, the choice would make perfect sense. Even though their relationship seems based on sexual behavior, it is clear that Nancy and Mike used to talk a lot and were closer to each other than to any one else at one time. Before Katie, Mike was the one Nancy could talk to, but he didn't approve of what she was doing. Nancy needed somebody not to approve of what she was doing but to accept her anyway. Down deep, she was very frightened at not being stopped.

THE MOTIVES BEHIND NANCY'S UNHEALTHY BEHAVIOR

Sexual Activity

Often early sexual activity can be seen as a symptom of an overall problem. The reason Nancy gets involved sexually at such a young age has little to do with sex and everything to do with her sense of rejection and wanting to be acknowledged and loved. Although Nancy is getting physical affection and some kind of positive experience from her sexual behavior, the sexual relationship isn't an especially healthy one because she lets her boyfriend do whatever he wants to do to her. Nancy shows little concern for herself and what she wants. When Mike breaks up with her, she says she hopes he realizes how difficult it will be for him to find someone who will let him do the things she let him do to her. This statement suggests that she wasn't too thrilled by all of their sexual activities, but she participated just to please Mike and keep him as her boyfriend. This is not to say that she didn't enjoy some of their sexual relationship, but she was evidently doing it for him rather than for her. If anything, her sexual involvement seemed to be a release for all of her pain. There is also a defiant aspect to her sexual acting out as there is with so many adolescents.

Cutting

Unless a person has experienced intense emotional pain, it is difficult to understand Nancy's enjoyment in cutting her arms and making them bleed. For Nancy, "[p]hysical pain is comforting and . . . now it has become a habit. Like the drugs" (p. 1). According to one theory, the cutting produces endorphins or hormones produced by the brain that have pain-killing and tranquilizing ability. Perhaps the cutting relieves some of Nancy's emotional pain. Nancy indicates that the cutting externalizes her pain—it puts the pain outside of her; it becomes something that she can see. In that way, Nancy can focus on something else besides her anguished feelings. She doesn't have other ways to communicate her feelings or her dilemma, even to herself.

The person who cuts is in control by making his or her own pain. Nancy says, "[p]hysical pain relieves mental anguish" (p. 33). She ties it to when she was little and got upset. Think about how her mother used to slap her when she cried: "to give [her] a good reason" (p. 6) to cry. From that childhood experience, Nancy learned that she needs a reason to break down. As an older child, she rationalizes that she cannot cry unless there is a reason so she cuts herself. Her focus is directed on the pain of the cut and not on the inner pain. The cutting then, in some strange way, relieves her pain for awhile.

Bulimia

Nancy's inner pain was so horrible that she also becomes bulimic, which is also related to control. Nancy cannot control how or what she feels, but she can control whether or not she vomits. All of Nancy's self-destructive behaviors are her attempts to change how she feels, to change her mood. Nancy succeeds in changing her mood since the vomiting that occurs with bulimia also releases endorphins. The stress on her body because of this behavior, as well as taking 24 aspirins at a time, may effect her physically in ways that she never considered.

WHAT WE CAN LEARN FROM NANCY'S STORY

Readers can feel Nancy's pain and the tension in her family but may not realize how much Nancy has to teach us all about alcoholism and its effect on families. *Crosses* validates that having alcoholic parents is a serious problem that has multiple effects on the family, especially children. Nancy's behavior, like any human behavior, is not random; it is fueled by something. In Nancy's case, it is fueled by her reaction to the rejection, distrust, shame, neglect, and fear her alcoholic parents have created in her life. Teachers know that some teenagers carry around tremendous burdens at school. When some of them act out, they are not necessarily trying to be "discipline problems" but are acting out their pain, fear, confusion, and anguish. Teenagers, parents, teachers, and therapists can learn a lot from Nancy's story. This book says to kids, "You're not the only one feeling like you do, and you have some legitimate reasons for feeling this way."

Middle and secondary school teachers may be confused and troubled by all of the "acting out" that is done in school. Certainly teachers must get used to a certain level of misbehavior, but it is the attention-getting behavior that goes beyond "normal adolescent angst" that becomes difficult to deal with or understand. For teachers who do not know that the rebelliousness and defiance are not usually a deliberate, conscious choice by the student, dealing with the teenager must be very frustrating. The truth is that "acting out" is often a behavioral way to express the conflicts that the person (of any age) is dealing with. Most people, if given a real choice, would choose to talk about their feelings and conflicts. In the case of alcoholics and their families, all experience negative feelings but do not have a cognitive way to express them in words. Because much of this confusion and turmoil are swirling around at an unconscious level, a person acts out and doesn't even know why. More often than not, students simply cannot tell anyone what is wrong because they don't know themselves.

Nancy frequently expresses concern that she and Katie can get away with anything and seems worried about not being stopped. Again, subconsciously, she desperately wants to be caught and stopped. Nancy wants somebody to do something for the pain she is in and the fear that she experiences. Instead, her family, the other kids, and teachers say, "We'll give you another chance." Sometimes, however, it can be very detrimental to give troubled teenagers another chance. Their problems won't magically disappear, and they interpret the one-more-chance message as "I really get away with everything because nobody cares." When youngsters feel this way, they have a horrible view of the world. Because they can really mess up and put something over on every adult at home and in school, they figure that nobody is either smart enough or has the energy to deal with them. As a result, troubled teenagers eventually begin to feel hopeless since adults can't or won't help them figure it out; there evidently is no way out of their pain. Nancy's problems escalate until hospitalization is necessary, and then she is finally stopped.

NANCY'S TREATMENT

Nancy represents a real kid with real problems. She is an appealing candidate for therapy for many reasons. She is bright and at the end of the book she is motivated to change. Ideally, treatment for Nancy's substance abuse will begin in a hospital where she will receive information about the nature of the disease of alcoholism, will be required to attend group therapy meetings focused on substance abuse, and will involve work with the family as a whole. Part of the educational aspects of the treatment will validate her experiences growing up in an alcoholic family. This will help her to understand that she was reacting to a very troubled environment that no one acknowledged at the time. Although the therapy she receives at this point should be both supportive and educational, Nancy should also experience enough confrontation so that she can see the seriousness of her problems. Nancy's symptoms—alcohol and drug abuse, cutting, disordered eating, depression, poor self-esteem, school truancy, sexual acting out, a major drop in grades in school, cigarette smoking, and her poor relationship with parents—are all manifestation of her alcoholic family. The focus of Nancy's treatment at this point should be on her abstinence and should provide her with the necessary tools to help her stay alcohol and drug free.

Nancy will need individual work for her substance abuse, her depression, her eating problems, and her poor self-esteem. Nancy needs to understand the reasons for her feelings, what caused them, and that she was not alone nor was she solely responsible. Individual therapy will help her sort out her own thoughts, feelings, and sense of self and to clarify what her wishes are for her life. There are developmental losses for children of alcoholics that leave an adolescent without the tools to negotiate adolescence successfully. Children of alcoholics characteristically have no stable sense of self, few relationship skills, no information about how to manage stress or anxiety, no language to talk about feelings or relationship issues, few problem-solving skills, and have little ability to trust what one experiences as truth. Without the appropriate treatment, these adolescents grow to adulthood without the tools to live an emotionally comfortable and healthy life. These are the tools that can be provided by psychotherapy, education, and Alcoholics Anonymous (AA).

When Nancy was no longer acutely suicidal or using drugs, hospitalization would no longer be necessary but a therapist would still have to work with Nancy in an outpatient program. Upon discharge, Nancy should attend several AA meetings a week, continue in ongoing individual psychotherapy, and meet at least weekly with her family in family therapy. Nancy will be helped to understand that she must now be responsible for participating in her own as well as her family's healing.

Her Family's Treatment

To successfully treat alcoholism, we must treat each of the members as well as the family unit. The problems in this family go well beyond the substance abuse and must be dealt with directly. Fortunately, Nancy's family seems ready and motivated for recovery. Nancy's parents' efforts at sobriety are begun out of concern for her. This hopefully indicates that they are each motivated to remain abstinent, to work on healing the related family problems, and mend their relationships with each other.

Family therapy provides members with the opportunity to talk about the problems that they presently have, the painful feelings—anger, guilt, shame, and sorrow—each experienced during the active phases of the alcoholism, and the relationship problems that exist. The therapist can help the family put into words their feelings. Being able to talk about what one feels and experiences is a powerful tool in the healing process. One of the ways that we deal effectively with painful feelings is that we talk about them to someone who is interested, cares, and is involved with us emotionally. The ability to put feelings and experiences into words helps dissipate the pain all by itself. Feelings heard by someone else can have the effect of changing the emotional experience. The feelings can become less painful. This family has a great deal of pain. Each of the people has behaved in ways that they regret or feel shame about. It appears that they have only begun to be open with one another. They have many years of history together during which the substance abuse was active that will need to be talked about. There was no intent to hurt or to ignore, but no one could express even the caring feelings much less the unpleasant ones. Healing can take place as they learn the skills to openly communicate with one another. Alateen and Alanon meetings, for family members and friends of alcoholics, are also helpful for individuals to learn how each was affected by the alcoholism.

Nancy's Prognosis with Treatment

Although Nancy is a pretty disturbed teenager with little to no self-esteem by the book's end, she has a good chance of being happy and healthy because she's dealing with her problems while she is still young. More often than not, adolescents in similar situations usually look like they are doing just fine. They somehow manage to get through college and fall apart later, often in their late twenties. Some people, like Nancy's mother, who also was the child of an alcoholic, never get to the point where they deal with their own pain. They struggle with the alcoholism for the rest of their lives in some form or another and usually pass the problems along to their own children. While Nancy's mother clearly states that she does not want Nancy to be like her, she doesn't know how to help. Nancy's mother, lacks the tools and skills that a parent must have to raise a healthy child. Parenting skills can be developed in individual therapy sessions, and Nancy's mother would certainly benefit from Adult Children of Alcoholics (ACOA) meetings.

Healthy emotional development cannot go on with heavy substance abuse because users stop growing emotionally. Even if the substance abuse stops, the person is still emotionally stuck—at least in some ways—where they were when the abuse started. In other words, people who never address their issues, never grow past them. Bright students might get through the system and graduate, but they can't grow emotionally because they lack the raw material they need to grow. By and large any teenager who starts abusing drugs and alcohol in high school never goes beyond where they were emotionally when they started in high school until they stop abusing. Nancy, for example, was using drugs or alcohol almost every day. Kids like this sometimes just stop. A 25-year-old who was heavily involved in drugs or alcohol at age 15 and then stops using at 25, is emotionally more like a 15-year-old than a 25-year-old. That person is going to have very important issues that have not been dealt with that were there when they started using. One has to open up the pain, deal with it, and stop trying to medicate it away in order to go forward.

CONCLUSION

By the book's end, it is unfortunate that Nancy is still on her own and is struggling to get her life back on track without much support or guidance. Although her mother is more supportive than she has ever been and even denies herself a drink, Nancy now has to deal with Katie's death and her guilt will not go away as fast as this book makes it seem. The psychiatrist helps Nancy in the hospital but not enough. Nancy and her family are prematurely discharged with no tools to deal with any of this. It is obvious that the family does not have the requisite skills or enough understanding at this point to make it.

Growing up in a family with alcoholic parents has deep, long-term negative effects. Alcoholism in a family damages the members in profound ways, actually stunting their emotional growth. Hopefully, those who read *Crosses* and the information provided in this chapter will seek help if necessary. Perhaps teachers will feel better equipped to recognize the source of their students' problems and know where to seek additional help. Since many of the children from alcoholic homes go into helping professions, perhaps teachers who grew up in alcoholic families will feel prompted to get help for themselves! The nonfiction books that follow are recommended to validate the experiences of adolescents, provide information about alcoholism, and to suggest ways to get help.

RECOMMENDED READINGS

Fiction

4.01.   Adler, C. S. (1980). *In our house, Scott is my brother*. New York: Macmillan. 139 pp. (ISBN: 0–127–00140–7). Middle School (MS).

Jodi, a 13-year-old girl, has been living alone with her father since her mother's death three years ago. When her father marries Donna, who brings her son, Scott, into the family, Jodi's life is completely disrupted by her alcoholic stepmother and son.

4.02.   Adler, C. S. (1990). *With Westie and the Tin Man*. New York: Macmillan. 194 pp. (ISBN: 0–020–41125–1). High School (HS).

Greg's mom is an alcoholic. Following his release from jail for shoplifting, he finds she hasn't had a drink in the year he's been gone. Greg has to learn to cope with his mom's new friend and learn to tell the truth.

4.03.   Arrick, Fran. (1984). *Nice girl from a good home*. New York: Bradbury. 199 pp. (ISBN: 0–02–705840–9). HS.

Since he has lost his job, Dory's father has developed a drinking problem while her mother shops compulsively. As the family spins out of control, 16-year-old Dory is unsure of what to do.

4.04.   Birdseye, Tom. (1990). *Tucker*. New York: Holiday. 120 pp. (ISBN: 0–8234–0813–2). MS.

Even when alcoholism doesn't lead to violence and physical abuse, it still has its effects on a family. Just ask 11-year-old Tucker, who lives with his alcoholic father, when his estranged sister decides to visit.

4.05.   Brooks, Bruce. (1989). *No kidding*. New York: Harper & Row. 207 pp. (ISBN: 0–06–020722–1). MS, HS.

In this 21st century society, 14-year-old Sam is allowed to decide the fate of his family after his mother is released from an alcohol rehabilitation center.

4.06.   Bunting, Eve. (1990). *A sudden silence*. New York: Fawcett/Juniper Books. 105 pp. (ISBN: 0–449–70362–2). HS.

It's bad enough when a drunk driver kills Jesse's deaf brother, but then he's faced with the realization that the girl he is involved with is the daughter of the drunk driver.

4.07.   Carter, Alden R. (1991). *Up country*. New York: Scholastic. 256 pp. (ISBN: 0–590–43638–4). HS.

Sixteen-year-old Carl Staggers is doing his best to make something of himself in spite of his alcoholic mother and his involvement with stolen car stereos. Carl sees education as his ticket out of his miserable life, but then his mother is arrested for her drunken behavior and he is placed in the care of an aunt and uncle who live nowhere near his school district.

4.08.   Conley, Jane Leslie. (1993). *Crazy lady*. New York: HarperTrophy. 180 pp. (ISBN: 0–06–440517–0). MS.

A boy struggling in school is helped by Maxine, a crazy lady who drinks. Through this connection, Vernon gets to know and care about Maxine's retarded son. Vernon has trouble believing what this boy has to go through when Maxine is drunk. Vernon hopes he can help, but eventually Maxine can no longer take care of her son.

4.09.   Daly, Niki. (1995). *My dad: Story and pictures*. New York: M. K. McElderry Books. 32 pp. (ISBN: 0–689–50620–1). E, MS.

In this picture book which teens could read to younger siblings, a father's drinking causes pain and embarrassment to his family until he begins to attend Alcoholics Anonymous meetings.

4.10.   Deaver, Julie Reece. (1995). *Chicago blues*. New York: HarperCollins. 170 pp. (ISBN: 0–06–024675–8). HS.

Seventeen-year-old Lissa becomes responsible for her 11-year-old sister whenever her mother goes on a drinking binge. These children are unable to trust what their mother promises, but both desperately want to believe her.

4.11.   Fosburth, Liza. (1990). *Cruise control*. New York: Bantam. 224 pp. (ISBN: 0–553–28441–X). HS.

Gussie "deals" with his mother's alcoholism by getting out of the house and cruising in his mom's car. When his mother has another breakdown, Gussie realizes that the family must face their problems together if they are to survive.

4.12.   Fox, Paula. (1986). *Moonlight man*. New York: Dell. 179 pp. (ISBN: 0–440–20079–2). MS, HS.

Fifteen-year-old Catherine experiences confusion during a visit with her father, a man she has never really known or understood since her parents' divorce. It doesn't take long before Catherine discovers that alcohol is directing his life and messing things up. He is a sensitive, fun, and caring father during the day but a drunken, delirious stranger at night.

4.13.   Grant, Cynthia D. (1992). *Shadow man*. New York: Atheneum. 149 pp. (ISBN: 0–689–31772–7). HS.

Gabe, a charming but reckless 18-year-old alcoholic, smashes his truck into a tree and dies, sending waves of shock and grief through his small town. In alternating chapters told by different narrators—his girlfriend, brother, uncle, father, and others—this powerful book examines the impact of his death. Gabe's voice, through journals he's written for his English teacher, is also heard as he reveals the forces in his family contributing to his alcoholism.

4.14.   Haddix, Margaret Peterson. (1996). *Don't you dare read this, Mrs. Dunphrey.* New York: Aladdin Paperbacks. 108 pp. (ISBN: 0–689–80097–5). MS.

In a journal she writes for her English class, Sarah chronicles what is happening in her life since her abusive, probably alcoholic, father returns home after a two-year absence. Sarah then has to scramble to provide for her younger brother when her mother leaves them alone and without money while she tries to find the husband who once again abandons the family. Secretive and desperate, Sarah finally allows her teacher to read the journal and in this way asks for help.

4.15.   Halvorson, Marilyn. (1986). *Cowboys don't cry.* New York: Dell. 160 pp. (ISBN: 0–440–91303–9). HS.

When Shane was ten, his mom was killed in a car accident caused by his inebriated father, who continues to deal with the pain of feeling responsible for her death. The road to sobriety for his father is not an easy one, and Shane has many difficult times during the years his dad still drinks.

4.16.   Hamilton, Dorothy. (1984). *Joel's other mother.* Scottsdale, PA: Herald Press. 120 pp. (ISBN: 0–8361–3355–2). MS.

Joel used to be proud of his mother, but everything changes when she becomes an alcoholic. Joel is so ashamed of her that he no longer lets anyone come over to his house, not even his best friend. Finally, Joel unknowingly does something that helps his mother see herself as others see her.

4.17.   Hautman, Pete. (1996). *Mr. Was.* New York: Simon & Schuster. 216 pp. (ISBN: 0–689–81068–7). HS.

Jack accompanies his mother to visit his dying grandfather, a man he has never known. On his deathbed, Jack's grandfather tries to strangle him. Before the funeral, Jack dreams of a door to the past and begins to search for it in his grandfather's house. Although he finds the door, Jack waits to open it until horrifying events in his life involving his alcoholic father prompt him to look inside.

4.18.   Howe, Fanny. (1987). *Taking care.* New York: Avon Flare. 160 pp. (ISBN: 0–380–89864–0). HS.

Sixteen-year-old Pamela has decided that "if you can't beat them, you might as well join 'em." Pamela, like her alcoholic parents, has a drinking problem. Pamela learns by chance that the choices she makes, she makes for herself.

4.19.   Kehret, Peg. (1991). *Cages*. New York: Dutton Children's Books. 160 pp. (ISBN: 0–525–65062–8). MS.

Being raised by an alcoholic stepfather has its negative effects on Kit. After being caught shoplifting, Kit is ordered to perform community service as part of her sentence. Kit helps in an animal shelter where she learns some things that only animals can teach a person.

4.20.   Koller, Jackie French. (1995). *A place to call home*. New York: Simon & Schuster. 250 pp. (ISBN: 0–689–80024–X). HS.

Anna is the typical older child of an alcoholic parent who assumes responsibility for the family when necessary. When Anna's mother disappears again, Anna assumes she's on another drinking binge and makes plans to stay home from school to care for her 7-month-old brother and 5-year-old sister. When Anna discovers her mother is dead, she hides the fact for fear of what will happen to the three of them. Anna demonstrates that she has learned well that secrets must be kept.

4.21.   LeMieux, A. C. (1996). *Do angels sing the blues?* New York: Avon Books. 215 pp. (ISBN: 0–380–72399–9). MS, HS.

Boog and Theo are best friends when they are kids, and their relationship gets even tighter when they play in a band together in high school. Theo's heart is captured by Carey, a girl who dresses very differently, and Boog tries not to dislike her in spite of the fact that she has come between him and Theo. After a tragic death, there is the realization that Carey is actually a very troubled young woman mainly because of her alcoholic father.

4.22.   Levy, Marilyn. (1988). *Touching*. New York: Fawcett. 165 pp. (ISBN: 0–449–70267–7). HS.

Eve's father is an alcoholic, and her mother deserted the family to become a "porno queen." Her father is generally okay when he is sober, but life gets pretty intolerable when he's drunk and that's when Eve stays at a friend's house. The night her father in a drunken stupor mistakes her for her mother and approaches her, is the night that Eve decides she must leave for good.

4.23.   Lynch, Chris. (1996). *Mick (blue-eyed son #1)*. New York: Harper-
Collins. 146 pp. (ISBN: 0–06–447121–7). HS.

Mick, at 15, starts questioning the ways of his family and the us-
against-the-world attitude his Irish, blue-collar neighborhood has always
displayed. Mick's parents are usually in an alcohol-induced haze, and his
older brother Terry enjoys terrorizing anyone who is not white. Mick takes a
new look at the alcohol his family consumes, the prejudices they display,
and the cruelty of his older brother.

4.24.   Lynch, Chris. (1996). *Blood relations (blue-eyed son #2)*. New
York: HarperCollins. 216 pp. (ISBN: 0–06–447122–5). HS.

Life for Mick has become increasingly intolerable. He is beaten up
and bloodied by his Irish comrades for mixing with people who aren't Irish
or white and thus not part of the "family." His own drunken brute of a
brother, Terry, assaults Mick when he refuses to be a part of the drinking,
partying scene. Mick eventually moves in with his best friend's family
where he has stayed over the years when his alcoholic parents forgot about
him. His friends Toy, Sully, and Evelyn continue to help him in the hope that
Mick can get his life together.

4.25.   Lynch, Chris. (1996). *Dog eat dog (blue-eyed son #3)*. New York:
HarperCollins. 136 pp. (ISBN: 0–06–447122–5). HS.

Because Mick just cannot believe that no one in his alcoholic family cares about him, Mick once again becomes entangled in his family's
mess. Now Terry is into finding dogs to fight other dogs to the death. In a
shocking and brutal ending, Mick finds out what he needs to know about his
family in order to move on with his life. This series shows the hold that alcohol and clan-like approval can have on people's ability to remain mired in
their narrow-mindedness.

4.26.   Marino, Jan. (1991). *The day that Elvis came to town*. New York:
Little, Brown. 208 pp. (ISBN: 0–316–54618–6). MS.

Set in the Sixties in Georgia, Wanda copes with her alcoholic father
by befriending a boarder who is a jazz singer.

4.27.   Mazer, Norma Fox. (1997). *When she was good*. New York: Scholastic. 234 pp. (ISBN: 0–590–13506–6). HS.

Em's divorced father is an alcoholic, her mom can barely hold her life together, and her older sister is mentally ill and violent. When their dad remarries, 18-year-old Pamela drags Em away so they can live together on their own. Em thinks she's finally free when her sister suddenly dies, but then she has to learn how to cope with Pamela's voice that Em carries in her head.

4.28.   McAfee, Carol. (1992). *Who's the kid around here, anyway?* New York: Ballantine Books. 153 pp. (ISBN: 0–449–70411–4). MS, HS.

By 16 years of age, Maddie has become an enabler to her mother's alcoholism by assuming the roles of mother to her brothers, caretaker of her father, and maid of the house. When Maddie wins the award of her dreams and no one in her family gives her any support, she becomes depressed and engages in self-destructive behavior. With the help of a savvy guidance counselor and a disaster which motivates her mother to seek help, Maddie overcomes her enabling behavior and starts assuming responsibility for her own actions.

4.29.   McKenna, Colleen O'Shaughnessy. (1992). *The brightest light.* New York: Scholastic. 191 pp. (ISBN: 0–590–45347–5). MS.

Anticipating the best summer of her life, 16-year-old Kitty begins a full-time babysitting job and becomes involved with a family torn apart by alcoholism.

4.30.   Osborne, Mary Pope. (1986). *Last one home.* New York: E. P. Dutton. 180 pp. (ISBN: 0–8037–0219–1). MS.

Bailey's mother left her family three years ago to be institutionalized for alcoholism and now lives in Florida. Now that Bailey's father is about to remarry, 12-year-old Bailey begins having temper tantrums and behaving like a small child.

4.31.   Reading, J. P. (1989). *The summer of Sassy Jo.* New York: Houghton. 182 pp. (ISBN: 0–395–48950–4). MS.

Sara Jo is spending the summer with her estranged mother, Joleen, who abandoned the family when Sara Jo was five. Joleen was once an extremely depressed alcoholic who could not even take care of herself much less her daughter. Joleen is a recovering alcoholic who wants to win her daughter's love back. Slowly this happens but not without pain and much explanation.

4.32.   Reaver, Chap. (1994). *Bill*. New York: Delacorte. 216 pp. (ISBN: 0–385–31175–3). MS.

Jessica lives alone with her father in the backwoods of Kentucky. Jessica's only companion is her dog, Bill, since her father is gone on frequent trips to distill and sell bootleg liquor. Because her father will not stop drinking and making moonshine, he is caught and jailed and Jessica must focus on changing the circumstances of her own life.

4.33.   Rodowsky, Colby. (1994). *Hannah in between*. New York: Farrar, Straus & Giroux. 152 pp. (ISBN: 0–374–32837–4). MS, HS.

Hannah knows her mother is drinking too much. She has found the liquor bottles her mother has hidden around the house and has seen her mother make a fool of herself in front of strangers. What Hannah doesn't know is what to do about it.

4.34.   Stevenson, James. (1995). *The bones in the cliff*. New York: Bantam Doubleday Dell. 119 pp. (ISBN: 0–440–22032–7). MS.

Eleven-year-old Pete is required by his alcoholic father to meet every ferry boat that comes to the island. In that way, Pete can warn him if a bad man comes to kill his father. Pete, as a child of an alcoholic, knows he can expect little from his father and is very self-sufficient.

4.35.   Wagner, Robin S. (1975). *Portrait of a teenage alcoholic*. New York: Ballantine Books. 120 pp. (ISBN: 0–345–31165–5). HS.

Sarah is a 15-year-old alcoholic who has been drinking for two years because of difficulties resulting from her parents' divorce. Sarah resents her stepfather and drinks to feel better about things, especially since she sees him and her own mother drinking practically every night. Eventually, she begins to do things that are destructive to herself and people around her. No one, especially Sarah, wants to admit that she has a drinking problem until she is hospitalized after a bash. Help is available but is effective only if she and her parents are willing to acknowledge the problem; Sarah eventually does.

4.36.   Winthrop, Elizabeth. (1978). *Knock, knock. Who's there?* New York: Holiday House. 192 pp. (ISBN: 0–823–40337–8). HS.

As two boys mourn the death of their father, their mother seems to be slipping out of touch with reality. The boys learn about her longtime problem with alcoholism that gets much worse after the father's death. The sons seek help for her, but she refuses the help that threatens to break up the family.

4.37.   Wood, June Rae. (1994). *A share of freedom*. New York: Putnam. 256 pp. (ISBN: 0–399–22767–9). MS.

Thirteen-year-old Freedom struggles to deal with a new family situation when her alcoholic mother is sent to a rehabilitation center. Little does she know that in spite of the difficulty of living with her arch enemy while her mother is away, one of her dreams will come true—to know the identity of her father.

Nonfiction

4.38.   Anderson, Louie. (1989). *Dear dad*. New York: Viking Penguin. 209 pp. (ISBN: 0–670–82939–0). HS.

In this series of letters written to his alcoholic father, comedian Louie Anderson explores the pain and guilt of living with an alcoholic parent. Often humorous, always painful, the letters deal with the feelings the author buried for years.

4.39.   Black, Claudia. (1987). *It will never happen to me*. New York: Ballantine. 183 pp. (ISBN: 0–345–34594–0). HS.

Written for adult children of alcoholics, three chapters are especially pertinent to teens: Chapter Two focuses on the roles different members of the family play, Chapter Three focuses on the "don't talk, don't trust, don't feel" syndrome and Chapter Five focuses on children who live with alcoholics.

4.40.   Coffey, Wayne. (1988). *Straight talk about drinking: Teenagers speak out about alcohol*. New York: New American Library. 164 pp. (ISBN: 0–452–26061–2). MS, HS.

Fifty alcoholic teenagers or teens living with alcoholic family members share their insights about this substance that "pollutes" the body and destroys the mind. Facts about the physiological and psychological effects of alcohol as well as an explanation on how teens with alcoholic parents can "help by not helping" are also included.

4.41.   David, Jay. (Ed.). (1994). *The family secret: An anthology.* New York: Morrow. 263 pp. (ISBN: 0–688–12067–9). HS.

Although alcoholic parents die early and their children are commonly abused, children of alcoholics are prone to abuse alcohol and drugs themselves. Information on how families hide the disease from others is also provided.

4.42.   Hall, Lindsey & Cohn, Leigh. (1988). *Dear kids of alcoholics.* Illustrated by Rosemary E. Lingerfelter. New York: Gurze. 96 pp. (ISBN: 0–936077–18–2). E, MS.

Aimed at the seven- to ten-year-olds, this story is told in first person by the young son of an alcoholic. The story is a blow-by-blow description of the progress of the child's father from an abusive man to a recovering alcoholic. The intervention in which the family members confront the father is carefully described.

4.43.   Hyde, Margaret O. (1988). *Alcohol: Uses and abuses.* Hillside, NJ: Enslow Publishers, Inc. 96 pp. (ISBN: 0–89490–155–9). MS.

Much background is provided about alcohol, but the chapter on children of alcoholics is especially helpful. Information is also provided about where to get help.

4.44.   Langsen, Richard C. (1996). *When someone in the family drinks too much.* New York: Dial Books. 32 pp. (ISBN: 0–8037–1687–7). E, MS.

This book explains the signs of alcoholism and the emotions one might feel living in a home where someone suffers from this addiction. The author gives advice on how to cope with the disease and suggests ways to get outside help. Use of teddy-like bears helps distance readers from their own emotionally charged situations at home.

4.45.   Leite, Evelyn. (1987). *Different like me: A book for teens who worry about their parents' use of alcohol and drugs.* Minneapolis: Johnson Institute Books. 110 pp. (No ISBN; privately published). HS.

Suggestions and advice for teens with alcohol- or drug-dependent parents are offered in this book, which helps teens recognize they are not alone in their struggles and that help is available for them.

4.46.   McCoy, Kathy & Wibbelman, Charles. (1996). *Life happens*. New York: Berkley/Perigee. 224 pp. (ISBN: 0–399–51987–4). HS.

Although this book focuses on the feelings and emotions involved in many kinds of common crises, one of the topics covered is having alcoholic parents. Since this book reduces each subject to manageable proportions without oversimplifying, it is particularly effective.

4.47.   McFarland, Rhoda. (1990). *Coping with substance abuse*. New York: Rosen. 160 pp. (ISBN: 0–8239–1135–7). HS.

McFarland, a certified alcoholism and drug abuse counselor, looks at the effects of chemical abuse on the body, the person, the family, and society. She is especially strong in discussing the implications for the family when a parent is addicted. Her exploration of the different roles children may take—hero, scapegoat, mascot, lost child—is especially insightful.

4.48.   O'Sullivan, Carol. (1989). *Alcohol*. San Diego, CA: Greenhaven Press. 22 pp. (ISBN: 0–89908–634–9). E, MS.

The book describes different points of view on issues involving alcohol. The most helpful chapter for teens is one called "Alcoholism Is a Disease" which explains the physical and emotional effects of alcohol.

4.49.   Porterfield, Kay Marie. (1985). *Coping with an alcoholic parent*. New York: Rosen Publishing Group. 134 pp. (ISBN: 0–8239–0662–0). HS.

Written for a teenage audience, the author addresses the problems of being raised by an alcoholic parent. Teenagers who have an alcoholic mother or father often feel trapped, guilty, and angry. The reader is given helpful information on how to understand and deal with the numerous problems while growing up in such a family.

4.50.   Rosenberg, Maxine B. (1988). *Not my family: Sharing the truth about alcoholism*. New York: Bradbury. 97 pp. (ISBN: 0–02–777911–4). HS.

Eight children and six adults tell what it is like growing up in the shadow of alcoholism. Based on real-life experiences—from the shocking news to attempts at denial and escape to lessons learned—these revelations provide hope, encouragement, and solutions.

4.51.   Ryerson, Eric. (1985). *When your parent drinks too much: A book for teenagers.* New York: Warner. 168 pp. (ISBN: 0–446–14692–6). HS.

Ryerson shows how family members may unintentionally aid the alcoholic in getting liquor, how to stop that behavior, and how to find ways to detach oneself from someone else's problems. As the son of an alcoholic, the author explores the disease of alcoholism and the limits of responsibility that a teenager has for that disease.

4.52.   Scales, Cynthia. (1990). *Potato chips for breakfast: The true story of growing up in an alcoholic family.* New York: Bantam Books. 192 pp. (ISBN: 0–553–28166–6). HS.

Scales tells what it was like surviving in a family where both parents were alcoholics. The message is clear: Children do not have to wait for their parents to stop drinking before they can help themselves to a better life.

4.53.   Shuker, Nancy. (1990). *Everything you need to know about an alcoholic parent.* New York: The Rosen Publishing Group. 64 pp. (ISBN: 0–8239–1076–8). MS.

This short book offers advice on how to deal with an alcoholic parent and where to go for help so children no longer feel alone and without hope.

REFERENCES

American Academy of Child and Adolescent Psychiatry. (1995, November). *Facts for Families, 17.*
Facts about COA's. (1995, November). In *National Association for Children of Alcoholics.* [Online]. Available: www.health.org/nacoa/coa3.html [1997, May 5].
Joint Committee to Study the Definition and Criteria for the Diagnosis of Alcoholism. Definition of Alcoholism. (1990, February 25). In *National Council on Alcoholism and Drug Dependence.* [Online]. Available: www.ncadd.org/defale.html [1997, May 5].
Kaywell, Joan F. (1993). *Adolescents at risk: A guide to fiction and nonfiction for young adults, parents, and professionals.* Westport, CT: Greenwood Press.

CHAPTER 5

Delinquency
and Family Conflict

Barbara L. Stanford & Roger D. Herring

INTRODUCTION

Although adolescents are becoming increasingly involved in delinquent activity, fortunately it is only a relatively small number of them who are serious or repeat offenders. Youth under the age of 21 account for about 30% of police arrests in the United States (U.S. Department of Justice, 1991). This number does not, however, reveal how many youth have committed crimes but have not been caught, how serious their crimes are, or whether many or few are responsible for them (Henggeler, 1989).

The lay perception is that most of these crimes are committed by males with a childhood history of antisocial behavior. Indeed, teenage females accounted for 25% of all juvenile arrests in 1995 according to a study conducted by the Office of Juvenile Justice and Delinquency Prevention analyzing female crime from the 1980s through 1995 (Hedges, 1996). The same study, however, also revealed that for every 100,000 females (ages 10 to 17), 121 were arrested for a violent crime compared with 786 boys. Boys may commit more crimes, but the rate of female youth crime has grown faster than that of male arrests. Young women are joining male gangs as subsidiary members and also forming all-female gangs. With the teenage population expected to rise 17% in the next decade and the trends of juvenile delinquency expected to increase accordingly, the prevention and remediation of this population deserves national attention.

I would like to thank my graduate students, Carmelita King, Malinda Pitts, and Derek Groff for assistance with the annotations.

CAUSATIVE FACTORS OF JUVENILE DELINQUENCY

Causative factors contributing to acts of juvenile delinquency can be found within two primary areas—family and peers. Even these two areas of influence are developmentally connected. Other factors include other non-peer and nonfamilial influences. A brief discussion of these factors follows.

Effects of Family Environment

A consistent factor related to delinquency is a family environment low in warmth, high in conflict, and characterized by lax and inconsistent discipline (Snyder & Patterson, 1987). Such forms of child rearing promote antisocial behavior. Research indicates that the path to chronic delinquency unfolds through the following steps (Patterson, DeBaryshe, & Ramsey, 1989):

Step 1:   Early childhood is characterized by a conflict-ridden home with lax and inconsistent disciplinary patterns, generally resulting in the child displaying conduct problems.

Step 2:   Middle childhood is characterized by rejection by normal peers and academic failure. The child sees commitment to deviant peer groups as the only viable alternative.

Step 3:   Adolescence is characterized by delinquency and membership in a violent gang without appropriate intervention.

Hence, the substantive causes for adolescent gang membership are primarily found within the family. If emotional and social needs of adolescents are not met through interpersonal relationships in the family, youths may turn to the gang to fulfill status needs that would otherwise go unfulfilled (Rice, 1993).

Effects of Peer Pressure

Peer conformity is greater during adolescence than at younger or older ages, and adolescents are most likely to surrender to peer pressure for antisocial behavior (Brown, Clasen, & Eicher, 1986). Interestingly, most adolescent peer pressures do not conflict with important adult values. Peers have the greatest influence on short-term, day-to-day matters; whereas, adults have more impact on long-term values and educational plans. Young people who feel worthwhile are less likely to succumb to peer pressure. In addition, authoritative child rearing, which fosters high self-esteem, social-moral maturity, and a positive view of parents, is related to greater resistance to unfavorable peer pressure (Baumrind, 1991).

Nonfamilial and Nonpeer Factors

Factors related to chronic delinquency include minimal verbal skills, poor school performance, peer rejection in childhood, and membership in antisocial groups. Social class and ethnicity are also strong predictors of arrest records; however, these factors are somewhat related to teenagers' self-reports of biases in the juvenile justice system. Specifically, low income, ethnic minority youths tend to be arrested, charged, and punished more often than middle-class, European-American and Asian youths (Fagan, Slaughter & Hartstone, 1987).

Nonfamilial or nonpeer factors also influence the adolescent's choice of antisocial gang membership and delinquency. Schools that fail to meet appropriate developmental needs have student populations that display higher rates of crime, even after other influences are controlled (Hawkins & Lam, 1987). Such schools are characterized by large classes, rigid rules, and poor-quality instruction. Poverty-stricken areas with high crime rates, fragmented community ties, and adult criminal subcultures also contribute to delinquency (Berk, 1993; Hawkins & Lam, 1987).

COMMON WARNING SIGNS OF DELINQUENCY

The following warning signs of delinquency have been adapted from Woititz's (1995) *Healing Your Sexual Self*:

- **Education:** begins to take school work less seriously and ends up with increasingly poor grades, increased suspensions, expulsions, and even dropping out of school; skips classes and does not complete homework assignments; becomes disinterested and gets angry at teachers.
- **Social:** has a change in friends or becomes isolated from friends; avoids people (not just friends) who are usually encountered; ignores family members; becomes aggressive, obnoxious, provokes arguments, and picks fights with family and friends to get them to leave; associates with younger children.
- **Drugs and Alcohol:** begins using drugs and alcohol which impair one's ability to think clearly and rationally (this tends to quiet one's conscience); usage of intoxicants increases, possibly to daily use; starts spending needed money on drugs; has blackouts; uses alone; and sells drugs.

- **Leisure:** has never developed appropriate leisure skills and activities; has not participated in any hobbies or interests that were important; leisure activities include excessive TV, drinking, and driving aimlessly around; avoids social activities and family.
- **Health and Physical Appearance:** does not keep up hygiene; dresses sloppily and wears the same clothes for days; eats little or just eats junk food, losing or gaining a lot of weight.

PREVENTION AND REMEDIATION

The ideal situation would be that all delinquent behavior could be prevented with appropriate and multiple interventions. Sadly, that is not currently the reality of this social dilemma. Consequently, educators and parents have to be prepared to help those adolescents who succumb to delinquent behaviors.

Preventive Efforts

Any effort to combat adolescent delinquency gang membership needs to emphasize prevention. McEroy (1990) maintains that some measures to combat gang activities have failed and some have even made matters worse. Practices that have not worked include "get-tough" law enforcement measures, increased police presence on school grounds, strong suspension programs, attempts to suppress gang involvement, and refusals to confront gangs. McEroy's alternatives include creating opportunities for gang members to transfer allegiance and loyalties to more acceptable groups, involvement in other extracurricular activities that provide success beyond the classroom, peer-assisted programs where select students receive guidance and training in helping peers, and gaining access to gangs by having storefront schools on their own turf.

Characteristics of Effective Programs

The following characteristics of effective programs have been adapted from Manning and Baruth's (1995) *Students at Risk*. Effective programs

- involve law enforcement officers working cooperatively with school officials, community leaders, and social service agencies.
- provide for law enforcement officers teaching, counseling, and advising students about illegal activities and also provide opportunities to participate in athletic events and other school functions.

- incorporate the use of technology and developmentally correct computer software to make at-risk students aware of appropriate and inappropriate behaviors.
- emphasize social skills as well as academic skills.
- employ educators with suitable professional backgrounds who want to work with children and adolescents.
- involve parents and families in planning and implementing appropriate suitable awareness and preventive experiences.

Other preventative strategies include identifying students who may be predisposed to getting in trouble, assisting parents in learning more effective parenting skills, helping parents to use authoritative parenting techniques, ensuring more effective education, and providing economic and social conditions necessary for healthy development (Rice, 1993). Prevention must begin early and be incorporated at multiple levels of development. When interventions are required or needed, they must address the multiple aspects that contribute to antisocial behavior or they are generally ineffective (Henggeler, 1989). Interventions that are lengthy, intensive, and use problem-focused methods that teach cognitive and social skills needed to overcome family, peer, and school difficulties are recommended (Goldstein, 1990).

Educators must remember that positive behavior changes typically do not last once youths return to the settings that contributed to their difficulties in the first place (Quay, 1987). Consequently, prevention strategies need to revitalize community and governmental efforts to improve socioeconomic opportunities. For example, a feasible intervention could be placing antisocial youth into groups of prosocial peers (such as day camps) where their behavior is influenced positively.

Remediative Efforts

A plethora of strategies exist for mental health specialists and educational personnel to remediate delinquent youth. Individual, group, and family therapy avenues are options. Long-term residential facilities with clinical psychological testing are other alternatives. Confrontation therapy will be needed for families in extreme denial, excessive blame, and inconsistencies. The delinquent adolescent must own responsibility for the behavior and its effect(s) on the victim(s). Pre-offense patterns, feelings, behaviors, and actions should be emphasized. In addition, family therapy should focus on anger control, communication skills, social skills, motivation, victim empathy, and safety plans (Carnes, 1993).

Social Interactions

Counselors and other helping professionals can assist students who are having social difficulties by arranging classrooms or small group situations in ways that will help them improve their social skills. Peer interaction can be encouraged through ethnically- and culturally-integrated small groups, toys and materials involving more than one ethnic child, and activities such as puppets and sociodramatic play (Herring & Runion, 1994). Ethnic minority students can be taught specific behaviors that will help them interact positively with peers. In particular, the use of cooperative learning and peer-tutoring activities have proven to increase peer acceptance and reduce rejections among these students (Slavin, 1995).

Bibliotherapy

The process of bibliotherapy is designed to help individuals solve problems or better understand themselves through their responses to literature or media (Bodart, 1980). Usually students at risk are less apprehensive about discussing situations involving storybook characters than about discussing actual situations that involve themselves. Bibliotherapy provides them the opportunity to explore their own feelings while discussing story outcomes, behavioral consequences, and alternative behaviors (Webb, 1992). Borders and Paisley (1992) appraise the role of bibliotherapy in this way:

> Counselors are ideal facilitators for discussions of stories, since they have professional skills in active listening, clarification of content, and reflection of feeling. The power of the literacy transaction between children and story, coupled with the interaction between a skilled counselor and children, has the potential to become bibliotherapy at its best. (p. 138)

An excellent example of the use of bibliotherapy with delinquent adolescents exists in S. E. Hinton's (1989) *The Outsiders.*

THE OUTSIDERS BY S. E. HINTON (156 pp.)

Synopsis

Fourteen-year-old Ponyboy Curtis is a parentless adolescent who lives with his two older brothers, 16-year-old Soda and 20-year-old Darry. Since their parents' deaths, Darry and Soda have tried to provide financial support to enable Ponyboy to be the one to stay in school. Their friends include Two-Bit, an almost-19-year-old wisecracker who shoplifts and carries a switchblade; 16-year-old Johnny, who's the gang's pet with a violent home life; Steve, a 17-year-old car mechanic and racer; and Dally, a 17-year-old tough guy with a police record. Together they belong to the Greasers, poor East-side boys who often rumble with the Socs (short for Socials), the jet set of the rich West-side kids. Ponyboy's loyalties to his brothers and the Greasers are challenged by the harsh realities of gang life, and he is caught in violence between the two gangs. When Johnny knifes and kills a Soc who was drowning him, he and Ponyboy flee and go into hiding.

Themes

At-risk adolescents may be able to identify with several of the common themes of juvenile delinquency apparent in this story: (1) Ponyboy's efforts to stay in school despite pressures from gang members; (2) the premature parenting role that prevents Ponyboy's brother Darry from attending college on a football scholarship, and Darry's concurrent fear of losing another person he loves; (3) the two nonnegotiable rules of the gang, stick together and don't get caught; (4) the dangers of hero worship as exemplified by Johnny's relationship with Dally; (5) the fact that all adolescent gangs have problems regardless of social class status, as revealed by Cherry; and (6) the ultimate reality of dealing with three unnecessary deaths within a very brief time.

Intervention Possibilities

A teacher or counselor could take this story and have students identify the central themes and causative factors throughout the plot and discern how the plot might have shifted if some character had reacted differently. At-risk students could list the negative and positive attributes of gangs and select those qualities of the characters that most resemble their own personalities and actions. The realization that the story's characters and plot resemble their own lives is possible. Ultimately, the goal is for at-risk students with a propensity for delinquent behavior to identify with the characters and gain insight by which to change their own antisocial and negative behaviors.

Therapy for the Outsiders

Could bibliotherapy have made a difference for the outsiders? Would it have made a difference to them to have read and discussed books about people and situations similar to their own? Perhaps. After all, Ponyboy is an avid reader and pays attention to what is going on in school. He is constantly asking questions about the reasons for violence and for the hostility that exists between the two groups. Ponyboy might have gained the insight he needed and wanted had he been asked to read about others in similar situations. Other Greasers still attending school might acquire more positive attitudes toward school if they were asked to read about people similar to themselves and in situations that they recognize. By increasing their engagement and success in school, they would become less prone to violent behavior. Randy and Cherry, two apparently good students who are both upset and remorseful when they realize that their behavior has led to violence, might be the ones to benefit the most from bibliotherapy. By seeing themselves in characters and recognizing their behavior in books, they might have had the foresight to change their roles.

Bibliotherapy is likely to be more successful if literature discussions are combined with a violence prevention or conflict management training program (Stanford, 1995). These programs teach concepts and communication skills that are quite appropriate for study in an English class. Such an approach helps readers focus on key "choice points" in the literature and then in their own lives. Their altered behavior often makes a difference and helps them learn skills.

Prothrow-Stith (1993) emphasizes that in typical teen violence, there is little difference between victim and aggressor. The difference between a teen who ends up either dead or in prison or becomes a successful adult is often attributed to an identifiable choice point. Prothrow-Stith's suggested curriculum helps students recognize risk factors associated with violence and helps them to make choices to avoid violence. For example, in the opening incident in *The Outsiders*, Ponyboy knows that he is taking a risk when he chooses to walk home alone from the movie. Had he bothered to call for a companion, the whole chain of events in the book might never have happened. A recent class discussion of risk factors associated with being alone in a dangerous neighborhood and the choices one has if ever found in that predicament might have altered Ponyboy's decision to take that chance.

Prothrow-Stith also emphasizes the role of alcohol and the responsibility of friends to protect friends from committing violence or making unwise decisions. Recent readings and class discussions on these issues might have helped Cherry and Bob recognize the roles they were playing in promoting violence and their responsibility for stopping it.

Several conflict management curricula teach verbal skills in dealing with conflict such as active listening and assertive confrontation. These skills probably would not have been useful in the violent confrontations in this particular book, and students from rough neighborhoods are usually quick to point out that using such tactics in violent confrontations would be interpreted as a sign of weakness; this might create more confrontation. Nonetheless, these strategies might have helped Ponyboy's relationship with Darry. If Ponyboy had used active listening when Darry confronted him about his being late, their conflict might not have escalated to the point that Darry felt compelled to hit him and might have prevented his running away. If Ponyboy had not run away, he would not have been in the park where he was attacked in the fight that led to Bob's death.

Many schools have peer mediation programs in which young people are trained to help other young people resolve conflicts before they lead to violence. Peer mediation has sometimes been successful in defusing conflicts like the one the boys have over Cherry at the drive-in. Peer mediation is only useful if both sides want to resolve the conflict. The evidence in the book suggests that Bob wanted an excuse to fight, not a resolution to the conflict. Many adolescents with tough exteriors do respond positively in the privacy of a peer mediation session. By actively listening to the other person's side of the story and then reciprocating the courtesy to problem-solve a solution, a "cease-fire" agreement is often reached with some recognition of the humanity of the former enemy.

CONCLUSION

The ongoing conflict between the Greasers and the Socs, or their equivalent, goes on in almost every high school. Conflict management, peer mediation, cooperative learning, and other programs designed to build a school community across peer divisions cannot eliminate all conflicts, but they can help build enough of a relationship that the kinds of attacks leading to serious injury may decrease. More and more schools need to coordinate the multi-pronged efforts of teachers, social workers, and counselors to promote positive changes in individual students, groups, and in the overall school environment.

RECOMMENDED READINGS

Borders and Paisley (1992) and Thompson and Rudolph (1988) offer annotated bibliographies of books and helpful resources for students with special needs. Journals such as *The ALAN Review*, *Hornbook*, and *The School Library Journal* also contain current reviews of young adult (YA) titles for consideration.

Fiction

5.01.   Arrick, Fran. (1983). *Chernowitz.* New York: New American Library. 192 pp. (ISBN: 0–451–15350–2). Middle School (MS), High School (HS).

Bobby Cherno responds to anti-Semitic abuse with a clever plan for revenge but discovers that revenge does not have the results he hoped for.

5.02.   Bennett, Jay. (1991). *Skinhead.* New York: Franklin Watts. 139 pp. (ISBN: 0–531–11001–X). HS.

Jonathan does not understand why he is drawn into a murder involving Skinheads until he discovers that his father is Jewish. This mystery has some good characterization of the Skinheads and an excellent description of Jonathan's reactions to a violent environment.

5.03.   Block, Francesca Lia. (1992). *Cherokee bat and the goat guys.* New York: HarperCollins. 116 pp. (ISBN: 0–06–020270–X). MS, HS.

In this tale of magical realism, Cherokee Bat, Raphael, Witch Baby, and Angel Juan form a rock band. Magical gifts and talents are spinning them out of control and tempting them to violence and danger.

5.04.   Bunting, Eve. (1990). *Such nice kids.* New York: Clarion Books. 120 pp. (ISBN: 0–395–54998). MS, HS.

Jason innocently tries to help a friend by loaning him his mother's car without permission. That dishonest choice point begins a series of conflicts and more bad choices that lead to a car wreck, an armed robbery, two arrests, and the death of his friend.

5.05.   Butterworth, William. (1980). *Leroy and the old man.* New York: Scholastic. 168 pp. (ISBN: 0–590–42711–3). MS, HS.

In this YASD Best Book for Young Adults, Leroy flees from a Chicago gang after he witnesses a murder. Leroy goes to rural Louisiana where he gets to know his grandfather and learns a positive and new set of values. When his father, who had deserted him a few years earlier, offers him a job as a numbers runner in New York, he has to choose which set of values to live by.

5.06.   Cormier, Robert. (1986). *The chocolate war*. New York: Dell. 191 pp. (ISBN: 0–440–94459–7). HS.

After his mother's death, Jerry defies both faculty tradition and a secret school society which brings on social torment and physical danger. Jerry ends up trapped in a power struggle between cruel students and a corrupt faculty. (An American Library Association [ALA] Notable Children's Book, A Best of the Best Books for Young Adults, a *School Library Journal [SLJ] Best Book of the Year, and a New York Times* Outstanding Book of the Year)

5.07.   Cormier, Robert. (1985). *Beyond the chocolate war*. New York: Dell. 288 pp. (ISBN: 0–440–00580–X). HS.

Archie continues to maintain power and domination through the Vigils, the secret school society that ruthlessly destroys dreams and lives. Archie and Obie tempt death with a guillotine, but even though they escape unscathed and graduate, their legacy of terror continues.

5.08.   Cormier, Robert. (1991). *We all fall down*. New York: Delacorte Press. 193 pp. (ISBN: 0–385–30501–X). HS.

Buddy had been drinking when he followed his friends to commit vandalism, resulting in a girl's serious injury. Buddy later falls in love with the injured girl's sister but loses her when she finds out about his involvement.

5.09.   Crutcher, Chris. (1989). *Chinese handcuffs*. New York: Greenwillow Books. 202 pp. (ISBN: 0–588–08345–5). HS.

Dillon witnesses his older brother's suicide and single-handedly confronts a motorcycle gang that he blames for Preston's death. When Dillon learns that his friend Jen is being sexually abused by her stepfather, he is tempted to murder him but finds a smarter and more effective revenge.

5.10.   Duncan, Lois. (1975). *I know what you did last summer*. New York: Pocket Books. 198 pp. (ISBN: 0–671–73589–6). HS.

This horror story is about a group of teenagers who are stalked by an unknown person seeking revenge for their involvement in a hit-and-run death. The choices these young people make to conceal their crime lead them to further danger.

5.11. Dygard, Thomas J. (1986). *Halfback tough*. New York: William Morrow. 210 pp. (ISBN: 0–688–06925–2). MS, HS.

After Joe is forced to leave his old school and friends where he had a tough-guy reputation, he decides to play football where being tough is welcomed. Joe has problems when his old friends get involved in vandalism, and his team members don't seem to accept him.

5.12. Dygard, Thomas J. (1996). *Running wild*. New York: Morrow Junior Books. 172 pp. (ISBN: 0–688–14853–0). MS, HS.

A police officer gives Pete a choice between staying at the police station or joining the football team. Pete is surprisingly good and enjoys the sport, but he has to make a choice between his football team's rules or hanging around with his old friends. The series of choices Pete makes and the reasons he makes them provide a good illustration of a boy working his way out of delinquency.

5.13. Greene, Bette. (1991). *The drowning of Stephan Jones*. New York: Bantam. 217 pp. (ISBN: 0–553–07437–7). HS.

Carla is disturbed when her boyfriend Andy begins to harass a couple of gay men. When his harassment leads to one of their deaths, Carla is the only witness who can testify against him.

5.14. Guy, Rosa. (1979). *The disappearance*. New York: Dell. 246 pp. (ISBN: 0–440–92064–7). HS.

After being recently acquitted of murder, Imamu Jones is thrown out of the house by his alcoholic mother and is taken in as a foster child by a middle-class family. Imamu's sense of self-respect is challenged by the rules of his new home and by the tragic disappearance of the youngest daughter. Imamu is immediately suspected and must solve the mystery to clear his name. (An ALA Best Book for Young Adults)

5.15. Hernandez, Irene Beltran. (1995). *The secret of two brothers*. Houston, TX: Arte Publico Press. 181 pp. (ISBN: 1–55885–141–0). MS, HS.

Beaver returns to the barrio after a three-year prison stay and tries to get his own life back on track while supporting his younger brother, who's been abused by their father. The old pitfalls are still around, but neighbors and a probation officer rally to help the young men succeed.

5.16.   Hewett, Lorri. (1996). *Soulfire*. New York: Dutton Children's Books. 231 pp. (ISBN: 0–525–45559–0). HS.

Todd and his best friend Zeke are caught in a web of violence between Todd's older brother Marcus and their cousin Tommy. Marcus is deeply involved with a gang, and Tommy is a "wannabe" gang member. Zeke is frustrated by his father's failure as a respected minister to confront gang violence, and Zeke almost gets himself killed when he confronts the situation himself.

5.17.   Hinton, S. E. (1989). *Rumble fish*. New York: Dell. 111 pp. (ISBN: 0–440–97534–4). MS, HS.

Rusty-James and Steve go from one fight to another. Rusty is attracted to the thrill of fighting and wants to be just like his detached older brother who is drifting away from sanity. Steve is so psychologically caught up in violence that he cannot rescue himself until he breaks all connections.

5.18.   Hinton, S. E. (1988). *Taming the star runner*. New York: Bantam Doubleday Dell. 181 pp. (ISBN: 0–440–20479–8). HS.

After being released from juvenile hall, Travis is sent to live with his uncle on a ranch. There, he works on his skill as a writer and develops a meaningful relationship with a girl who works with horses; meanwhile, his old friends become involved in a robbery and murder.

5.19.   Karas, Phyllis. (1995). *The hate crime*. New York: Avon. 181 pp. (ISBN: 0–380–78214–6). HS.

After a local temple is defaced, Zack is threatened and almost injured before he finds out why a member of his lacrosse team would commit a hate crime.

5.20.   Kerr, M. E. (1989). *Fellback*. New York: Harper & Row. 181 pp. (ISBN: 0–06–023292–7). MS, HS.

In this mystery involving a secret school society and an apparent suicide, the author describes in some detail the series of choices made by some students that lead to violence and crime.

5.21.   Lynch, Chris. (1996). *Mick (blue-eyed son #1)*. New York: Harper-Collins. 146 pp. (ISBN: 0–06–447121–7). HS.

Mick does not like the lines in his checkerboard neighborhood that separate the Irish from the Cambodians, Blacks, and Hispanics. After he unwillingly participates in violence to defend the lines he despises, Mick becomes a victim when he tries to cross the lines.

5.22.   Martinez, Victor. (1996). *Parrot in the oven*. New York: HarperCollins. 216 pp. (ISBN: 0–06–026704–6). MS.

Manuel's father treats him badly, so Manuel seeks initiation into a gang to get the acceptance and respect he so desperately wants.

5.23.   Mowry, Jess. (1997). *Babylon boyz*. New York: Simon & Schuster. 188 pp. (ISBN: 0–689–80839–9). HS.

Dante needs a heart operation and Pook, who is gay, wants to be a doctor. The both know that there is little chance that their dreams will come true in the ghetto. When they find a case of cocaine, they must choose between their values and the money they could get to fulfill their dreams. They are drawn into a violent drug culture where they struggle to survive and support each other.

5.24.   Murphy, Barbara Beasley. (1977). *No place to run*. Scarsdale, NY: Bradbury Press. 176 pp. (ISBN: 0–87888–116–6). HS.

Billy follows his tough friend, Milo, in harassing a tramp and then is horrified to hear that the tramp has died and the police know that he was involved.

5.25.   Myers, Walter Dean. (1988). *Scorpions*. New York: Harper & Row. 160 pp. (ISBN: 0–060–24365–1). MS, HS.

When Jamal's brother, the leader of the Scorpions, is sent to prison, he asks Jamal to take over the gang and use the money they get from selling drugs to pay for his appeal. Jamal cares for other things more than gang life, and the other Scorpions would rather fight than accept him as leader. (A Newbery Honor Book and an ALA Notable Children's Book)

5.26.   Myers, Walter Dean. (1992). *Somewhere in the darkness*. New York: Scholastic. 168 pp. (ISBN: 0–590–42411–4). MS, HS.

Jimmy is drifting away from school when his father, who has just escaped from prison, finds him and takes him on a journey to his own youth.

Jimmy discovers the road that led his father to prison as his father tries to make peace before he dies.

5.27. Peck, Richard. (1993). *Bel-Air Bambi and the mall rats*. New York: Delacorte Press. 181 pp. (ISBN: 0–385–30823–X). MS.

This is a humorous, satiric story of a Hollywood family who confronts a small-town gang that keeps terrorizing the two sisters, Buffie and Bambi.

5.28. Tolan, Stephanie. (1990). *Plague year*. New York: Morrow Junior Books. 198 pp. (ISBN: 0–688–08801–5). HS.

Bran Slocum was immediately rejected at Ridgewood High because of his weird dress, but the hostility of the town becomes vicious and dangerous when a reporter reveals that he is the son of a serial killer. David, who narrates the story, tries to respond to the mob hysteria but fails to prevent tragedy.

5.29. Tolan, Stephanie. (1996). *Welcome to the ark*. New York: Morrow Junior Books. 250 pp. (ISBN: 0–688–13724–5). HS.

In a group home, four youths—Miranda, Doug, Taryn, and Elijah—try to use paranormal abilities to make a difference in a violent world by making it a place worthy to call home.

5.30. Voigt, Cynthia. (1987). *Sons from afar*. New York: Atheneum. 214 pp. (ISBN: 0–689–31349–7). HS.

James and Sammy Tillerman search for the father they have never known and encounter his world of violence. After getting caught in a bar fight and learning more about their father's violent behavior and irresponsibility, they find hope by working together.

5.31. Voigt, Cynthia. (1994). *When she hollers*. New York: Scholastic. 177 pp. (ISBN: 0–590–46714–X). HS.

Tish is definitely over her violent, sexually abusive stepfather and her mother who is trapped in denial. For awhile a knife seems to be the solution, but Tish continues to look for other ways out.

5.32. Williams-Garcia, Rita. (1995). *Like sisters on the homefront*. New York: Lodestar Books. 165 pp. (ISBN: 0–525–67465–9). MS, HS.

When street-wise Gayle gets pregnant a second time, her mother sends her and her baby to live with an aunt in rural Georgia. Gayle learns a new set of values from her dying great-grandmother.

Nonfiction

5.33.   Abner, Allison & Villarosa, Linda. (1995). *Finding our way: The teen girls' survival guide.* New York: HarperCollins. 308 pp. (ISBN: 0–06–095114–1). MS, HS.

This practical, realistic, and readable guidebook for teenage girls includes topics ranging from beauty and pregnancy to violence and gangs. The chapter, "It's Rough Out There," includes the dangers and temptations that face ordinary girls and has stories of young women caught in violence and the way they coped. Another chapter deals with violence and abuse within the family.

5.34.   Atkin, S. Beth. (1996). *Voices from the streets: Young former gang members tell their stories.* Boston: Little, Brown & Co. 121 pp. (ISBN: 0–316–05634–0). MS, HS.

Through stories and photographs, the author helps eight young people from a variety of backgrounds and ethnic groups tell their stories of how they got involved in gangs and why they chose to get out of them. Some of the people and programs that help young people get out and stay out of gangs are identified, and the ways some of them are now working in gang-prevention programs are presented. (A *Booklist* Editors' Choice, an ALA Best Book for Young Adults, and a *Hungry Mind Review* Book of Distinction)

5.35.   Bode, Janet & Mack, Stan. (1996). *Hard time: A real life look at juvenile crime and violence.* New York: Delacorte Press. 183 pp. (ISBN: 0–385–32186–4). HS.

The authors interview teenagers who have been imprisoned and tell the actual stories behind their delinquency.

5.36.   Chaiet, Donna. (1995). *Staying safe while shopping.* New York: The Rosen Publishing Group. 55 pp. (ISBN: 0–8239–1869–6). MS, HS.

This is one book in a series written for adolescent girls that helps them learn coping strategies for potentially violent situations and avoiding their becoming a victim of violence. Other books in the series include safety on dates, at home, at school, at work, on public transportation, on the streets, and while traveling.

5.37.   Chavis, Melody Ermachild. (1993). *Altars in the street: A neighborhood fights to survive.* New York: Bell Tower. 251 pp. (ISBN: 0–517–70492–7). HS.

Ms. Chavis describes the struggles of a neighborhood going against violence and drugs, and her own personal struggle to build a family and to live up to her Buddhist values.

5.38.   Gardner, Sandra. (1992). *Street gangs in America.* New York: Franklin Watts. 92 pp. (ISBN: 0–531–11037–0). MS, HS.

The author describes gang life, history and structure of gangs, gangs in the media and gang intervention programs in this factual book.

5.39.   Hubner, John & Wolfson, Jill. (1996). *Somebody else's children: The courts, the kids, and the struggle to save America's troubled families.* New York: Crown Publishers. 309 pp. (ISBN: 0–517–59941–4). HS.

This series of case studies of young people in California's Santa Clara County's Juvenile Court System describes the situations or behavior that led to their involvement with the court. The reasons behind the judges' decisions, the procedures of the court, and the institutions where young people can be placed are discussed. The authors follow a number of young people through the system and describe the outcomes of the cases.

5.40.   Korem, Dan. (1994). *Suburban gangs: The affluent rebels.* Richardson, TX: International Focus Press. 256 pp. (ISBN: 0–9639103–1–0). HS.

The author, an investigative journalist, provides a detailed but readable study of suburban gangs both in the United States and Europe. Korem compares suburban gangs with inner-city gangs and makes a distinction among delinquent gangs, ideological gangs, and occult gangs. The final section provides strategies for helping youth disengage from gangs.

5.41.   Oliver, Marilyn Tower. (1995). *Gangs: Trouble in the streets*. Springfield, NJ: Enslow Publishers. 107 pp. (ISBN: 0–89490–492–2).
HS.

Oliver includes a survey of factual information on the history of
gangs, characteristics of gangs, and consequences of gang life.

5.42.   Prothrow-Stith, Deborah. (1991). *Deadly consequences: How violence is destroying our teenage population*. New York: HarperPeren-
nial. 203 pp. (ISBN: 0–06–016344–5). HS.

An emergency-room physician studies the risk factors that have
created an epidemic of violence and proposes ways of resolving them. One
chapter describes her violence prevention curriculum that is widely used in
high schools.

5.43.   Sparks, Beatrice. (Ed.). (1996). *Almost lost*. New York: Avon. 239
pp. (ISBN: 0–380–78341–X). HS.

Sam was on the streets for several months as a gang member. When
he finally returns home, physically and emotionally traumatized, he returns
to the therapist who had begun working with him before he ran away. This
book is the edited transcripts of Sam's therapy sessions; it not only shows
the thought processes that led Sam into and out of delinquency, but shows
the therapy process at work.

REFERENCES

Baumrind, D. (1991). The influence of parenting styles on adolescent competence
and substance use. *Journal of Early Adolescence, 11*, 56–95.
Berk, L. E. (1993). *Infants, children, and adolescents*. Boston: Allyn & Bacon.
Bodart, J. (1980). Bibliotherapy: The right book for the right person at the right
time and more. *Top of the News, 36*, 183–188.
Borders, S. & Paisley, P. O. (1992). Children's literature as a resource of class-
room guidance. *Elementary School Guidance & Counseling, 27*,
131–139.
Brown, B. B., Clasen, G., & Eicher, S. (1986). Perceptions of peer pressure, peer
conformity dispositions, and self-reported behavior among adolescents.
Developmental Psychology, 22, 521–530.
Carnes, P. (1993). *Out of the shadows*. Minneapolis, MN: CompCare.
Fagan, J., Slaughter, E., & Hartstone, E. (1987). Blind justice? The impact of race
on the juvenile justice process. *Crime & Delinquency, 33*, 259–286.

Goldstein, A. P. (1990). *Delinquents on delinquency.* Champaign, IL: Research Press.

Hawkins, D. J. & Lam, T. (1987). Teacher practices, social development, and delinquency. In J. D. Burchard and S. N. Burchard (Eds.), *Prevention of delinquent behavior.* Newbury Park, CA: Sage, 241–274.

Hedges, M. (1996, December 4). Girls rapidly closing the crime gender gap, study says. *Arkansas Democrat Gazette,* 1A, 12A.

Henggeler, S. W. (1989). *Delinquency in adolescence.* Newbury Park, CA: Sage.

Herring, R. D. & Runion, K. B. (1994). Counseling ethnic children and youth from an Adlerian perspective. *Journal of Multicultural Counseling and Development, 22,* 215–226.

Hinton, S. E. (1989). *The outsiders.* New York: Dell.

Macbeth, F. & Fine, N. (1995). *Playing with fire: Creative conflict resolution for young adults.* Philadelphia: New Society Publishers.

Manning, M. L. & Baruth, L. G. (1995). Programs and efforts addressing societal and personal conditions. *Students at risk.* Boston: Allyn & Bacon, 287–318.

McEroy, A. (1990). Combating gang activities in schools. *The Education Digest, 55* (2), 30–34.

Patterson, G. R., DeBaryshe, B. D., & Ramsey, E. (1989). A developmental perspective on antisocial behavior. *American Psychologist, 44,* 329–335.

Quay, H. C. (1987). Institutional treatment. In H. C. Quay (Ed.), *Handbook of juvenile delinquency.* New York: Wiley, 244–265.

Rice, F. P. (1993). *The adolescent: Development, relationships, and culture.* Boston: Allyn & Bacon.

Slavin, R. E. (1995). *Cooperative learning* (2nd ed.). Boston: Allyn & Bacon.

Snyder, J. & Patterson, G. R. (1987). Family interaction and delinquent behavior. In H. C. Quay (Ed.), *Handbook of juvenile delinquency.* New York: Wiley, 216–243.

Stanford, B. (1995). Conflict and the story of our lives: Teaching English for violence prevention. *English Journal, 84* (5), 38–42.

Thompson, C. L. & Rudolph, L. B. (1988). *Counseling children* (2nd ed.). Pacific Grove, CA: Brooks/Cole.

U.S. Department of Justice. (1991). *Crime in the United States.* Washington, DC: Government Printing Office.

Webb, W. (1992). Empowering at-risk children. *Elementary School Guidance & Counseling, 27,* 96–103.

Woititz, J. (1995). *Healing your sexual self.* New York: Health Communication.

CHAPTER 6

When Divorce Comes to Class

Bonnie O. Ericson & Shari Tarver-Behring

INTRODUCTION

Tolstoy is well known for commenting that happy families are all alike, but families in trouble are unhappy in many different ways. Extending the comment, divorces, too, are unique. Interestingly, divorce does not play a major role in Tolstoy's work or in other classic literature. Single parents, unhappy parents, and parentless children exist in the classics, but such situations are usually explained by death, illness, or social conditions other than divorce.

Divorce itself is a relatively recent phenomenon and is one that warrants attention when the following statistics (Levine, 1995) are noted:

- One in every two marriages currently ends in divorce in the United States.
- Every year a million new children will experience a family breakup because of divorce.
- Forty-four percent of all children of the 1990s will be children of divorce.
- Only fifty percent of fathers ordered to pay child support provide the full amount.
- Eighty percent of divorced parents remarry within five years of divorce.

These are staggering numbers, especially when considered from a teacher's or school counselor's perspective. A high school teacher might expect almost half of her students to be coping with the aftermath of divorce, including perhaps a reduced standard of living or adjustment to a blended family. An upper elementary or middle school teacher might expect a number of his students to be in the critical period when parents are separating and determining new life courses. Further, sometimes we forget that divorce impacts not only a single family, but the friends and extended family of the divorcing family as well. Cousins, friends, and neighbors also must adjust to breakups resulting from divorce.

While not present in classic literature, the recent pervasiveness of divorce is reflected in the literature available for youth. A search of a local public library's computerized card catalog system using the subject heading "divorce fiction" yielded 191 entries. Of these, all but five entries were juvenile or young adult (YA) books. Of the 186 non-adult books, the vast majority had been published since the mid-1970s, paralleling both the rise of divorce and the onset of realistic adolescent fiction. In contrast, nonfiction books about divorce were available in approximately equal numbers for adults and youth. Clearly, children and adolescents have books available to them featuring divorce.

EDUCATOR MEETS COUNSELOR

In our initial meetings to talk about the topic of divorce and books about divorce, we two authors experienced some difficulty remaining directly focused on the topic at hand. Instead, our talk was circular and markedly personal. "I have *got* to talk about this parent!" exclaimed Tarver-Behring of a book character at the beginning of one of our meetings. Our own families and adolescent years, as well as our experiences with our respective adolescent daughters, were at first as pressing as how this chapter might be organized or exactly what resources might be recommended.

These discussions correspond with both Louise Rosenblatt's reader response theory (1978) and Anderson's schema theory (1984). Reader response theory recognizes that each reader's "transaction" with a text, particularly a work of fiction, is unique and colored by personal associations and experiences. Similarly, schema theory notes the importance of a reader's bringing and connecting previous knowledge and experience with new information. These types of connections marked our conversations both about psychological issues and the divorce fiction. Tarver-Behring's psychological insights clarified and crystallized Ericson's understanding of key psychological concepts for discussing adolescence—such as identity development, depression, and the term "parentified"—by providing a more precise vocabulary. On the other hand, talking about children's and YA literature provided cases which exemplified key issues related to divorce—issues which we address in this chapter. It seems essential that all readers and learners have the opportunity to connect their own related knowledge and experiences in discussing divorce as a topic or divorce as it pertains to literature.

Our meetings also revealed a common passion for working with children and adolescents, including those from divorced or divorcing families. But what can teachers do? How might they be more sensitive and responsive, even proactive in helping students in their classes who are coping with divorce? What is "over the line" in terms of what teachers have the capacity to achieve? We address these questions below, beginning with a discussion of typical responses of children and adolescents experiencing divorce. We also examine a "case study" of divorce based on Cynthia Voigt's *A Solitary Blue*. Later, we provide a number of suggestions that are appropriate for teachers and describe student behaviors which would indicate the need for referral to a specialist. Finally, we provide an annotated bibliography of fiction, non-fiction, and videos appropriate for children and adolescents.

HOW CHILDREN AND ADOLESCENTS RESPOND TO DIVORCE

Literally thousands of studies in the past decades have enabled researchers and practitioners to better understand how children and adolescents respond to divorce. The central effect of divorce on adolescents is the impact it has on their development (Wallerstein & Kelly, 1980). Marital separation and divorce can be similar emotionally to the death of a loved one; however, it should be noted that not all teens experience significant difficulty with family divorce (Kelly, 1993). If divorcing parents have high conflict or poor communication, it is more likely that children and teens will experience difficulties that interrupt or even cause regression (reversal) in normal development. Conversely, children and adolescents whose divorcing families resolve differences and living arrangements in a healthy manner may well make adjustments with minor, temporary disruptions in developmental functioning. Additionally, the role of gender and cultural differences associated with developmental needs must be taken into account when considering the impact of divorce.

The developmental areas that may be impacted by separation and divorce include cognitive or intellectual development, identity development, social development, and emotional development. Children of differing ages may experience

- grief, sadness, loneliness, or depression over the loss of familiar family relationships or a particular parent;
- anger with one or both parents;

- lowered self-esteem associated with negative family behavior;
- conflict of loyalties regarding the parents;
- anxiety about how basic needs will be met, about finances, and about real or potential abandonment;
- withdrawal from friends and social activities;
- denial that the divorce is really happening;
- blame or guilt at being the cause of the break-up.

Such responses may take forms clearly observable in classrooms. A student's schoolwork may deteriorate rapidly, for example, or a student may appear inattentive and unmotivated in class. Students who are angry with parents may exhibit impulsive, antisocial, or conflictual behaviors with the teacher or with classmates. Some adolescents may also appear to move toward maturity more quickly because they feel that they must fend for themselves while parents are absorbed with the divorce. When parents are dysfunctional, some students may become "parentified" adolescents, caring for a distraught parent. This premature assumption of caring behaviors may actually accelerate normal adolescent conflict and result in the development of marginal skills required for independence in adulthood. Children and adolescents need parental guidance and support while learning to make independent judgments and to establish interpersonal relationships (Robson, 1993).

Many other changes can occur in a divorcing family that may temporarily interrupt normal development. Living arrangements and school placements may change, which can interfere with academic stability and the peer relationships so central to children and teens. For adolescents, economic resources may lessen at a time when they desire greater financial support in order to learn economic decision-making. With support and open, healthy communication with parents, most adolescents recover smoothly from these changes. But when parents are fighting and not communicating well with each other or the children, teachers and school counselors may become involved because of problems occurring in the school setting. Children's and YA literature can effectively portray what the experience of divorce is like.

INSIGHTS INTO SEPARATION AND DIVORCE: CYNTHIA VOIGT'S *A SOLITARY BLUE* (307 pp.)

With its compelling characters and beautifully written prose, Cynthia Voigt's *A Solitary Blue* is an extraordinary example of a YA novel about separation and divorce. The story spans ten years in the life of the protagonist, Jeff—from the time his mother Melody leaves him and his father, through his senior year in high school. Many changes occur during these years. The story realistically captures, over this period of time, the negative developmental effects that Jeff experiences as a result of his parents' difficult relationship. The characters in *A Solitary Blue* are richly developed and so encourage readers' empathy and caring.

Jeff's Story

At the beginning of the book, Jeff returns home from second grade one day to find a note from his mother telling him that she is leaving because she has to help other little boys who don't get enough to eat. Although she is saddened by her choice to leave, her commitment to other people who need her is greater than her commitment to her young son. Thus Jeff's mother leaves him and her husband in Baltimore to live with her grandmother in Charleston, South Carolina. Jeff and his father, a history professor who prefers things "regular and neat," manage for the first few years with the assistance of a series of male student housekeepers. Jeff, however, lives in constant fear that his father, who he calls "the Professor," will abandon him just like his mother did. Jeff has no idea where she is and dares not ask. It takes a very serious illness and the help of a friend named Brother Thomas to partially awaken Jeff's dad to his responsibilities as a caregiver for his son.

Several years later, Jeff unexpectedly hears from his mother and goes to spend the summer with her. He is overwhelmed by her warmth, talkativeness, and passion for a variety of causes; similarly, he is fascinated by the family stories of his great-grandmother. After Jeff returns home to his father, he writes to his mother regularly over the next year but she doesn't respond—not even at Christmas. Meanwhile, Jeff and his father have a breakthrough in communication, partly centered around a beautiful old guitar the Professor buys for him. Jeff returns to Charleston the next summer, but is deeply hurt when his mother goes away for weeks at a time with her boyfriend. And, to make matters worse, his great-grandmother has suffered a stroke so he no longer feels welcome in the house. Left to his own devices, he buys a rowboat and explores the outlying waterways. There he grows accustomed to seeing blue herons, a kind of water bird called the "solitary blue." Near the end of the summer Jeff and his mother have a terrible argument, and she tells him that had he been a girl she would have taken her baby with her when she left. After this terrible confrontation, Jeff spends his last night on an island's sandy beach seeking solace in the beauty of nature.

Jeff returns to Baltimore and is so pained by the memory of his mother's hurtful comments that he withdraws into himself and his fantasy island, fails his classes, and spends his time visiting an amusement park for the thrill of the rides. With Jeff's school failure and because his father has written and sold a book, the two of them leave Baltimore and move to the Chesapeake Bay area where they convert an old cabin into a comfortable home they both love. During this time, the two continue their slow healing and gradual improvement in communication.

Jeff makes two new friends at school, Phil and Andy, and meets Dicey Tillerman and her family. Though Dicey is a few years younger, she is fiercely independent and is a survivor like Jeff. At one point in the story, Jeff is reminded of the blue heron when he thinks of Dicey and Dicey is thinking exactly the same of him. When Jeff's mother learns that the Professor has sold a book, Melody decides to seek a divorce and custody of Jeff. Jeff is appalled but is supported by his father, who's handling all of the legal aspects. Still, Melody simply appears one day at the house, and Jeff must tell her it's his decision to live with his dad. It's a blunt telling, and Jeff experiences tremendous guilt to the extent that it is difficult for him to make college plans.

Melody later returns when Jeff, as the sole male descendent, inherits the entire estate of his great-grandmother. Jeff gives his mother a large diamond ring that he has received, even as she plans to leave for South America with her boyfriend to chase her dream of helping the poor. Jeff has reached a sad conclusion about his mother: She doesn't really understand anything about love. Further, Jeff realizes that his relationship with his father will continue to possess a certain awkwardness. By the book's end, however, Jeff has attained personal peace while recognizing the value of family and friends.

PSYCHOLOGICAL INSIGHTS ABOUT JEFF AND HIS PARENTS

From the age of seven until well into adolescence, Jeff wonders what he has done wrong to drive his mother away and cause his father to be emotionally distant. In fact, Jeff's parents are in a very dysfunctional marriage. The father has not learned how to express his feelings and later is deeply depressed over the loss of his relationship with his wife. The mother projects caring but in fact is quite selfish and immature, spending money excessively and avoiding emotional intimacy by professing passion for environmental and social causes. (In counseling, we might refer to her as having a narcissistic personality disorder.) None of this is known by Jeff because of his age and the family's poor communication. Jeff, not surprisingly, shows many of the signs of maladjustment linked to a dysfunctional divorce situation.

Low Self-Esteem

Jeff has very low self-esteem. When he is younger, he feels he is "bad" and has caused his parents' separation. He blames himself and fears abandonment by his father. Such responses are typical in situations where the parents do not communicate clearly the reasons for their divorce or their desire to maintain stable, supportive relationships.

Social Isolation

Jeff is socially isolated and withdrawn, most likely as a result of his low self-esteem. He has no school friends, nor is he friendly with any of his teachers. Additionally, there is a lack of involvement and good role-modeling by his parents which is essential for promoting positive social development.

Parentified Child

Jeff shows many signs of a "parentified child" who must care for himself and a parent. After his mother leaves, Jeff cooks for his dad and is often solely responsible for himself and for household tasks. The unhealthy aspects of assuming responsibilities typical of an adult at such a young age become glaringly apparent when Jeff becomes ill and his father does not know what to do to help him. Because Jeff is a child, he is too young to know how or when to see a doctor; this is the parent's job. Jeff also shows many gaps in social skills development because of his "parentified child" status.

Depression

After his second visit to Charleston, Jeff also appears to be suffering from childhood depression; lethargic and despondent, he feels worthless. At this time, Jeff shows signs of developmental regression at school when his grades drop dramatically. He starts to daydream in school, fails to complete assignments, and he skips classes.

Resentment

Initially, Jeff has some underlying resentment toward his father because he feels his father was never invested in the relationships with his mother or himself. One sign of the anger and lack of closeness or connection in their relationship is that Jeff calls him "the Professor" instead of "Dad." At a later age, Jeff learns about his mother's parenting limitations through his visits with her. When Jeff realizes his dad has remained committed as a parent in ways his mother never has, he develops anger towards Melody and ultimately rejects her.

Healing

But there are signs of healing as well. The father's friendship with Brother Thomas leads to improvements in communication between father and son. Later, Jeff's friendships with Phil, Andy, and Dicey indicate social growth, and his strong schoolwork similarly shows a more normal developmental pattern. Jeff's empathy and understanding of his parents, his friends, and Dicey and her family point to his emotional recovery; however, it is likely that anger toward his mother or father may well resurface in the future.

JEFF'S THERAPY

If Jeff were an actual child or teen who was entering counseling, he would benefit from several types of interventions. Ideally, Jeff's family should have been in family therapy when initial problems emerged. Jeff's parents may have learned how to communicate with each other in an adult-only portion of the therapy session and may have avoided divorce or at least could have received guidance about how to explain their separation to Jeff so that he would not feel responsible. Suggestions could also be offered by the therapist for promoting a healthy, stable environment after the parents' separation. A separate time for Jeff to express hurt and anger alone with the therapist could also be available.

If intervention were to occur at a later point, Jeff's parents could receive parent education about how to set normal expectations for a child as opposed to the excessive expectations experienced by the "parentified" child. Similarly, they could receive help on ways to promote social success and advice about home/school communication and educational progress. For example, Jeff might benefit from a tutor to maintain academics during periods when he needed such help. The information gleaned and the skills learned could be used consistently by Jeff's parents even though they were not living together.

Because Jeff witnessed a divorce by two dysfunctional parents, he is exhibiting depression and low self-esteem. Jeff could join a group for children whose parents are divorced to gain insights from others who are in similar situations and to observe ways that others successfully cope with divorce. Groups also minimize the potential for social isolation and maladjustment. Jeff would also benefit from individual counseling where he could learn to separate the cause of divorce from himself, express anger about the divorce and his parents, and develop coping skills to deal with the pain of divorce.

Individual counseling, parent education, and peer groups are sometimes available through counseling services in schools. Community outpatient clinics, churches, and self-help programs also offer some services. Jeff's situation might have been markedly different had a teacher or school counselor recognized and been more sensitive to his problems.

SUGGESTIONS FOR TEACHERS WITH STUDENTS INVOLVED IN SEPARATION AND DIVORCE

The behaviors of students in divorcing families may be much more understandable to teachers once knowledge about the impact of divorce, as described above, is acquired. Aware that a student is experiencing divorce, teachers can provide support and understanding to the student in the school setting. Many students benefit from a simple acknowledgment of the emotional stress of the divorce experience. The student may want this recognition to occur in a private manner to avoid embarrassment in front of peers; a written comment on a paper or a brief, discrete conversation are appropriate venues.

Teachers may also express understanding that academic work may be harder to complete at this time and temporarily offer modifications to work quantity or extend due dates for assignments until work returns to pre-divorce output levels. Outside academic resources, such as tutoring, can also be identified for the student at a time when parents may be less available or desirable as help to the student. Additionally, teachers must recognize that students respond differently to divorce. Teachers should not always expect difficulties in children and teens experiencing divorce. For some students, no change in the level of expectations for schoolwork is needed or desirable.

Academic Activities

Academic activities that allow the student an opportunity to express feelings about the divorce can be healing. Literature assignments can include books about adolescents' experiences in divorcing families. These books can "normalize" the reactions of adolescents and help them to feel they are not unusual or alone in their feelings. Strategies for coping with divorce exemplified by characters can be identified and evaluated. Writing assignments encouraging personal reactions can give students additional opportunities to identify and articulate feelings about divorce. Group discussions of book characters and themes may also lead to self-disclosure about being from a divorced family by a number of students and further opportunities to feel one is not alone in this experience. In addition, students from intact families will have the opportunity to empathize with students from divorced families.

Specific Ideas for the Classroom

Establish a Safe Classroom. Establish a structured, stable, and safe classroom environment. Routine and feelings of "safety" at home may be in transition; all students will appreciate a classroom that is consistent and supportive.

Talk. Talk individually with any student exhibiting recent behavior problems to identify the reasons for withdrawal or acting out. While maintaining high expectations, make individual arrangements as necessary and appropriate as the student adjusts to the changes at home. Talk individually with any student experiencing family divorce, simply to acknowledge the inevitable changes and to offer an expression of support.

Develop Teaching Units. Develop a "Growing Up," "Families," or "Pressures" (Hurwitz, 1994) unit. In this unit, individuals or small groups in a class could read books about a variety of topics, including divorce, and write book reviews for a school or even a local newspaper; research facts about a related topic, including divorce, and develop a pamphlet or bookmarks for the counselor's office (Hurwitz, 1994); part of this project might involve interviewing a school psychologist or counselor (Kaywell, 1994).

Develop and conduct a school-wide survey on unit topics, including divorce. With administrators' approval, students might create and publish a school profile regarding family living arrangements (single parent, blended family, etc.) based on this anonymous survey.

Collect and respond to "Dear Ann" or "Dear Abby" letters which address the unit topics, including divorce; do the same with cartoons. (For example, a series of Garry Trudeau's *Doonesbury* comic strips in December 1996 addressed communication and relationships among divorced parents and their daughter.)

Write dialogues between two characters, such as Jeff and his father or Jeff and his mother, at key story points; role-play a situation prior to reading or in response to reading a particular scene; or draw characters' heads with "bubbles" depicting the characters' thoughts and feelings at different points of a story.

Have Regular Writing. Make journal writing a regular part of the classroom routine. Some journal entries might be "free choice" to allow expression of personal feelings. Students can be given the option to fold over and staple any entry they would like to remain private. Even when they elect this privacy, individuals benefit from the opportunity to articulate their thoughts and feelings.

Utilize Peer-Counseling Groups. Provide information and encourage discussion about divorce with peer-counseling groups that may already exist at the school.

Establish a Peer Problems Book Club. Establish a "Peer Problems Book Club" for interested students that meets during lunch or after school once or twice a month. The group might be led by a school counselor and an English language arts teacher working in tandem, and the books read by the group might address a variety of problems faced by youth including divorce.

Provide Reading Information. Provide other opportunities during the school year for reading a book that involves divorce, through independent reading, literature circle (cooperative small group) reading, or whole class reading. Students might also view a video in which divorce plays a role. In discussing a book or video, students should analyze the characters' situations, predict their decisions, evaluate their behavior, and consider their alternatives. Students might also be encouraged to write a sequel, looking into a character's future in five or ten years. At the very least, make a number of the books annotated in the final section available in a classroom library and recommend certain titles for independent reading that may appeal to individual students.

SUPPORT SERVICES FOR STUDENTS

Teachers will also want to be familiar with counseling services available in the school for those adolescents who require support services beyond the scope of what a classroom teacher or peer support group can provide. Teachers can recognize students who need additional help in a number of ways. First, teachers can observe the emotional caliber of the student's responses in class; that is, does the student appear to be reacting more strongly than is typical to content material, especially when it is about divorce or families? Reactions in class that appear repeatedly and include crying or sadness, strong avoidance of material, anger which seems out of context, or emotional and behavioral outbursts, may indicate the need for counseling. In addition, the student may make statements that suggest the need for counseling such as "I feel so sad when I read this book" or "I just don't have any energy to get my schoolwork done."

A number of other indicators of student distress are important to monitor, including academic deterioration, decline in hygiene and dress, fatigue, weight loss, irritability, social difficulties, and inattentiveness or daydreaming. Finally, the student may indicate a need to talk about personal experiences more than is possible in the context of classroom activities.

Students who exhibit any of these signs, especially when the signs appear repeatedly, may benefit from an opportunity to continue to explore their feelings in counseling. The teacher who recognizes these indicators may want to consult with the school counselor or school psychologist about available counseling services and determine whether parents should be contacted to express concerns and request permission for services. Not all adolescents whose families are experiencing divorce will show adjustment problems or need referrals for counseling; however, those students who are experiencing difficulties are at risk for long-term problems in a number of areas, including social adjustment problems and underachievement. As a caretaker who spends a great deal of time with students but is not directly embroiled in the emotional impact of divorce, a teacher can be a safe and responsive lifeline to other services needed for the recovery of healthy adolescent developmental patterns and long-term adjustment.

While not usually as life-changing a problem as, for example, incest or a parent's severe drug abuse, divorce is so common an occurrence that teachers and school counselors should develop ways to work together to help students through what may be a difficult time. Counselors and teachers may draw on literature that provides poignant examples of what the experience of divorce is like. And, while sensitivity in the classroom will be enough for many students, referral for support services available outside the classroom may be necessary for some.

RECOMMENDED READINGS

Fiction

6.01.   Bauer, Marion Dane. (1994). *A question of trust*. New York: Scholastic. 130 pp. (ISBN: 0–590–47915–6). Middle School (MS).

Brad and his little brother are so sad and angry when their mother moves out that they won't answer her calls or visit her; their dad retreats to his study. It takes a stray cat and her kittens to help the boys reestablish contact and trust with both of their parents.

6.02.   Betancourt, Jeanne. (1986). *Puppy love*. New York: Avon Books. 96 pp. (ISBN: 0–380–89958–2). MS.

Aviva has adjusted to the changes brought by her parents' divorce and the joint legal custody arrangements. Then she learns more changes are in store when her father moves in with his girlfriend, and her mother remarries and becomes pregnant.

6.03.   Blume, Judy. (1972). *It's not the end of the world*. Scarsdale, NY: Bradbury Press. 160 pp. (ISBN: 0–87888–042–9). MS.

Sixth-grader Karen tries to get her separated parents back together again before their divorce is finalized. The story depicts reactions to the divorce from her brother and sister, her mom and dad, an aunt, and her grandfather.

6.04.   Brooks, Bruce. (1986). *Midnight hour encores*. New York: Harper Keypoint. 263 pp. (ISBN: 0–06–447021–0). High School (HS).

Sibilance "Sib" Spooner is a gifted cellist who was raised by her unorthodox father. When Sib and her dad travel to San Francisco to meet the mother who gave her up at birth, both are in for surprises.

6.05.   Brooks, Bruce. (1984). *The moves make the man*. New York: HarperCollins. 252 pp. (ISBN: 0–06–447022–9). HS.

Jeremy and Bix share friendship and a love of basketball, but the similarities end there. Jeremy is African American, bright, and living happily with his single mother; Bix, on the other hand, is Caucasian and living unhappily with his stepfather while his mother is in a mental hospital.

6.06.   Brooks, Bruce. (1992). *What hearts*. New York: HarperTrophy. 194 pp. (ISBN: 0–06–447127–8). MS, HS.

As a kindergartener, Asa adjusts to his parents' separation. As he grows older, he must cope with his manic-depressive mother and his stepfather. Changes over the years are depicted in this thought-provoking book. (Newbery Honor Book)

6.07.   Christopher, Matt. (1996). *The comeback challenge*. Boston: Little, Brown. 151 pp. (ISBN: 0–316–14152–6). MS.

Mark is the center on his school's soccer team, but how can he play to his potential during his parents' divorce?

6.08.   Cleary, Beverly. (1984). *Dear Mr. Henshaw*. New York: Dell. 133 pp. (ISBN: 0–440–41794–5). Elementary (E), MS.

Sixth-grader Leigh Botts writes to his favorite author. When the writer responds, Leigh has an outlet for discussing the issues in his life, including his feelings of abandonment by his father. (Newbery Medal Book)

6.09.   Cleary, Beverly. (1991). *Strider*. New York: William Morrow. 192 pp. (ISBN: 0–688–09900–9). E, MS.

In this sequel to *Dear Mr. Henshaw*, Leigh Botts is still adjusting to his parents' divorce. Through his journal entries we experience his joining the track team and acquiring joint custody of his dog, Strider.

6.10.   Cole, Brock. (1989). *Celine*. New York: Farrar, Straus, & Giroux. 216 pp. (ISBN: 0–374–31234–6). HS.

A mature 16-year-old, Celine is often on her own as her father and mother travel and her young stepmother follows her own interests. With all the "adults" away, Celine cares for a young neighbor, Jacob, and she helps him come to terms with his parents' divorce; at the same time, she learns something about herself.

6.11.   Conrad, Pam. (1997). *Holding me here*. New York: HarperTrophy. 184 pp. (ISBN: 0–064–47166–7). HS.

Because Robin's parents divorced when she was 14 years old, she tries in earnest to reunite a new boarder with her husband and children. Unbeknownst to Robin, Mrs. Walker left an abusive situation and Robin learns that divorce is sometimes necessary even if children initially suffer.

6.12.   Cooney, Caroline B. (1990). *Family reunion*. New York: Bantam Starfire. 176 pp. (ISBN: 0–553–285–73–4). MS.

Shelley lives with her father, a man who has remarried again into a "perfect" family whose attitudes about life and living drive her crazy. (A YASD Recommended Book for Reluctant Readers)

6.13.   Corcoran, Barbara. (1978). *Hey, that's my soul you're stomping on*. New York: Atheneum. 122 pp. (ISBN: 0–689–30617–2). MS, HS.

Sixteen-year-old Rachel learns about life, love, and death during a stay with her grandparents in Palm Springs while her parents are deciding about their divorce back home in Massachusetts. She ultimately decides to live with her mother, though it appears Rachel will be the more mature of the two.

6.14.   Danziger, Paula. (1982). *The divorce express*. New York: Delacorte. 148 pp. (ISBN: 0–440–02035–2). MS.

The title refers to the bus that journeys from Woodstock to New York City, filled with kids visiting their other parent for the weekend. There's a great deal of humor in this story about Phoebe and her friend Rosie as they discover important truths about family, friendship, and adjusting to change.

6.15.   Danziger, Paula. (1985). *It's an aardvark-eat-turtle world*. New York: Dell Laurel Leaf. 132 pp. (ISBN: 0–440–94028–1). MS.

Rosie and Phoebe are now sisters because Phoebe's dad and Rosie's mother have married; Phoebe's mother has also remarried. Told from Rosie's perspective, we learn that Phoebe struggles to handle the continuing changes; Phoebe eventually agrees to see a counselor. (An IRA/CBC Children's Choice)

6.16.   Ferris, Jean. (1993). *Relative strangers*. New York: Farrar, Straus, & Giroux. 229 pp. (ISBN: 0–374–36243–2). HS.

Seventeen-year-old Berkeley receives an invitation to tour Europe from a father she rarely sees, and then discovers—at the airport—that her new stepmother and stepsister will be joining them. While she desperately wants her father's love and acceptance, Berkeley comes to see her father's strengths and weaknesses and to appreciate her good relationships with her mother and boyfriend Spike.

6.17.   Fine, Anne. (1996). *Step by wicked step*. Boston: Little, Brown & Co. 138 pp. (ISBN: 0–316–28345–2). E, MS.

When five kids riding together on a school trip learn that they are all from divorced families, they share their stories about family breakups, step siblings, and half siblings. The characters are not fully developed, but their emotions are real as they tell of their experiences with divorce and its aftermath.

6.18. Fox, Paula. (1986). *Moonlight man*. New York: Dell. 179 pp. (ISBN: 0–440–20079–2). MS, HS.

When her mother remarries, it's decided that Catherine will spend her vacation from a boarding school with her father. Unfortunately, her father is an alcoholic, a fact which causes difficult moments. This is a serious book and a thoughtful story with complex characters. Readers will understand how Catherine and her father can love each other but will probably not see each other again. (An American Library Association [ALA] Notable Children's Book)

6.19. Haynes, David. (1992). *Right by my side*. Minneapolis, MN: New Rivers Press. 179 pp. (ISBN: 0–89823–147–7). HS.

When 15-year-old Marshall Field Finney's mother leaves, he and his father Sam eventually adjust, but then must adjust again when she returns. Marshall's white friend Todd actually has more family problems. Charming and poignant, this book yields insights about family and friendship. (An ALA Best Book for Young Adults, 1994)

6.20. Holland, Isabelle. (1987). *The man without a face*. New York: Harper. 157 pp. (ISBN: 0–694–05611–1). HS.

Fourteen-year-old Charles Norstadt is so distraught over living in a house full of females with no father that he will do anything to get out—even if that means studying all summer to pass a boarding school's entrance exam. His physically and emotionally scarred tutor teaches him more than just academics. A movie, starring Mel Gibson, is also available. (An ALA Best of the Best Books for Young Adults)

6.21. Klass, Sheila Solomon. (1995). *Next stop nowhere*. New York: Scholastic. 81 pp. (ISBN: 0–590–46686–0). MS.

When her mother remarries, 14-year-old Beth is not at all pleased because she is shipped off to live with her artist dad in a small Vermont town. The story chronicles Beth's "burying the hatchet" in her relationship with her father, whom she calls Pablo.

6.22. Klass, Sheila Solomon. (1986). *Page four*. New York: Bantam Books. 167 pp. (ISBN: 0–553–26901–1). HS.

Seventeen-year-old David and his mother are both devastated when David's father abandons the family to live in Alaska with a younger woman.

Slowly they learn that time and friends can help heal the hurt and anger. The title refers to the essay David needs to write for his college applications.

6.23. Klass, Sheila Solomon. (1981). *To see my mother dance*. New York: Charles Scribner's Sons. 154 pp. (ISBN: 0–684–17227–5). MS, HS.

Jessica's dad has raised her since she was a baby when they were abandoned by her mother. Now Jessica's dad intends to marry Martha but Jessica is opposed. A wise Martha takes Jessica to California to meet her mother, but what Jessica finds is hardly the woman of her fantasies.

6.24. Latiolais, Michelle. (1990). *Even now*. New York: Farrar, Straus, & Giroux. 211 pp. (ISBN: 0–374–14993–3). HS.

Even though Lisa is 16 and her parents have been divorced for several years, the problems persist. Now her mother is seeing an old boyfriend, and her father has a new girlfriend. No matter which parent she is with, Lisa feels uneasy, tense, and downright miserable.

6.25. LeMieux, A. C. (1993). *The TV guidance counselor*. New York: Avon. 184 pp. (ISBN: 0–380–72050–7). HS.

Michael Madden has a horrific sophomore year: His parents get a divorce, his mother has to sell their home and move into a "shack," he is expelled from school, and he thinks maybe he should end it all when a silly prank almost turns into a tragedy.

6.26. Maloney, Ray. (1987). *The impact zone*. New York: Dell Laurel-Leaf. 256 pp. (ISBN: 0–440–94013–3). MS, HS.

Jim doesn't care for his stepfather or his life in California so he decides to run away to his real father in Hawaii. There he receives a rude awakening from his surfer dad. (The Third Annual Delacorte Press Prize for Outstanding First Young Adult Novel)

6.27. Mazer, Harry. (1990). *Guy Lenny*. New York: Dell Laurel-Leaf. 144 pp. (ISBN: 0–440–93311–0). MS.

Twelve-year-old Guy's life was chaotic enough after his parents' divorce and he went to live with his father. It gets beyond complicated, however, when his father finds a new mother and his biological mother returns and wants him to live with her and her new husband.

6.28.   Mazer, Norma Fox. (1996). *Missing pieces*. New York: Avon Flare. 137 pp. (ISBN: 0–380–72289–5). MS.

There's conflict between Jessie and her mother concerning what Jessie needs to know about her dad, who left when she was a baby. When he unexpectedly arrives in town, Jessie meets him face-to-face but can't bring herself to talk with him or ask him her many questions. Readers are left thinking that they will meet again.

6.29.   Mazer, Norma Fox. (1981). *The taking of Terri Mueller*. New York: Avon Flare. 190 pp. (ISBN: 0–380–79004–1). MS, HS.

Kidnapped by her father at age four, Terri has begun asking questions about her mother and family. Terri ultimately learns that her mother did not die in a car accident, and she is reunited with her understandably overjoyed mother. Terri has a difficult decision to make about whether to live with her mother or father.

6.30.   Miller, M. J. (1992). *Me and my name*. New York: Puffin Books. 128 pp. (ISBN: 0–140–34374–1). MS.

Erin has an important choice to make and her biological father hasn't made it any easier: Will she let her stepfather adopt her and change her last name now that her mother is expecting his twins?

6.31.   Pardo, Gina. (1995). *Jason and the losers*. New York: Clarion. 120 pp. (ISBN: 0–395–70160–0). MS.

After his parents' divorce, Jason's mother sends him to live with her sister and husband and their son, who Jason considers a real loser. Cousin Everett may drive Jason crazy, but Everett is all he's got for the time being while his mother works nights and his father is out of the country.

6.32.   Peck, Richard. (1988). *Father figure*. New York: Dell. 182 pp. (ISBN: 0–440–20069–5). MS, HS.

Jim is a junior in high school and Bryon is eight when their mother commits suicide, forcing them to live with a father who deserted them when Bryon was just a baby. Jim has always been the "father figure" for his little brother since their parents' divorce, and he resents Bryon's immediate attachment to "Dad." (An ALA Best Book for Young Adults)

6.33.   Peck, Richard. (1991). *Unfinished portrait of Jessica*. New York: Delacorte. 176 pp. (ISBN: 0–385–30500–1). MS, HS.

When Jessica's parents divorce, she blames her mother and worships her photographer father who has moved to the Mexican house of her uncle, a famous painter. Jessica has yet to complete her journey toward self-identity, but during a visit with her father she discovers he is not so worthy of her admiration. Jessica returns to her mother and a new and stronger relationship is forged.

6.34.   Pullman, Philip. (1992). *The broken bridge*. New York: Knopf. 218 pp. (ISBN: 0–679–91972–4). HS.

Ginny has been led to believe by her father that her mother, a black Haitian artist, is dead. When Ginny discovers that her father has lied, she is determined to learn the truth. Ginny locates her mother but finds that her father was protecting her from the cold truth: She was unwanted by her mother. (An ALA Best Book for Young Adults, 1993)

6.35.   Skinner, David. (1992). *You must kiss a whale*. New York: Simon & Schuster. 94 pp. (ISBN: 0–671–74781–9). MS.

After Evelyn's parents separate, she and her mother and sister move to the desert where her mother is working on a secret project. Evelyn finds a story her father wrote long ago, in which a character receives a letter saying he must kiss a whale. While adjusting to the new living arrangements, Evelyn attempts to learn what the message means.

6.36.   Stolz, Mary. (1992). *Go and catch a flying fish*. New York: HarperKeypoint. 213 pp. (ISBN: 0–06–025868–3). MS, HS.

Taylor Reddick has two problems: her parents argue more and more frequently, and she's terribly nervous about beginning high school in the fall. Gradually, she comes to accept that her parents' choices are outside of her control and that she will be able to adjust to changes in family and school.

6.37.   Talbert, Marc. (1991). *Pillow of clouds*. New York: Dial Books. 204 pp. (ISBN: 0–8037–0901–3). MS.

Chester must decide whether to live with his alcoholic and needy mother in Iowa or his bookstore-owning father in New Mexico. The cold and warm climates in the two states mirror Chester's relationships with his parents. After he makes his decision, Chester wonders how he'll ever be able to tell his mother.

6.38.   Van Leeuwen, Jean. (1996). *Blue sky, butterfly*. New York: Dial Books. 125 pp. (ISBN: 0–8037–1972–8). MS.

Twig's father leaves. Even though she still has her mother and older brother, Twig is very lonely as they all cope with the changes in their lives.

6.39.   Voigt, Cynthia. (1983). *A solitary blue*. New York: Scholastic. 307 pp. (ISBN: 0–590–47157–0). MS, HS.

This book chronicles the life of Jeff from the time his controlling, "cause-happy" mother leaves him when he is seven through his senior year in high school. Complex characters and changes over time make this compelling story the choice for further attention in this chapter. (An ALA Best of the Best for Young Adults, an ALA Notable Children's Book, a Newbery Honor Book, & a Boston Globe/Horn Book Honor Book)

6.40.   Willey, Margaret. (1993). *The Melinda zone*. New York: Bantam Books. 135 pp. (ISBN: 0–553–09215–4). MS, HS.

Melinda is so busy being the peacemaker between her divorced parents that she never has time to be herself. When she goes to spend the summer with her aunt, uncle, and cousin, she comes to important realizations about herself and finds the courage to confront her parents with her needs.

6.41.   Wilson, Nancy Hope. (1994). *The reason for Janey*. (1994). New York: Macmillan. 160 pp. (ISBN: 0–02–793127–7). MS.

Philly lives with her mother and brother, but she makes monthly visits to her "couch-potato" dad who lives in Boston. Rounding out her family at home, however, is Janey, a mentally retarded adult. Philly learns a great deal about what "family" means over the course of the book.

Nonfiction

6.42.   Boeckman, Charles. (1980). *Surviving your parents' divorce*. New York: Franklin Watts. 133 pp. (ISBN: 0–531–02869–0). MS.

This book presents information about child support, custody, feelings about changes that come with divorce, and other related topics. Case studies bring these topics to life and provide a realistic yet hopeful view for the future.

6.43.   Goldentyter, Debra. (1995). *Teen hot line: Parental divorce*. Austin, TX: Raintree Steck-Vaughn Publishers. 80 pp. (ISBN: 0–8114–3817–1). MS, HS.

Questions and answers introduce chapters about why parents divorce, the legal process, remarriage and new families, among other topics. Also included are interviews which present brief case studies.

6.44.   Krementz, Jill. (1984). *How it feels when parents divorce*. New York: Knopf. 115 pp. (ISBN: 0–394–54079–4). MS, HS.

Kids from 10 to 17 years of age tell their individual stories about divorce, explaining how their parents acted, what the difficulties were, economic changes, and how they've coped over the years. Pictures of the child or teen with a parent show how most of these youths have adjusted.

6.45.   LeShan, Eda. (1986). *What's going to happen to me? When parents separate or divorce*. New York: Macmillan. 144 pp. (ISBN: 0–689–71093–3). MS.

This book describes the feelings that accompany separation and divorce, including feelings before, during, and after the divorce.

6.46.   Levine, Beth. (1995). *Divorce: Young people caught in the middle*. Springfield, NJ: Enslow Publishers. 112 pp. (ISBN: 0–894–90633–X). MS, HS.

The author presents brief cases of families in the midst of divorce, as well as numerous statistics that put the scope of divorce into perspective. Eight chapters focus on a variety of divorce issues, from before the divorce to disappearing dads.

6.47.   List, Julie A. (1980). *The day the loving stopped: A daughter's view of her parents' divorce*. New York: Seaview Books. 215 pp. (ISBN: 0–872–23559–9). HS.

In this poignant first-person account, the author describes how divorce impacts children. Her diary entries and letters reveal feelings connected to the separation and changes in living arrangements.

6.48.   McGuire, Paula. (1987). *Putting it together: Teenagers talk about family breakup*. New York: Delacorte Press. 167 pp. (ISBN: 0–440–50242–X). MS, HS.

This book's author interviewed numerous children, teenagers, and counselors about their experiences with divorce. Her findings strongly suggest that most kids and families cope remarkably well, and that life is often better than before the divorce once adjustments have been made.

6.49.   Richards, Arlene Kramer & Willis, Irene. (1986). *How to get it together when your parents are coming apart*. Summit, NJ: Willard Press. 170 pp. (ISBN: 0–961–53490–7). HS.

Case studies help depict the various aspects of divorce, including legal issues and reasons for outside help or counseling. Direct and easy to read, this book will answer the questions teens have.

6.50.   Rosenberg, M. B. (1990). *Talking about step families*. New York: Bradbury Press. 160 pp. (ISBN: 0–027–77913–0). MS, HS.

After interviewing step-parents, natural parents, and step-children, the author concludes that perspectives about the same events and issues can be markedly different. Readers will learn about typical feelings about step-parents and blended families.

6.51.   Worth, Richard. (1992). *Single parent families*. New York: Franklin Watts. 127 pp. (ISBN: 0–531–11131–8). MS, HS.

This book describes the reasons for the large numbers of single parent families, including divorce, and explores the effects on families. The author also presents common problems and ways to deal with the stress.

RECOMMENDED VIDEOS

6.52.   Garces, Marcia, Williams, Robin, & Williams, Marcia Radcliffe. (Producers). (1993). *Mrs. Doubtfire*. Twentieth Century Fox Film Corp. Fox Home Video. (ISBN: 0–7939–8588–9). PG-13.

Daniel Hillard, played by Robin Williams, misses his children terribly following his divorce. Dressed in a wig, dress, and make-up, he applies for—and is given—a position as his own children's housekeeper. Often hilarious and frequently touching, the film shows how Daniel is able to develop nurturing behaviors and respect for women, attitudes that were foreign to him as a man.

6.53.   Jaffe, Stanley R. (Producer). (1979). *Kramer vs. Kramer*. Columbia Pictures. A Columbia Tri-Star Film. RCA/Columbia Pictures Home Video. [No ISBN]. PG-13.

Adapted from the novel by Avery Corman, this film garnered eight Academy Award nominations and won five Academy Awards. Dustin Hoffman plays a selfish New York advertising executive who is suddenly left to care for his young son when his wife leaves. The early parts of the video portray the growing closeness of the father and son; the last part depicts the heart-rending custody battle that ensues when the mother, played by Meryl Streep, returns.

REFERENCES

Anderson, R. C. (1984). Role of the reader's schema in comprehension, learning and memory. In R. C. Anderson, J. Osborn, & R. J. Tierney (Eds.), *Learning to read in American schools: Basal readers and texts*. Hillsdale, NJ: Erlbaum, 243–257.

Brandt, A. (1991, October). Children of divorce: From hurt to healing. *Parenting*, 119.

The Family Center of the Conciliation Court. (1992). *Children and divorce*. Tuscon, AZ.

Hofferth, S. L. (1987, February). Implications of family trends for children: A research perspective. *Educational Leadership, 44* (5), 78.

Hurwitz, Sharon. (1994, Winter). Using literature and technology to relieve adolescent problems. *The ALAN Review, 21* (2), 33.

Kaywell, Joan F. (1993). *Adolescents at risk: A guide to fiction and nonfiction for young adults, parents, and professionals*. Westport, CT: Greenwood Press.

Kaywell, Joan F. (1994, Winter). Using YA problem fiction and nonfiction to produce critical readers. *The ALAN Review, 21* (2), 29–32.

Kelly, J. (1993). Current research on children's post-divorce adjustment: No simple answers. *Family and Conciliation Courts Review, 31* (1), 29–49.

Levine, Beth. (1995). *Issues in focus: Divorce: Young people caught in the middle*. Springfield, NJ: Enslow Publishers.

Robson, B. (1993). Changing family patterns: Developmental impacts on children. In J. Carlson & J. Lewis (Eds.), *Counseling the Adolescent: Individual, Family, and School Interventions*. 2nd Ed. Denver, CO: Love Publishing Co., 149–165.

Rosenblatt, Louise M. (1978). *The reader, the text, the poem: The transactional theory of the literary work.* Carbondale, IL: Southern Illinois University Press.
Wallerstein, J. S. & Kelly, J. B. (1980). *Surviving the breakup: How children and parents cope with divorce.* New York: Basic Books.

CHAPTER 7

Adam and Eve and Pinch-Me: Issues of Adolescents in Foster Care

Cynthia Ann Bowman & Jennifer Fike

INTRODUCTION

FOSTER PARENTS NEEDED
Training, daily reimbursements,
and intensive support to those who
wish to provide a loving home
for abused and troubled youth.

Ads such as this one appear in newspapers across the country at alarming rates as more and more children are removed from their homes and placed in foster care. According to the Child Welfare League of America, of the adolescents who entered foster care in 1990, more than 50% were for protective services reasons; an additional 21% due to parental illness, death, handicap, or financial hardship; another 11% because of the youth's delinquent offenses; and 2% in cases where the adolescent has a disability or handicap (Tatara, 1993). Most dramatic are the increasing numbers of children infected with HIV and children who are medically fragile and/or physically handicapped who are being placed in foster care. Adolescents in such abusive and troubling environments are at risk of emotional, behavioral, and developmental problems including conduct disorders, depression, difficulties in school, and impaired social relationships.

At-risk students know alienation, loneliness, and a loss of hope. They are at risk of being left behind, losing identity, making poor choices, and engaging in destructive behavior. "Children who feel rootless or caught in conflict at home find it difficult to pay attention in school. Once they begin to miss out on learning, they feel lost in the classroom, and they begin to seek acceptance elsewhere" (Bronfenbrenner, 1976, p. 432). Today's society places more and more students at risk, at risk of developing a poor self-image manifested as "I don't care," "I give up," and "I can't do it" as well as an inability to ask questions and a weak sense of direction. At-risk students are below average for their ability, exhibit behavior problems, have no established goals, possess low self-esteems, appear disenfranchised and uninvolved in school activities, and are frequently tardy and truant. Adolescents placed in foster care are vulnerable and at risk of drug and alcohol abuse, pregnancy and sexually transmitted diseases, and suicide. The faces of adolescents featured on segments of local news programs, "Wednesday's Child" or "Adopt a Child" are haunting. Their educational, emotional, and social needs are even more troubling. Research has indicated that these young people achieve less and are academically behind their peers who are not in foster care by at least one year (Ohio Department of Human Services, 1987; Jones & Moses, 1984; Festinger, 1994).

EDUCATOR MEETS COUNSELOR

As we began our discussion, we discovered that our roles were inextricably bound. Teachers focus on counseling issues as well as content as we help our students with goal setting, decision-making, and behavior problems. Improved literacy skills, likewise, have the potential to open up new doors for counselors and therapists. Identification with a protagonist can have a powerful effect on an adolescent. Literature can help students understand themselves in relation to others and their position in life; can reach a student when a parent, teacher, and counselor cannot; and provide a sense of community. True learning requires personal connections or engagement with others. Louise Rosenblatt (1983) reminds us that the personal, social, and cultural contexts of literature provide such a sense of belonging. We all yearn for a community, an extension of the bonds of family and friends. The essence of human life is one's connection to others, and adolescents in foster care lack these integral connections.

Collaboration between literacy experts and therapists can have a strong therapeutic value for adolescents at risk. As an educator of English education collaborating with a counselor for this chapter on foster care issues, I envisioned wonderful teaching strategies in the therapy plan my co-author had for counseling Sara Moone, the protagonist in *Adam and Eve and Pinch-Me* by Julie Johnston. My co-author perceived new opportunities for therapy in my teaching activities and class discussions. We both identified overlapping issues and roles in our understanding of Sara Moone, we both recognized the significance of school as a major focus of life for adolescents, and we both found a strong affinity for this young adult (YA) novel.

I was originally drawn to *Adam and Eve and Pinch-Me* because I *knew* Sara Moone. I knew and understood what it was like to escape from pain, unhappiness, and even life, through a book. I recognized the solace of living someone else's life, dealing with someone else's problems, experiencing joy and freedom, leaving my world behind for a few hours. As Sara said, "I get involved in books to the point where it becomes embarrassing. When I read *The Secret Garden*, I began to sound quite snotty. When I read *The Color Purple*, I developed a Southern drawl. I'm not safe around books" (p. 7). My co-author was just as enthusiastic about the novel as it supports her research with bibliotherapy and the power of narrative in counseling.

ADAM AND EVE AND PINCH-ME BY JULIE JOHNSTON (180 pp.)

Synopsis

Adam and Eve and Pinch-Me is the story of Sara Moone as told by Sara through the journal she keeps on her computer. Fifteen-year-old Sara is a ward of Children's Aid and is preparing to leave yet another foster home. Sara was given up for adoption at birth, but her adoptive parents were killed in a fire when she was young. Since then, she has been in more foster homes than she wants to remember. She has spent the last two years with the Koscyzstins, an older couple who needed the help she could provide around the house. When Mrs. K. becomes ill, Sara's social worker, Ruth, arranges for Sara to go to the Huddleston's farm. Mr. K. gives Sara his old computer, saying, "Maybe you'll relate to it, because God knows you don't relate to people" (p. 3). The computer is the only friend she has, the only thing she relates to. Sara herself writes, "Of course I don't relate to people. Why would I? I'm not related to anybody and nobody's related to me" (p. 3). When the story begins, Sara is writing in her computer journal, "I can blank out people. Click. Erase. Gone" (p. 1). The ride with Ruth to the Huddlestons reveals even more of Sara's character and the protective walls she has built around herself. She is quiet and unemotional. As Ruth tries to get Sara to talk about her feelings, Sara withdraws and rationalizes, "If you don't want your heart broken, don't let on you have one" (p. 6). It is apparent that Ruth genuinely cares for Sara as she encourages her to respond to the letters and inquiries her biological mother has sent, but Sara claims to want no part of the woman who left her feeling as though she was disposable. Sara and Ruth argue over Sara's uncommunicative manner and when Ruth lights a ciga-rette, the flame causes Sara to react hysterically and they end up in a ditch. From there, they walk to a small diner, Fran's Ee-Lite Café, which is the gathering place for the people in the small town of Ambrose, Ontario, in or-der to telephone the Huddlestons.

Sara is greeted warmly by the Huddlestons, a childless couple who regu-larly take in foster children. Hud is a wise and understanding man who doesn't say more than is absolutely necessary and works hard on his farm. Ma loves to talk, cook, and care for her family. Already with the Hud-dlestons are Nick and Josh. Nick, in his early teens, is a bitter, cynical, and sneaky boy who is constantly in trouble. Josh is a four-year old who loves to be with people, likes affection, and enjoys looking at catalogs. The family has also taken in a stray dog, Edith Ann, who lets people get just so close, only to then turn on them. Throughout the story are strong parallels between Sara and Edith Ann. Ma Huddleston has fixed a room for Sara, and it looks as though Sara has every opportunity to finally be happy. Sara's own per-sonal boundaries and aloofness preclude her from this family and this com-munity. She realizes the strong connections that exist in this rural area: "I was thinking about the way everybody around here takes a personal interest in everybody else's affairs. They seem to be spread over half the county and yet they're linked, somehow, like short stories in a book I just finished read-ing" (p. 60).

The element of story permeates the novel as Nick and Sara make up hurt-ful and hateful stories of mothers who don't want them. Another story of pain is the thread created by the riddle about "Adam and Eve and Pinch-Me." As Josh tries desperately to get close to Sara, she asks him, "Adam and Eve and Pinch-Me went down to the river to bathe. Adam and Eve fell in, and who do you think was saved?" (p. 37). When Josh responds with "Pinch-Me," Sara pinches his arm. Josh leaves Sara's room with none of his typical spirit and enthusiasm, and Sara watches the little boy put up the same walls she had constructed when someone tricked her. The episode puts a crack in her wall, though, as she searches for Josh that evening to ex-plain to him that the next time someone tries to hurt him he needs to say, "Pinch-Me Not." Later in the story Josh, indeed, says it to the social worker who makes him go back to his abusive biological mother. Sara is reminded of this pain she caused Josh when she notices similar expressions on the faces of those people who care for her.

Sara's greatest retreat from others is her plan to run away when she turns sixteen. "Picture me as something like a little hyphen on a blank screen. A cursor. Unattached to anything before or after. I move along and down, along and down, until finally I get to page sixteen. That's when the story starts" (p. 8). She begins to plan her escape by working part time at the café, the one place where, interestingly enough, "conversation is communal property" (p. 59). It is truly ironic that she finds herself employed in a place where "it's almost as if they're all connected somehow. They make me think of the inside of my computer" (p. 62). When he learns that she is trying to save some money, Matthew Bellington, who has been sitting next to her on the school bus, offers her work typing the manuscript of Grainger Cleary, an author staying at his family's bed and breakfast. The manuscript is a collection of ghost stories and history, and Grainger tells Sara, "I think you'll find that memories, fears, longings, strong passions, all that sort of thing, are related to ghostly emanations" (p. 64).

Matt obviously likes Sara and is undaunted by her uncaring, uninterested attitude. He talks to her of his plans for college, his hopes and dreams, and his love of history. This is a painful topic for Sara who says, "I am one of a kind, first person singular, taking up not quite sixteen years of time and space. Less, actually, when you think about it, considering my blank early childhood. I cannot attach myself to a history. I stand alone in the present tense" (p. 96). However, life at the Huddlestons as well as Matt's promise to always be there for her are slowly changing Sara as she begins to see connections in life. As she marvels at her newfound curiosity, she ponders Matt's discussion of history, "I have always thought of history as chunks of time, eras, something connected to reigns, or wars, or movements. But the way he said that made me think of ordinary people linked together, going back and back and back. Or even forward" (p. 58).

The influence of nature is also helping to break down Sara's walls. While on the farm, Sara assists with the birth of baby sheep and the May planting. Unwittingly, she describes herself in a field of wildflowers. "It was one of those flowering weeds you see but don't notice until you look closely. The flowers were exquisite. When I closed my hand around it, I got a fistful of prickles" (p. 107). When a strange woman comes to town in search of the daughter she had given up at birth and Matt asks Sara if she will speak with her, Sara replies, "[She t]hrew out a real live person, a thinking, feeling, hurting person. I hate her!" (p. 106). The woman, who is never given a name or a real identity, tries to convince Sara that her daughter would have a nice life in the city if she would go with her. Sara comes to a personal realization that she actually has connections in the community, a bond with the Huddlestons and the people of Ambrose. She enjoys working on the farm and says to Hud, "I like this kind of work. You can see where you are going and you can see where you've been. Making your mark on the land. . . . Chip off the old block, Hud said, just as if I was related to him" (p. 121).

The descriptions of the Canadian countryside become more vivid as Sara's relationships become more authentic. Authenticity requires integral connections and responsibility as well as a vulnerability, or opening up to others. Such authenticity is frightening, especially for someone who has protected himself or herself from vulnerability. Sara tells us, "Not a specific fear, just a fear without end" (p. 109). Even the dog, Edith Ann, runs away after allowing Sara to pet her. When Sara learns that Nick has read her journal from her computer screen, she writes, "Printed words are so present, so vulnerable. If I printed this stuff, anybody could read my words, study them, give meaning to them. Concrete evidence that I exist" (p. 155). Sara certainly does exist and has found a home with the Huddlestons. She realizes the power of community, "I finally get to be a free agent and I find I'm tied, tethered, and bound to every living creature in the entire county" (p. 173). She shares with Josh, "If I have to be related to anybody, I wouldn't mind being related to you, you little blister. . . . Brother and sister, Pinch-Me and Pinch-Me Not" (p. 163). When Hud gets sick, she realizes, "I had broken my own rule about not letting on I had a heart. Now I had a pain in it. I was involved. I felt not so much trapped, as tangled up in these other lives, a participant, not merely a captive audience" (p. 143).

The turning point for Sara in her search for belonging and personal identity is the night she calls Hud in the hospital. She telephones to ask him if he is still willing to teach her to drive his truck, remembering that she had once denied she would be with them when she turns sixteen. Knowing it is her way of reaching out, Hud tells her she is the salt of the earth. That night Sara witnesses an eclipse of the moon. Earlier in the novel, "the moon was not very big and just hung there, uselessly, partly shrouded in mist" (p. 105). Now, "at first the moon seemed to be disappearing piece by piece. I was so sad I nearly cried (a habit I seem to be getting into). And then, the strangest thing! The moon became a sphere. A ball. Not just a flat disc hanging in the sky" (p. 149). So, too, evolved Sara *Moone*.

TEACHING STRATEGIES

Adam and Eve and Pinch-Me not only deals with issues of adolescents in foster care but issues of all adolescents—belonging, sexuality, relationships, trust, jobs, money, friendship, loyalty, and identity. It lends itself to a variety of strategies to engage students in reading, writing, listening, speaking, and viewing.

Journals

I would encourage students to write in a journal as Sara does and provide the option to keep a private journal or an interactive one with a peer or myself. We would discuss the many computer and composition metaphors Sara uses to express her feelings and emotions and brainstorm a list of other metaphors to describe Sara as well as ourselves.

Genealogy

Sara's last name is symbolic as well as descriptive, and I would have students explore the genealogy of their names and create a family tree. They could illustrate any interesting facts they learn or research an interesting ancestor. For adopted students or students in foster care, they would see that they are not void of a background or identity.

Natural or Unexplained Phenomena

Nature plays an important role in the novel as Sara describes herself with images from nature. Students could brainstorm in small groups the elements of nature which best describe them as a pre-writing activity for creative works.

The ghost stories Grainger Cleary is collecting could also generate interest as students collect stories from family and friends, unexplained phenomena, and legends in order to compile an album of "local color."

Role-Playing

Much of the novel's activity takes place in Fran's Ee-Lite Café. By discussing the setting choice in popular television shows such as the bar on *Cheers* or the coffeehouse on *Friends*, students could begin to brainstorm gathering places in their area and create a series of skits reflecting the community. I would insert an "outsider" in the activity to encourage students to think about the difficulties of being new to a community and how to make someone feel welcome.

The Ending

The ambiguity of the ending will be problematic for many students. In cooperative learning groups, I would have students discuss their perceptions and write or perform their versions of the ending and explain why they came to those conclusions.

RECOMMENDED THERAPY FOR SARA

We both enjoyed the novel for its fair and realistic portrayal of the foster care system and the adolescents the system serves. Most states have foster care agreements to provide care, custody, and rehabilitation needs of children removed from their families and procedures to eventually reunite families. Each of the three children in the Huddleston's care has a unique history and set of problems. Josh was taken from his abusive mother by the courts, yet she occasionally wants him back and tries to bribe him with desserts or treats only to beat him while under the influence of drugs and alcohol. Nick's mother was a drug addict who didn't want him at all; the numerous foster homes cannot provide the stability to keep him from lying, stealing, and cheating. Even the Huddlestons, with all their love and patience, are at a loss as to how to be a positive influence. Sara's pain is internal; she has closed herself completely off to others. She has a difficult time talking to people and has a poor self-image. "With a computer you don't need a voice" (p. 26).

The issues, which Sara experiences, are very typical for adolescents who are given up for adoption or placed in foster care for unforeseen circumstances. She shares the Huddleston's home and attention with Josh and Nick. Often the children who are placed in foster care are not the only child in the setting. At times, entire families are made up of a number of foster children taken in by foster parents who are willing to assume the responsibility. In focusing from a psychotherapeutic viewpoint to help Sara work through her many feelings and difficulties, I suggest the following areas of concentration during therapy:

- Assist Sara in improving her self-concept.
- Increase Sara's responsibility to herself and to other members of her foster family.
- Improve Sara's interaction patterns with her foster parents, biological parent, peers, and foster brothers.
- Provide support and inspiration and improve social skills and insight into problem solving for Sara.

Sara seems to have found a friend in writing, a process that can prove to be very therapeutic for some individuals. In Sara's case, it appears that when she is upset or needs to talk about something, she allows the computer to be her voice. She shares with Matt that she is not good at expressing herself verbally and communicates her feelings by writing him a letter. As a therapist, I would be negligent if I were to ignore the powerful impact that writing and literacy has had on this adolescent through her many years in foster care. Integrating the use of journal writing and giving Sara recommended readings during therapy would be of great benefit to her continued growth.

The most favorable way to help Sara expand her self-awareness and self-concept is to provide her with a setting in which she would have the opportunity to talk about herself and the environment in which she is living, with assistance in her search for her identity. Physical, sexual, social, religious, and moral changes all contribute to an adolescent's struggle for identity. Sara would benefit in an atmosphere that is supportive of discussions on these topics and other common problems of everyday life. She needs to be able to explore her feelings regarding relationships and life experiences.

Group therapy is something that I recommend for Sara as well as other youth in foster care, more so than individual therapy, for it provides opportunities to grow and share with one another. There is an element available in group therapy that is not available in individual psychotherapy—the element of common ground. Communicating with others who are experiencing similar ordeals often lessens their struggles; therefore, the recommended mode of psychotherapy for Sara is an adolescent therapy group which would consist of members who live in foster care placements. Sara finds this commonality, to a certain extent, with Nick and Josh. She and Nick both understand the feeling of abandonment. Likewise, Sara attempts to protect Josh from some of the pain and frustration she has experienced in foster care. In this type of group therapy, adolescents have an opportunity to participate in psychoeducational discussion topics, engage in problem solving, and talk about personal experiences through group sharing. Unfortunately, group therapy is often difficult to find for adolescents in foster care.

If Sara were to participate in an adolescent group designed to serve children and adolescents who are placed in foster homes, she would be introduced to a short-term psychoeducational form of support group. The primary goal of these groups is to provide a safe environment in which adolescents can explore their feelings and discuss issues relating to self-concept, school, sexuality, and friends. Oftentimes adolescents are not open to sharing, as Sara has revealed in her aloof attitude toward those involved in her life. This group provides an outlet for sharing and receiving feedback and is led by an expert trained in facilitating group interaction. Sara is experiencing all of the normal teenage problems of growing; however, her world may be changing even faster than that of the average teenager. The group session topics progress in hierarchical fashion so as to move through the levels of intimacy. This hierarchical presentation allows risk-taking behavior to develop among the peers in the group. The most important function of the group is to develop community among its participants.

Although this group would give Sara the opportunity to share her frustrations, problems, and other feelings, it is equally important that she be exposed to the psychoeducational dimension of therapy which provides a more structured method of presenting information to these adolescents regarding teenage issues. The psychoeducational portion of a group setup would give Sara the freedom to share openly and honestly, but would also be structured enough that direction would be provided to guide the conversations among the group members. Sara, Nick, and Josh often had difficulty communicating. Perhaps this is one avenue that would facilitate opening the lines of communication among them.

A SAMPLE THERAPY SESSION

Allow me to share my experiences leading a group therapy session for adolescents in foster care. The first meeting of the group was led by two of us: a child psychologist and me. Since the members of the group were simultaneously in individual counseling with the child psychologist, it was appropriate for him to be a co-leader during the first session to set the participants at ease. As a group leader, I found myself attempting to be counselor, teacher, parent, mediator, facilitator, and referee all at once. More often than not, everyone in the group wanted to talk at the same time. Trying to keep order in the group and making sure that respect was maintained among the group members, in addition to keeping the members focused and on-task, made the group experience exciting, invigorating, and frustrating. The following portraits will better explain the dynamics of the group.

Individuals in the Group

Thomas

Thomas was a 13-year-old white male who came from a home where his parents felt as though they could no longer control his behavior. He was an outgoing young man involved in extracurricular athletics at school. Although he acted tough externally and pretended to be a behavior problem, he disciplined others in the group when anyone got out of line. He shared a foster placement with Lisa, and their relationship was that of a biological brother and sister with the usual bickering and teasing. He had other siblings who were still with their biological family.

Lisa

Lisa had been in foster care for two years after her abusive mother, an un-wed teenage mother with a drug habit, died. She came from an inner-city area and was placed in a rural foster family with her brother, Thomas. Thirteen-year-old Lisa was withdrawn and uninvolved in school activities. She often stole from her family to get attention. Like many adolescents in foster care, she desperately wanted to be adopted. Lisa responded well to writing in her journal about boys, fitting in, her biological mother, her foster parents, and other personal issues.

Ed

Ed was a very immature 12-year-old boy on medication for Attention Deficit Hyperactivity Disorder (ADHD). Ed came from a broken home in the inner city and shared a foster placement with Mark and Teddy. He was hesitant to express himself and was extremely withdrawn. He was uninvolved in extracurricular activities, excessively absent from school, and when he did attend was always in trouble.

Mark

Mark, at 14, was the oldest of the group. He had been placed in a mental health facility for depression and wanting to commit suicide. Mark was always talking about guns or cruelty to people and animals. In addition to his negative attitude, he had a felony record of shoplifting, theft, and stealing a car. Trust was a major issue for him and he was in constant need of attention. He had no participation in any school activities and was obsessively concerned about his future.

Teddy

Teddy, a 13-year-old African-American male, was highly athletic, polite, and respectful. He was on the school's basketball team and was proud of his academic accomplishments. Many of Teddy's relatives had been killed in gang-related incidents. He was quiet and shy and kept to himself.

Characteristics of the Group

All of these adolescents had a tendency to embellish and exaggerate what their life was like, where they came from, and who they were. This was their attempt to fit in with the rest of the world. All, however, were in the mode of trying to please the individuals who were involved in their placements: social workers, foster parents, and psychologists. School personnel did not appear to be on the list of those they wanted to please. To some extent these students were all loners.

The three boys who lived together in foster care—Mark, Ed, and Teddy—were very different in their outlooks on life, their maturity levels, and their school experiences. Mark made several comments during the course of the group concerning Ed's immature attitude. Mark told Ed that if he wanted to cure that sick mind of his and be healed, then he needed to come to the group. Ed was frequently absent and could not maintain a serious conversation, his way to escape from dealing with his problems. Teddy had to be encouraged to talk or he would just take it all in and say nothing.

Although Lisa and Thomas were two very different personalities, the closeness that existed between them was evident during the group sessions. Lisa, the older of the two, felt the need to mother Thomas, who teased her until she became angry and lashed out at him verbally or physically. Theirs was an unusual but productive relationship, similar to that of Sara and Josh.

The boys were much more willing to talk when there was an activity involved. Lisa, much like Sara, was a loner. A growing adolescent girl in the midst of four pubescent young men, Lisa kept to herself during the first few sessions. The boys often manipulated the conversation, and I had to specifically open the floor for Lisa during group. Through nonverbal cues and journal writing, Lisa and I found an outlet for communication. I watched her mature throughout the group experience. She became more verbal with all the boys and mothered them as she did Thomas. Lisa's strong will and persistence helped her stay ahead of the rest of the group. Just like Sara, Lisa frequently escaped into her own world in order to avoid any type of emotional attachment. Eventually it became increasingly difficult for Lisa to maintain her distance for long periods. She and Ed eventually became good friends, always coming to one another's rescue while learning what true caring really meant.

Recommended Activities

Some of the activities that I recommended for this group as well as for individual adolescents include the following.

Ungame

This board game, developed for persons five and older, is used to promote the sharing of personal issues in a non-threatening environment. In a non-competitive way, youth interact with peers and/or family members about feelings, relationships, schools, living situations, and values. Young people make progress around a board by answering questions about themselves or commenting on an issue presented on a card. For example, students might respond to questions such as these: If you could make one law that people would live by, what would it be? Say something about child abuse. What are you apt to do when you feel lonely? The textual cards allow the players to monitor the level of intimacy at which to share information with the other members of the group.

Basketball Game

This activity encourages self-disclosure as students share their feelings before attempting a foul shot. After the shot is made, the student passes the ball to a person he or she wants to hear from. This game builds the trusting environment to allow for more risk-taking and sharing.

Collage of Me

Another opportunity for self-expression is encouraged when group members make pictorial representations of themselves and their situations in life. They become creative and conversational with the inclusion of hobbies, interests, age, and goals. Each collage should show the person's name clearly so others can ask probing questions of why certain items were chosen.

Value Shields

The purpose of this activity is to encourage group members to evaluate and prioritize what is important to them. Students draw pictures to create a coat of armor that depicts their responses to the following questions:

- How did you feel when you first had to leave your family?
- What made you angry?
- What made you sad?
- How did you behave with your foster family?
- How do you feel (or how do you think you will feel) after you visit home?
- How do you feel now?

Through group sharing of individual shields, each person will see the commonalities of their experiences and notice the stages of grief and loss they have all experienced.

Skits

In dyads and triads, students write plays about various issues in their lives. In my experience, skits are usually about friendships, lying, stealing, cheating, and authority figures.

Movies

Both of us planned opportunities for our participants to view one of two films—*The Pinballs* or *Angels in the Outfield*—to see how other children react to being placed in foster care. The purpose of this activity is to give the adolescents exposure to characters with whom they may identify and who have similar issues. The focus is to promote the sharing of individual experiences and to involve everyone in a discussion. Often, it is easier for adolescents to speak in the third person when speaking of themselves. This serves as a springboard from the film, which is a depiction of reality, to reality itself.

The Pinballs. *The Pinballs* is the story of three foster children—Carlie, Thomas J., and Harvey—who have lived their lives as pinballs, constantly being bumped from one place to another. The one constant thing they all have to hold onto is each other. In the summer they spend at the Masons, they learn to tear down the walls they have hidden behind, to trust, to care, and to love. While searching for independence, they find the dependence they have lived without—a dependence on friendship and compassion. *The Pinballs* touches on the topics of child abuse, death, and dealing with a disability. It presents an optimistic view of a pessimistic situation.

Angels in the Outfield. Likewise, *Angels in the Outfield* is the story of three boys—Roger, J.P., and Miguel—who live with Maggie, a kind and understanding foster mother. Miguel is adopted early in the film, and J.P. and Roger become closer friends and more avid baseball fans, particularly when Roger's father says he will come for him when the Angels win the pennant. *Angels in the Outfield* is a hopeful film about love, friendship, and faith.

CONCLUSION

Both of us attempt to nourish connectedness through story and communication in the language arts class and the counseling group. Both of us attempt to promote responsiveness and sharing. Both of us attempt to create community through the power of literacy. Both of us believe in creating an environment conducive to an authentic sharing of ideas where every voice can be heard and valued.

Education and counseling both must embrace a spirit of community based on acceptance, affirmation, encouragement, support, and renewal where adolescents feel comfortable to explore the treasure within themselves. As Giroux (1987) reminds us, "Schools need to provide the opportunities for literate occasions for students to share their experiences, work in social relations that emphasize care and concern for others, to take risks, and to fight for a quality of life in which all human beings benefit" (p. 181).

As we work with adolescents in foster care, indeed, all adolescents who have been experiencing instability in their lives, we need to take to heart the words of Henri Nouwen (1975):

> Students cannot be molded into one special form of the good life, but are only temporary visitors who have been in many rooms before they came into ours. Our relationship with our students is first of all a relationship in which we offer ourselves to our searching students to help them develop some clarity in the many impressions of their mind and heart and discover patterns of thoughts and feelings on which they can build their own life. By a supportive presence we can offer the space with safe boundaries within which our students can give up their defensive stance and bend over their own life experience, with all its strong and weak sides, to find the beginnings of a plan worth following. As teachers we have to encourage our students to reflection which leads to vision—theirs, not ours. It is, however, only realistic to say that many students have become so tired of the demands of the educational institutions they have to go through and so suspicious of anyone who expects something new, that they can seldom respond to a really hospitable teacher and take the risk of trust. (p. 90)

Through the relationships possible with literature, the self-understanding that comes from writing, and the supportive communities of the English language arts classroom and/or the group therapy model, we can reach Sara Moone and other adolescents like her when our multiple roles begin to overwhelm us.

RECOMMENDED READINGS

Fiction

Foster Care

7.01.   Ames, Mildred. (1976). *Without hats, who can tell the good guys?* New York: Dutton. 133 pp. (ISBN: 0–525–43125–X). Middle School (MS).

Convinced he will never get used to his new foster family, a young boy dreams of the day his father will come to take him away.

7.02.   Angell, Judie. (1978). *Tina Gogo*. Scarsdale, NY: Bradbury Press. 196 pp. (ISBN: 0–878–88132–8). MS.

Living in a small resort town where her family runs a restaurant, 11-year-old Sarajane meets and befriends an unusual girl with a mysterious past.

7.03.   Calvert, Patricia. (1989). *When morning comes*. New York: Scribners. 153 pp. (ISBN: 0–684–19105–9). MS, High School (HS).

Fifteen-year-old Cat Kincaid, having failed to fit into a series of foster homes, is now stuck on a farm with an elderly female beekeeper. She secretly longs for a place where she can be herself, not somebody she has invented.

7.04.   Childress, Alice. (1981). *Rainbow Jordan*. New York: Conrad, McCann, & Geoghegan. 142 pp. (ISBN: 0–698–20531–6). MS, HS.

Fourteen-year-old Rainbow, her mother, and her foster guardian comment on Rainbow's return to a foster home for another stay.

7.05.   Cleaver, Vera. (1987). *Moon Lake angel*. New York: Lothrop, Lee, & Shepard. 135 pp. (ISBN: 0–688–04952–4). MS.

Kitty Dale, whose mother does not want to deal with a child or admit one into her new life, spends the summer with Aunt Petal and eventually learns to accept her mother's weaknesses.

7.06.   Cohen, Miriam. (1986). *Robert and Dawn Marie 4 ever*. New York: Harper & Row. 149 pp. (ISBN: 0–060–21396–5). HS.

A 14-year-old boy in Brooklyn, who has grown up in the foster care system, discovers respect and love with a parochial school girl and with an eccentric couple who take him in.

7.07.   Cresswell, Helen. (1982). *Dear shrink*. New York: Macmillan. 186 pp. (ISBN: 0–027–25560–3). MS, HS.

When the woman looking after them in their parents' absence dies suddenly, three children end up in foster care and must use all their courage and ingenuity to cope with the situation.

7.08.   Dorman, N. B. (1980). *Laughter in the background*. New York: Elsevier/Nelson Books. 158 pp. (ISBN: 0–525–66714–8). MS.

Twelve-year-old Marcie, who has tolerated her divorced mother's alcoholism for years, finally decides she cannot stand it any longer.

7.09.   Dunlap, Eileen. (1979). *Fox farm*. New York: Holt, Rinehart, & Winston. 144 pp. (ISBN: 0–030–49051–0). MS.

Through caring for a stray fox cub, a ten-year-old boy gradually accepts the fact that he does have a rightful place with his foster family.

7.10.   Eyerly, Jeannette. (1984). *Angel Baker, thief*. New York: J. P. Lippincott. 246 pp. (ISBN: 0–397–32096–5). HS.

Fifteen-year-old Angel, released on probation to a foster family after being convicted of shoplifting, is anxious to make a fresh start and to be accepted by her new family and friends.

7.11.   Guy, Rosa. (1979). *The disappearance*. New York: Dell. 246 pp. (ISBN: 0–440–92064–7). HS.

The disappearance of a seven-year-old girl casts suspicion on a juvenile offender from Harlem who has recently come to live with a Brooklyn family. (An American Library Association [ALA] Best Book for Young Adults)

7.12.   Hall, Lynn. (1982). *Tin Can Tucker*. New York: Scribner. 154 pp. (ISBN: 0–684–17623–8). HS.

A 16-year-old girl runs away from her foster home in Missouri, planning to make a name for herself on the rodeo circuit.

7.13.   Hill, Margaret. (1981). *Turn the page, Wendy*. Nashville, TN: Abingdon. 176 pp. (ISBN: 0–687–42700–2). MS, HS.

Wendy risks her position at Virginia Hall and her chance to become part of a real family in a good foster home when she impulsively runs away to search for the mother who deserted her at birth.

7.14.   Holland, Isabelle. (1996). *The promised land*. New York: Scholastic. 155 pp. (ISBN: 0–590–47176–7). MS, HS.

Annie and Maggie, now 10 and 15, were part of the orphan trains until an uncle comes to get them, disrupting their security with a good foster family.

7.15.   Myers, Walter Dean. (1982). *Won't know till I get there*. New York: Viking Press. 176 pp. (ISBN: 0–670–77862–1). HS.

After 14-year-old Stephen is caught writing graffiti on a train, he and his new foster brother and friends are sentenced to help out at an old-age home for the summer.

7.16.   Nixon, Joan Lowery. (1987). *A family apart*. New York: Bantam Books. 162 pp. (ISBN: 0–553–05432–5). MS, HS.

When their mother can no longer support them, six siblings are sent by the Children's Aid Society of New York City to live with farm families in Missouri in 1860.

7.17.   Paterson, Katherine. (1978). *The great Gilly Hopkins*. New York: Crowell. 148 pp. (ISBN: 0–690–03837–2). MS.

An 11-year-old foster child tries to cope with her longings and fears as she schemes against everyone who befriends her.

7.18.   Radley, Gail. (1991). *The golden days*. New York: Macmillan. 137 pp. (ISBN: 0–027–75652–1). MS.

Convinced that his new foster parents do not really want him, 11-year-old Cory decides to run away with his new friend, an old lady from the nearby nursing home.

7.19.   Samuels, Gertrude. (1988). *Yours, Brett*. New York: Lodestar Books. 165 pp. (ISBN: 0–525–67255–9). MS, HS.

When her father leaves home to marry another woman and her mother is unable to care for her, Brett spends several years in a variety of foster homes.

7.20.   Swetnam, Evelyn. (1978). *Yes, my darling daughter*. New York: Harvey House. 166 pp. (ISBN: 0–817–85782–6). MS.

An 11-year-old girl is slow to accept the love of her foster family.

7.21.   Wolitzer, Hilma. (1978). *Toby lived here*. New York: Farrar, Straus, & Giroux. 147 pp. (ISBN: 0–374–37625–5). MS.

Toby's hope to be reunited with her mother and sister on her 13th birthday is not realized, and she enters her teens in a foster home.

Adoption

7.22.   Beatty, Patricia. (1980). *That's one ornery orphan*. New York: William Morrow. 222 pp. (ISBN: 0–688–32227–1). MS, HS.

Based on the casual adoption practices in 19th century Texas, a 13-year-old girl is finally forced to face the placement she has tried so hard to avoid.

7.23.   Christopher, Matt. (1995). *Double play at short*. Boston: Little, Brown, & Company. 151 pp. (ISBN: 0–316–14267–0). MS.

Twelve-year-old Danny thinks that there is something very familiar about the girl who plays shortstop on the team he faces during the championship series, and his curiosity leads him to a surprising discovery about his own adoption.

7.24.   First, Julia. (1981). *I, Rebekah, take you, the Lawrences*. New York: Watts. 123 pp. (ISBN: 0–531–04256–1). MS.

Even after she has been adopted, 12-year-old Rebekah wonders if she wouldn't be better off back at the orphanage with her friends.

7.25.   Hamilton, Dorothy. (1981). *Holly's New Year*. Scottsdale, PA: Herald Press. 127 pp. (ISBN: 0–836–11961–4). MS.

In this sequel to *Christmas for Holly*, the protagonist examines her mixed feelings about being adopted even though she loves her foster family.

7.26.   Holland, Isabelle. (1991). *The house in the woods*. Boston: Little, Brown. 194 pp. (ISBN: 0–316–37178–5). MS, HS.

Feeling overweight, unattractive, and unloved, Bridget learns to put aside her escapist fantasies and live in the real world after uncovering the secrets of a mysterious house.

7.27.   Howard, Ellen. (1988). *Her own song*. New York: Atheneum. 160 pp. (ISBN: 0–689–31444–2). MS, HS.

When her adoptive father is hospitalized after an accident, Mellie is befriended by an owner of a Chinese laundry who holds the key to the events surrounding her adoption.

7.28.   Lifton, Betty Jean. (1981). *I'm still me.* New York: Random House. 243 pp. (ISBN: 0–394–84783–0). HS.

A history assignment to explore her roots propels a high school junior into a search for her biological parents.

7.29.   Lindbergh, Anne. (1983). *Nobody's orphan.* San Diego: Harcourt Brace Jovanovich. 147 pp. (ISBN: 0–152–57468–9). MS.

Martha, the only green-eyed member of a brown-eyed family, is convinced she is adopted but thinks she wouldn't mind so much if her parents would let her have a dog.

7.30.   Lowry, Lois. (1978). *Find a stranger, say goodbye.* Boston: Houghton Mifflin. 187 pp. (ISBN: 0–395–26459–6). HS.

Natalie, a 17-year-old girl who seems to have everything, goes in pursuit of her real mother.

7.31.   Sachs, Marilyn. (1992). *What my sister remembered.* New York: Dutton Children's Books. 122 pp. (ISBN: 0–525–44953–1). MS.

While visiting her younger sister, Beth confronts painful memories of the sudden death of her parents and subsequent adoption of the sisters by different families.

Nonfiction

7.32.   DuPrau, Jeanne. (1990). *Adoption: The facts, feelings, and issues of a double heritage.* Englewood Cliffs, NJ: Messner. 129 pp. (ISBN: 0–671–69329–8). MS, HS.

The legal and emotional aspects of the adoption process are discussed. The text also lists sources to consult if searching for biological parents and examines the current movement for giving the adoptee free access to the records of origin.

7.33.   Hyde, Margaret Oldroyd. (1982*). Foster care and adoption.* New York: Watts. 90 pp. (ISBN: 0–531–04403–3). MS, HS.

After a brief discussion of adoption issues, Hyde investigates the foster home care system which enables children from troubled families to be placed temporarily in other authorized homes.

7.34.   Krementz, Jill. (1983). *How it feels to be adopted.* New York: Random House. 187 pp. (ISBN: 0–394–52851–4). MS, HS.

Krementz relays interviews she had with adopted children and adoptive families about their experiences and feelings concerning adoption.

REFERENCES

Bronfenbrenner, Urie. (1976). Alienation and the four worlds of childhood. *Phi Delta Kappa, 76* (6), 430–437.
Byars, Betsy. (1977). *The pinballs.* New York: Harper & Row.
Festinger, Trudy. (1994). The foster children of California. Sacramento, CA: The Children's Services Foundation.
Giroux, Henry A. (1987). Critical literacy and student experience: Donald Grave's approach to literacy. *Language Arts, 64* (2), 175–181.
Johnston, Julie. (1994). *Adam and Eve and Pinch-Me.* Boston: Little, Brown, & Company.
Jones, M. & Moses, B. (1984). West Virginia's former foster children: Their experience and their lives as young adults. New York: Child Welfare League.
Nouwen, Henri. (1975). *Reaching out: The three movements of the spiritual life.* New York: Doubleday.
Ohio Department of Human Services. (1987). Children in out-of-home care. Columbus, OH: Division of Children and Family Services.
Rosenblatt, Louise M. (1983). *Literature as exploration,* 4th Edition. New York: Modern Language Association.
Tatara, Toshio. (1993). *Characteristics of children in substitute and adoptive care, fiscal year 1989.* Washington, DC: American Public Welfare Association.

CHAPTER 8

Eating Disorders in Young Adults' Worlds and Their Literature: Starving and Stuffing Families

Pamela Sissi Carroll, Mae Z. Cleveland, &
Elizabeth M. Myers

INTRODUCTION

Perhaps one of the most unusual issues involved in any discussion of ano-rexia nervosa is the reaction of families and society to its victims. Never have the victims of an emotional disorder been as maligned (perhaps with the exception of alcoholics) as those with anorexia nervosa. The anorexic's refusal to eat is an endless source of power struggles between the anorexic and her family and doctors. Her illness both angers and frightens those around her. It affords her no privacy since she wears it conspicuously on her limbs. Anorexics are often thought of as stubborn brats who could eat if they really wanted to. Frequently, they agree to play the brat role in which they are cast, so that no one can see the shame they feel over their anorexia—a life-threatening, irrational facet of their personalities (Levenkron, 1982, p. xvii).

ORGANIZATION

In this chapter, we discuss eating disorders that affect adolescents, par-ticularly anorexia nervosa and bulimia nervosa. The chapter is divided into three parts. First, we present Elizabeth Myers' personal struggle with ano-rexia then bulimia. Her further recollections are augmented by excerpts from her sister Anne's diary, a private journal that chronicles the younger sibling's attempts to follow her sister's example by starving herself to achieve perfection. By presenting both perspectives, we hope to demon-strate the devastating effects that the sisters' concurrent eating disorders had on what had been, during their childhood, an ideal sibling relationship. Their troubling truths about a relentless need to control their food intake, then the loss or fear of loss of that control, reveal some of the deeper battles with self-esteem and the quest for perfection that were at the core of their eating disorders. Through their stories we learn that eating disorders are not about food per se; instead, they are about control and loss of control, power and powerlessness. And they are often about self-loathing and attempts to transcend human limits. Through them, we learn that family and friends often are unable to reach the victim of an eating disorder in order to help her. As any teacher of high school students, Meyers wants adolescents to understand that they are not alone if they have eating disorders, and that they do not need to fear being labeled as "a failure," or as "crazy" by seeking help for anorexia nervosa or bulimia nervosa.

Second, we present facts about the primary eating disorders. Cleveland, who has worked in the fields of psychology and nutrition for 20 years, holds a Ph.D. in nutrition and serves on an eating disorders counseling team that includes physicians, nurses, and psychologists. The team works with university students who have, or are at risk of developing, eating disorders. Cleveland defines anorexia nervosa, bulimia nervosa, and other eating disorders, then outlines warning signs, and the dangers associated with eating disorders. This section closes with Cleveland's professional comments on the ways that characters in two popular young adult (YA) novels are portrayed; both have an eating disorder. Emily in *I Am an Artichoke* by Lucy Frank (1995) suffers from anorexia nervosa and is helped by her friendship with protagonist Sarah. In *Fat Chance* by Leslea Newman (1994), Judi, the narrator, is at risk of developing bulimia nervosa, but she realizes how harmful the disease is by watching its effects on her friend, Nancy, who has a full-blown case.

Third, we present annotations of other contemporary YA novels and nonfiction books that Carroll, a specialist in YA literature, believes may help parents, teachers, other adults, and the friends of those who have developed eating disorders better understand the kind of problems the person with an eating disorder may be trying to handle by him- or herself. Although we are strong advocates of YA literature, believe that the books reviewed herein are of high literary quality, and that they address issues that have been—for far too long—ignored, we add a strong note of caution here: We do not recommend that parents, teachers, or friends merely give the books discussed in this chapter as independent reading to an adolescent who shows some signs of developing or having one of the primary types of eating disorders.

Although we believe that reading is a positive activity, one that we heartily endorse for adolescents as a means of comparing their realities against those presented in fiction and as an assurance that they are not the only ones who have ever experienced such problems, we also recognize that the books do not provide cures for the diseases. A teen may read one and begin to understand the need to seek help for an eating disorder, and that is a positive result; however, we fear that a teen may read one and tell him- or herself, "Hey, I can do that!"

Almost without exception, the YA fiction books in which a character is either an anorexic or bulimic provide prescriptions—or "how-to" guides—that can easily be modified to fit a young teen's actual condition. For instance, many of the books will give teens who are already at risk of developing these serious problems some suggestions about how to hide their food; how to pretend that they have eaten when they have not; how to deceive coaches, teachers, parents, and even medical doctors and therapists; how to squeeze in another half hour of exercise when the family has gone to bed; and so on. The books that are exceptions to this generalization are discussed and recommended below. Despite this warning, we do see a definite need for parents, teachers, and friends to recognize and better understand the eating disorders. It is our hope that the fiction and nonfiction that we recommend will open up communication among teens and the adults with whom they interact. We all need to learn more about the potential for disrupting and perhaps destroying family relationships that accompanies the physical, emotional, social, and spiritual challenges of dealing with a child, sibling, student, or friend who has an eating disorder. The subject needs to be addressed seriously and sensitively by those who work closely with adolescents.

ELIZABETH'S STORY

Shy and chubby as a fifth grader, I tended to linger at the back of the line, letting others go first. But today we were running the 50-yard-dash, and I didn't want the boys to see my face distort with effort or watch my breasts bouncing in my tight gym suit. Unfortunately, I was not able to run faster than my classmates; nor was I able to run across the field and away from the school. That day, I had already endured the humiliation of being rounded up like one of 30 cows for the routine of public weighing, measuring, and body-fat measuring. When I stepped up to have my measurements taken by my teacher, one boy yelled out, "Watch it! Don't break the scale!" Though I was embarrassed, I was also momentarily hopeful; if the scale actually did break, I reasoned, no one would know how much I weighed.

At five feet tall and with size ten shoes, I was, without question, the largest girl in my fifth grade class. It was I who wore the largest cheerleading uniform, served as the base for pyramids, and played center halfback on the soccer team. It was during my fifth grade year that I began hearing girls giggle and make remarks behind my back. I was the one who stood in the corner to dress after gym class, trying to conceal myself, but feeling other girls' stares no matter how hard I tried to hide. The summer following the fifth grade, I started my first diet.

At the time, it seemed harmless, and my mother was delighted that I was taking a break from my usual fare of double cheeseburgers and fries. I perused fashion magazines, gathering "diet tips" and "celebrity health regimens." By the time I reached high school, I was a dieting expert, a label-reader extraordinaire, counting calories and analyzing the fat content of every morsel that went into my mouth. With each day that I adhered to a strict routine of diet and exercise, the girls' giggles and critical stares diminished and eventually they disappeared.

The first high point of my dieting career came when, as a sophomore, I landed my first real boyfriend—a senior who was six feet two inches tall, with blue eyes and blonde hair, and a swimmer on the school's team. Finally I had someone with whom I could attend ball games and dances, someone with whom I could walk at school and attract the attention—and envy—of popular girls. I assured myself that I would never have been dating the senior if I were still "fat Elizabeth." When our relationship ended later that year, I became convinced that there was something wrong with me. Therefore, I intensified my efforts to achieve perfection. I convinced myself that if I could become increasingly thinner, I would become increasingly perfect. Once I was perfect, I would be irresistible to him and to other guys, too!

All summer I worked toward perfection. I ran, danced, and followed a strict self-imposed diet. I returned to school for my junior year, thinner than ever. I was showered by compliments from girls who asked, "How'd you do it?" or "How can you be so disciplined?" My cross-country track coach praised me for the accomplishment of whittling my five-feet, eight-inch frame down to a lean 115 pounds. He explained that keeping my weight down would help me run longer and faster, and he held me up as an example of determination to the rest of the team when I pushed to run further and faster each day. I was a fuel-efficient machine; I could run six to ten miles a day while eating very little. At home, my parents were accustomed to seeing me eat small amounts so they did not worry. At school, I maintained an A+ average and studied harder than ever. I showed extraordinary physical and mental discipline through what I perceived to be exceptional organization. I kept a record of everything: how much I weighed, what I wore to school, which work I would complete first at night, and so on. I made rules for myself about all aspects of my life: how I must brush my teeth, how many times I must chew each bite of food, in what order I could eat different foods. Deviation from these rules was simply not allowed. I swore that I would never lose control or be fat again. Although they had never asked for it, I had become my parents' "perfect" child. And although I did not know the term for it at the time, I had developed an eating disorder that I now recognize as anorexia nervosa.

Things changed abruptly during my senior year. I developed shin splints due to running an excessive number of miles and was forced to curtail my daily six to ten mile regimen. My world began to crumble as I gained weight, unable to maintain my once rail-thin appearance. I hated myself for every ounce that I gained and felt ashamed after all of the compliments and praise for being skinny I had received the year before. To avoid people, I constantly made up excuses to not go out in public. I refused even to go to school as often as I could get away with it. When I did attend, I made every effort to be invisible. When the bell rang at the end of the day, I would rush home so that I could be alone. I'd head straight from the kitchen, stand in the open refrigerator door, and furiously stuff my face with as much food as I could find. After gorging, with my stomach stretched to its limit and overwhelmed with both nausea and guilt over what I had just done, I'd feel a strange mix of depression and elation. I would proceed to my bathroom, lock the door, expel the contents of my stomach, then go up to my bedroom and sleep for the remainder of the afternoon. This cycle became my new daily ritual. If someone were home after school, I would take off somewhere—a grocery store parking lot or the park—and devour the day's feast in my car. Gradually, I grew oblivious to the torture and abuse I imposed on my body. Nothing mattered but the ritual. It was as if some other force had taken control of my body and had left me completely powerless to refuse the binges. For the next five years, I persisted in a cycle of bingeing and purging. My parents never knew how unhappy or self-destructive I had grown as a former anorexic who had rebounded with bulimia nervosa. But my sister did.

Elizabeth and Anne: Two Sisters' Stories

My sister Anne has always been, and will always be, my best friend. While growing up, we were affectionately referred to as "the girls" by the rest of the family and we did everything together. Although two years my junior, Anne and I shared many "firsts": We got our ears pierced together and learned to drive at the same time. By the time we reached high school, we seemed inseparable; that is, until we both developed eating disorders. During the time that the two of us needed each other more than ever, we experienced the most intense and difficult times of our lives. While I developed bulimia, she developed anorexia nervosa. And I blamed myself for her disease.

In the passages that follow, my recollections move beyond concern with my own eating disorder to include my sister's; my remarks are interrupted by selected entries from her journal (in italics). Anne has generously allowed me to read and share excerpts from her journal. Until very recently, she has treated each entry as her own private writing. We hope that by sharing our personal experiences, caring adults including parents, teachers, and media specialists might gain insights into the effects of eating disorders on a family's relationships.

I remember arriving home one afternoon to find the door to the family room closed. Usually I wasn't expected home until evening, but my dance classes had been canceled and I was looking forward to spending a couple of hours in front of the television. While nearing the door, I heard the familiar pulsing tempo of my aerobic dance tape; even before entering, I knew that my sister was exercising—again. At that moment, I regretted ever having related to her my "dieting expertise" and the advice that an exercise routine of 20-to-30 minutes per day would guarantee "results." Now, after she had followed my advice for several months, I felt betrayed. We had agreed to help each other lose weight. I was still 20 pounds heavier than she, and Anne was gradually melting away.

As I reached for the doorknob, I felt my neck stiffen in anticipation. With one sudden movement, I flung open the door and caught her in "the act." Although visibly startled and annoyed, Anne ignored me and continued exercising despite my contemptuous glare. I noticed that she was wearing *my* shorts, and seeing them hanging loosely around her hips with the waistband folded over reminded me of the "perfect" body I once had and now envied. "AREN'T YOU SKINNY ENOUGH?" I shrieked, adding a few obscenities. I impulsively threw my school books against the wall and exited furiously.

After berating my sister, I retreated directly to the refrigerator where I hastily stuffed myself. Tears streamed down my face while my hands moved in a frenzy. When I finally paused, nauseous and disgusted, I was disoriented. I went to the bathroom upstairs and forced myself to throw up everything. If I didn't have the discipline to refrain from eating, I thought, at least I could have the discipline to get rid of it. I was growing tired of performing the exhausting ritual, and as I propped myself against the bathroom counter, I remember looking painfully at myself in the mirror, noting my puffy eyes and face. I couldn't recognize myself any longer, and more importantly, I couldn't understand how I could feel such hatred for my sister. "What has happened to us?" I wailed to myself.

Anne, I learned much later, was wondering what was happening to us, too. About that episode, she wrote the following journal entry:

Elizabeth exploded, AGAIN! . . . about her weight and mine. I'm sick of it! UGH!!!!! I wish she would leave me alone. Elizabeth is being a pain about dieting. If I say something about being full, she goes, "Oh, right, like I'm sure you're full" or if I say I'm not hungry, she'll do the same thing. But, she used to starve herself silly, so she doesn't have much room to talk. . . . I can see what she's doing. The only thing worse is that my friends see it, too. But, because Elizabeth lives with me, she WATCHES ME to see what I eat. You see, I started dieting at the beginning of the year by changing my eating habits and exercising. I went from being 5'4" and 135 lbs. to 105 lbs. It's not easy, TRUST ME!! But I don't think that I should have to deal with other dieters always on my case.

Indeed, there were times when my sister and I, "the girls" who had been inseparable as children, could hardly be in the same room together. We stopped riding to school together, and because of my frequent antagonism, Anne became increasingly withdrawn. I missed her, though, and made various attempts to talk with her to engage in other sisterly activities. But, with the relationship strained, my seemingly good intentions appeared to her to be interference. Anne felt imposed on and was reluctant to talk about her feelings with me or with anyone. She wrote the following entry about a need for sanctity:

I swear it makes me cry! Nothing of mine is sacred! I wish there was just one thing that I liked and cared about, that no one would try to take away or share! My sister is bad enough borrowing my clothes, jewelry, perfume, etc. It's going to ruin me! One day I am going to explode from frustration and anger and hate! . . . I agreed to go with Elizabeth to do some errands today, but on the way, she tried to "philosophize"; i.e., have a "meaningful" conversation about my life. I realize what she wants. She wants me to open up to her. I'm sorry. I just don't feel like it. . . . I'm not going to kill myself, I never would. I'm too smart, but I feel like I'll just shut down. . . . Elizabeth cried because I didn't open up to her, but there isn't anything she can do.

Later that year, our relationship and our eating disorders were further complicated by the presence of a boyfriend. I began dating someone and while my sister and I grew further apart, I spent almost all of my time with him. Anne, in turn, felt abandoned, forgotten, lonely. As a result, her refusal to eat, which had begun with the desire for a perfect body, evolved into an effort to waste away. She conveys the loneliness she felt as she observed my relationship:

Today at lunch, E. didn't sit with us. She sat with "Dave." But, if she can't go out with him tonight, tomorrow she may go to the beach and she can do stuff with K. [a friend] and me (thanks!!). . . . Today it hit me how lonely and unattached to the world I am. I was just thinking that if I wanted, I could go to another school right now and start over! It's not completely out of the question. . . . It's not so much that Elizabeth is with him all the time; it's more like now I have no one. I was counting on her to hold onto our goals, dreams, beliefs, but they're dashed! I do wish her the best, but I feel I'm being slowly discarded from her life.

The emotional distance that resulted from, and perpetuated, the eating behaviors was at an extreme by the time I graduated from high school. When I left for college, I feared that my move would increase Anne's feeling of being abandoned. The physical distance, however, actually helped us begin the road toward recovery, precisely because it provided us with a means to mend our relationship. Without seeing my sister, I ceased obsessing about her appearance and eating behaviors. While my parents continually bothered her about her eating and her weight, I seemed to be the only who could relate to her fears; therefore, I became, again, someone with whom she felt comfortable talking about her feelings. In trying to overcome her anorexia, Anne describes her fears of losing control, of not being able to talk to any of her friends at school, of being the target of teachers' sympathy, and of fighting with our parents:

I'm getting so irritated with everyone, especially T. and K. I mean, it might be me, but I've been listening to them and their lives without being able to tell them any of my problems. Even Ms. B. and Mrs. D. called me into the hall today and said they were concerned about my health. What bitches. I wish they'd leave me alone. After school Dad and I got into a fight about my weight. Mom had also bought lots of food—fatty food. It made me feel as though they were all against me. . . . I talked with Elizabeth today . . . nothing significant, really, but it just seemed like it. I mean, at least she understands what it's like. She came up from college this past weekend. Every time she comes up I realize it more and more. When she leaves I feel like I am starting from scratch again.

Anne and I have discovered recently, through the lenses of retrospect, what she hinted at in that journal entry—our relationship as sisters was essential in overcoming our disorders. Anne needed someone, as did I, to talk with—someone who could understand her fears and empathize with her feelings. Our parents' concerns, our teachers' questions, and our friends' comments all went unheard, but we finally began to hear *each other*. We had both dealt with the fear, guilt, confusion, and anger that those with eating disorders suffer. We understood each other. When in college, I also met other young women who were trying to overcome eating disorders. When we shared our stories, thoughts, fears, and feelings, friendships and trust emerged. Those friendships, built on trust and understanding, provided another means of coping.

The reasons that my sister and I developed eating disorders are difficult to pinpoint. In part, we believe that we both began to use dieting as a means of dealing with our belief that we were inadequate when compared with our peers. We wanted to be in control of our bodies so that we could be perfect. Our stories have many features in common with several of the adolescent characters portrayed in the YA fiction reviewed below.

EATING DISORDERS: DEFINITIONS, CHARACTERISTICS, AND SOME FRIGHTENING FACTS

Eating disorders most often appear in young adolescent females between the ages of 15 and 24. The outstanding features are an intense fear of gaining weight or becoming fat, a preoccupation and dissatisfaction with body shape or size, and obsessive or compulsive eating-related concerns. The primary types of eating disorders are anorexia nervosa, bulimia nervosa, and other recognized eating disorders that are not specified in the diagnostic guidelines for these two disorders.

The American Psychiatric Association publishes a comprehensive diagnostic and statistical manual (DSM) which lists the categories and criteria for currently recognized eating disorders.

Anorexia Nervosa

All of the following criteria must be met before a diagnosis of anorexia nervosa can be made:

- A refusal to maintain a minimally normal body weight, defined as 15% or more below a normal healthy weight for age and height.
- An intense fear of gaining weight or of getting fat even though underweight.
- A distorted image of size, shape, or weight of body, including a denial of the seriousness of a very low body weight.

- In women, amenorrhea, defined as the absence of at least three consecutive menstrual cycles.

The extreme weight loss is an obvious sign of anorexia nervosa. The desire to lose weight even though a person is not overweight and a dissatisfaction with one's body may not be recognized early as a sign because many women talk about the need to lose a few pounds or how they would like smaller thighs or hips. Professional, athletic, or fitness-oriented women may be particularly sensitive to their bodies and their weight and will express some dissatisfaction in conversation when the topic comes up. The girl who is developing an eating disorder, however, frequently brings up the topic and may seem obsessed about her weight, frequently making negative comments about some aspect of her body. She often tries to hide her body under loose or baggy clothing. One client who was an aerobics instructor with a lean and healthy body weight (about 5% below average for her height) refused to wear a leotard without a very loose-fitting tee shirt over it. She was convinced that her stomach and abdomen were fat and unsightly.

As an individual suffering with anorexia nervosa loses weight and gets comments that she is already thin enough and certainly doesn't need to lose any more weight, she may wear oversized clothing to hide under and avoid comments; she still believes, though, that she needs to lose more weight. Other deceptive behaviors may include ordering normal amounts of food, then busying herself with the food on the plate but actually eating only a tiny amount or leaving most of the food. There may be other food and eating rituals such as cutting food into tiny portions or separating foods so they don't touch. Socially, she begins to isolate herself so others won't be aware of her eating but also so she won't be as tempted to eat because she is very hungry and fears losing all control if she eats. Recurring episodes of binge eating may or may not occur during anorexia nervosa. Personality changes often observed include denial and anger when weight or eating behavior are discussed, and as mentioned above, deceptive behavior and avoidance of social interactions. Starvation affects mood and may lead to depression, irritability, crying, and difficulty sleeping.

Physical signs are more difficult to notice until the disorder has become well established. Feeling cold and wearing more clothing than would seem warranted in a given atmosphere, growth of fine body hair (on the arms and abdomen), and loss of hair from her head all can occur with extreme underweight and malnutrition. Initially the individual appears to have boundless energy and seems hyperactive as far as exercising, but eventually fatigue and lethargy occur as a result of starvation.

Bulimia Nervosa

All of the following criteria must be met before a diagnosis of bulimia nervosa can be made:

- Recurrent episodes of binge eating, characterized by both of the following:
  a. Eating in a discrete period of time a definitely larger amount of food than most people would eat in this time;
  b. Feeling of lack of control over eating during the binge-eating episode, e.g., cannot stop eating or control how much or what is eaten.
- Minimum average of two binge-eating episodes a week for at least three months.
- Undue influence of personal body shape and weight.
- Occurs independent of or during episodes of anorexia nervosa.
- Regularly engages in purging (e.g., self-induced vomiting, use of laxatives or diuretics) or uses strict dieting, fasting, or vigorous exercise to avoid weight gain or to lose weight after binge episodes.

A person with bulimia nervosa may have frequent and noticeable weight fluctuations, express dissatisfaction with body weight and size, and make self-deprecatory statements in general. She may constantly talk about food or make comments about others' eating behaviors. The individual may disappear after meals or excuse herself to go to her room or the bathroom in order to vomit. She may have tooth or gum complaints, puffy eyes, swollen parotid (salivary) glands in the jaws, or a sore throat and hoarseness as a result of frequent vomiting. Stomach complaints often occur with exhausting vomiting episodes or laxative abuse. The disappearance of food from cupboards and refrigerators is one sign of a binge eater.

Emotional fluctuations may be observed and range from blaming others to negative self-talk, or from expressions of anger toward others to depression and crying. Behavioral fluctuations may range from fatigue and over sleeping to hyperactivity and sleep disturbances.

Eating Disorder Not Otherwise Specified

Some most commonly observed variations in the above two disorders would be classified as Eating Disorder Not Otherwise Specified. This diagnosis is applicable when the following occur:

- All the criteria for anorexia nervosa are met except amenorrhea or abnormally low weight;

- All criteria for bulimia nervosa are met except eating binges are less fre-quent than the stated criteria or the individual does not engage in regular compensatory purge behavior (often referred to as Binge Eating Disorder).

A diagnostic manual can be very helpful, but the criteria certainly do not ac-count for all the variations in behaviors and symptoms.

About 5% of the total population suffers from an eating disorder which meets diagnostic criteria, but professionals recognize that disordered eating behaviors serious enough to interfere with normal living may affect up to 20% of the female population. A significant number of males also suffer from anorexia nervosa, bulimia nervosa and binge eating disorder. A rising number of males are obsessed with body image and abuse substances (such as ster-oids or diuretics) in an attempt to dramatically alter body shape or weight.

DANGERS ASSOCIATED WITH EATING DISORDERS

The physical dangers of an eating disorder are many and serious. Ulti-mately, of course, death can occur and does occur in an estimated 10% of cases. In anorexia nervosa, death is most often due to complications of star-vation, such as kidney or heart failure. Suicide brought on by depression and a feeling of hopelessness is another cause of death. With self-induced vomiting and laxative abuse, dehydration or loss of electrolytes, such as po-tassium or chloride, can lead to death. Continued vomiting can result in what is known as "rebound edema," fluid retention and the swelling of hands and legs. A danger is congestive heart failure. Laxative abuse can cause a bloated feeling, perpetuating the use of laxatives to "flatten the stomach." In addition to dehydration and electrolyte imbalance, vomiting causes tooth decay and inflammation of the throat and esophagus. Amenor-rhea leads to reduced bone mass and osteoporosis, which does not appear to be reversible when health is regained. Some women are unable to regain their normal menstrual cycle, and a possible danger may be reproductive failure. Binge eating disorder can lead to obesity, menstrual irregularities, and diseases for which one has a family history, such as type II diabetes mel-litus or hypertension. Other physical dangers due to underweight and mal-nutrition are anemias, thyroid abnormalities, and an inability to regulate body temperature. The excessive use of substances and dietary manipula-tions to increase body size or make a certain weight for a sports team may lead to a habitual and dangerous disordered pattern. In addition, liver and kidney enzyme abnormalities may occur. Other concerns are dehydration and, especially in susceptible individuals, hypertension.

Disordered eating behaviors usually begin innocently but quickly take a painful psychological toll. Calorie restriction is often learned at an early age from family members concerned about weight and image. Most often purging is taught by friends at school or learned from personal accounts written by someone with an eating disorder or even from a family member. The individual thinks this will be a quick way to lose weight and then she will be able to stop. However, for one who is susceptible to developing an eating disorder, the behavior becomes her only feeling of control over her body. As the disorder becomes more evident and obviously affects the individual's functioning, it becomes much more difficult to treat. The individual is unable to change even if she wants to, and the fear of losing all control takes over. Psychological dangers include an obsessive preoccupation with food and body weight and an inability to concentrate on other tasks; compulsive eating regimens or excessive exercise; not being able to willfully stop the self-induced vomiting or laxative use; depression, which could be exacerbated by or a result of starvation; and food phobias and increased fear of eating with others. All of these become more intense the longer the disorder continues. Early intervention can prevent some of these more serious and difficult to treat behaviors and thought processes.

Often, a young girl or boy who is developing an eating disorder may be a popular, good student who is active in clubs, sports, or volunteer work. While it can be difficult to notice an early disorder, some behaviors may be telltale. Change in eating preferences or habits; increased isolation, irritability or negative feelings about oneself; compulsive or excessive exercising; or an intense preoccupation with weight and body shape are all warning signs, if not of a developing eating disorder, perhaps depression or other need for help.

GETTING HELP

Although the diagnostic criteria for eating disorders center around weight control behaviors and body image, the true origin of the problem is not with eating and weight; it is a growing inner emotional conflict over which the individual feels no control and at the same time has no skills to express or resolve. The eating disorder becomes a coping mechanism. Rigid food restriction is one way of gaining some control over oneself and one's environment; binge eating numbs inner conflict; purging alleviates fear and guilt and gives a certain sense of peace or euphoria. These are, of course, temporary, dangerous, and ineffective mechanisms.

Therapy must be geared to helping the individual and family find and verbalize inner emotional struggles, learn constructive ways of relating while respecting each other's self, use honest and effective ways of communicating, and express unconditional respect and love for one another. A major factor in the perpetuation of an eating disorder is the individual's inability to make her true feelings known. Often this inability to express oneself is a result of the family pattern of not communicating honestly with one another, or parents making all decisions for a child, even into young adolescence when she or he should be developing a sense of an independent self with permission to make some decisions.

I AM AN ARTICHOKE BY LUCY FRANK (187 pp.)

Synopsis

" 'You can be fat or skinny or anything and I won't care. You're my friend, Emily. We're friends.' She clutched the teddy bear closer, and I thought I heard a little noise—a sigh, or it might have been a sob. Then she turned toward the wall. 'But Emily,' I said, 'I'm worried about you. Don't get any skinnier, Emily. Please' " (p. 74). *I Am an Artichoke* (1995) details the experience of 15-year-old Sarah during her summer job as a mother's helper to Florence Friedman, a recently divorced freelance writer and mother of 12-year-old Emily. Thinking that her position was merely to baby-sit a little rich girl, Sarah discovers an entirely different reason for her presence in the Friedman household. One day while they are out for breakfast, Emily, who is suffering from anorexia nervosa, informs Sarah that her purpose as "mother's helper" is to try to persuade her, by example, to eat, and also to prove to Emily that adolescent girls can enjoy their lives. Emily's parents hope that when she is around a "normal" teen, she may begin to become interested in eating and other activities again. We soon learn that Emily uses her refusal to eat as a means of controlling the family. Her parents, now living apart, are forced to communicate; they argue daily over the telephone about how to respond to Emily's resistance to food. Emily's father threatens her with hospitalization and criticizes his ex-wife for her inability to force Emily to eat. Emily's mother, in an effort to maintain custody and control of Emily, convinces herself that Emily is improving and growing out of a bad phase. She denies the seriousness of her daughter's physical and emotional conditions.

Florence plans a birthday bash for Emily, and invites classmates with whom Emily had been friends in the past, but whom she has alienated during months of refusing to go out of the house. Upset about the party, which her mother conducts against Emily's protests, and incensed when she suspects that her mother has found and read her diary, Emily runs away. Sarah finds Emily and takes her to her own parents' home. The next day, when Emily's mother and father arrive to take her home, it is Sarah who steps in to explain to them that Emily's illness is an attempt to control the family, an attempt to force her parents to cooperate. Once honest communication opens for Emily and her parents, and with the help of Sarah's friendship, readers are left with hope that Emily will be able to begin the struggle toward recovery.

Comments from the Perspective of a Nutrition Counselor

In *I Am an Artichoke*, Emily could not express herself in healthy ways. Her mother controlled rather than listened as illustrated when she removed Emily's exercycle, had her hair cut, and invited friends to a party despite Emily's protest. Emily may have agreed to some of these decisions had she been part of the decision-making process and then felt she was a real person whose feelings mattered. Instead, she used her disorder to gain a feeling of control in her life and even manipulate her parents. Readers are not privy to how her therapy sessions progressed, but we do know that her mother— rather than gain some reassurance—grew increasingly anxious that she was being blamed for Emily's disorder. She attempted to deal with her anxiety by reading Emily's journal, a devastating invasion of Emily's privacy. Elliott, Emily's father, resorted to threats of hospitalization or to blaming Florence in his helpless attempts to be effective. He needed some specific directives. When Sarah pointed out a few of her own observations, it appeared the whole family was ready for help and intervention, in spite of all their bluffing, blaming, and angry outbursts. The eating disorder was the problem, not Emily or Florence or Elliott, and it was exhausting all of them.

An important early therapeutic strategy is to have a family session as well as individual sessions with involved family members. Florence's history of disordered eating behavior is her attempt to cope with problems of her own. She could benefit from therapy to explore ways to replace her fear of being blamed, her own insecurities, and her manipulative attempts to control others with some positive and productive interactions. Both parents need to reconstruct their relationships with Emily, essentially to listen to her and help her find her own identity and to respect her boundaries.

Emily's therapy probably began with Sarah's unconditional and honest friendship, a relationship which fortunately everyone desires should continue. Emily should be encouraged in her journal writing, as it can be an important tool for her to gain insight into some of her true feelings. She wants to be her own person but fears she won't be able to cope. Her parents would probably find the book *Surviving an Eating Disorder* (Siegel, Brisman &

Weinshel, 1997) a helpful guide. It gives specific and practical help to families and friends of someone with an eating disorder. Included is a discussion of types of therapy and other treatments and what to expect. *Surviving an Eating Disorder* guides parents on how to improve communications and offers other ways to develop healthy relationships by relating to the person, not the disorder. Often, family and friends focus on the gaining weight, eating, stopping the compulsive exercising, or throwing up. Emphasis should be on "How can I help you express how you feel and not get angry or try to lay blame somewhere else?" Suggestions in this book can help families build healthy relationships; counselors will work with the disordered behavior.

Emily also needs physical follow-up. A blood chemistry analysis for signs of malnourishment and imbalances is essential in her current condition, especially if she is purging. Endocrine functions should be assessed. She could benefit from sound nutrition counseling to help with normalizing her eating. Although she promises to eat, phobias associated with foods and eating are difficult to change; she needs follow-up support and guidance.

FAT CHANCE BY LESLEA NEWMAN (224 pp.)

Synopsis

" 'Fine,' I said, and I shoved my entire supper into my mouth. Then later after I did all the dishes and made Mom her coffee I just went upstairs into my bathroom and threw up the whole thing. That'll show her. If she's going to make me eat like that, I just don't have a choice. I've simply got to get thin, and that's all there is to it" (pp. 98–99).

As the narrator of *Fat Chance* (1994), Judi Liebowitz relates her experiences through the diary she is required to keep for a class during the first semester of her 8th-grade year. The diary, assigned at the beginning of the year by her rotund English teacher, Ms. Roth, catalogues each day's events. Judi has three goals for the year: to figure out what she wants to be when she grows up, to have a boyfriend (the seemingly unattainable Richard Weiss), and to lose enough weight to be the thinnest girl in the entire 8th grade (except for, maybe, Nancy Pratt). Judi commences her diet with "operation fast"; she starves herself for three days until her mother intervenes. Judi tries to compensate for her mother's fattening dinners and her insistence that the teen eat, by skipping breakfast and lunch then exercising excessively each night before she goes to bed. Then one day during lunch period, Judi discovers Nancy Pratt—the most beautiful and most popular girl in the school—forcing herself to throw up in the school bathroom. Judi reasons that since "even Nancy Pratt does it" that she, too, will force herself to vomit her meals in order become thin. Judi is delighted to be armed with a secret weapon to thwart her mother's calorie- and fat-laden meals.

As she chronicles her weight fluctuations, Judi realizes that even when thinner, she is not happy. Throughout the novel, Judi seems unable to talk to her mother about her problems, her low self-esteem, and her conflicting attitudes about eating. Her mother frequently asks her what is bothering her but does not push Judi to answer. Judi withdraws more and more into herself. She finally gathers the courage to present her diary to her mother as a Hanukkah present. Through it, her mother, who has shown Judi caring and loving support throughout the novel and who has respected Judi's need for privacy, begins to understand the depth of her daughter's frustrations, confusion, and fear. Her mother writes Judi a letter conveying her support, and the novel closes with Judi and her mother visiting a therapist together. Judi is easing toward recovery with her mother at her side.

Comments from the Perspective of a Nutrition Counselor

Judi, the protagonist in *Fat Chance*, was certain the only way to be happy was to be thin. She learned purging behavior from a classmate, but this only made Judi more unhappy with herself. She was fortunate in having a teacher who encouraged, actually assigned, self-expression through a diary. Through her journal, Judi was able to recognize that her behaviors were not constructive. She and her mother love and respect each other but seem to live in their separate worlds; thus, they are not constructing a relationship that is helpful to each other. Judi feels her life is getting more and more out of control and thinks she is disappointing her mother. Her mother still seems to be mourning her husband's death, not tuning in to Judi's needs or allowing Judi to be a real part of her life.

Judi is fortunate in having a teacher, school officials, and a mother who do not look for who to blame but get down to solutions as soon as they are aware of a problem. At school, an assembly is held to discuss eating disorders after a classmate's hospitalization with anorexia nervosa. Judi's teacher listened to and helped her work out an action plan, and Judi took a step of her own in giving her diary to her mother to read. Her mother wasted no time in getting counseling for Judi, but Judi's mother also needs to find a way to build a happier life for herself that would include a real interactive relationship with her daughter. The book *Reviving Ophelia* (Pipher, 1994) would give her new motivation as well as insights into the world in which Judi lives. The author of *Reviving Ophelia* takes an open look at daughters and family relationships and discusses positive and creative ways of interacting without placing blame or looking for deep, hidden reasons for maladaptive or disruptive behaviors. Nearly any parent will find a situation to identify with, gain some understanding, and find ideas to initiate change in the family relationship.

SUGGESTIONS FOR PARENTS AND TEACHERS

Not everyone is as fortunate as Judi to have a teacher help her get early assistance or even as Emily who had Sarah to point out the reality of the family's ineffective circus-like behavior and inability to meet one another's emotional needs. Reading novels where the young adult can identify with the protagonist and see herself in the family scheme can help put words to feelings or gain insights into how to change. A set of questions or activities could be given to each person to write about and then used to discuss the realities of disordered behaviors. Some examples are these:

- Pretend you are the protagonist, or other character, with an eating disorder problem. Write a letter to "your" parents expressing how you feel.
- How do you think the family in the novel could improve how they relate to one another?
- Do you think the protagonist thought her attempt to lose weight would lead to the eating disorder? What are some indicators of concern?
- What are some ways our society keeps us focused on our bodies?
- Write about how you feel if someone makes a comment, positive or negative, about your body.
- How do you think it would affect someone else if you made some comment about another person's body? Why would you make the comment?
- How does it affect you when your parents or someone you know is always on a diet or other program to lose weight?
- What are some things you wish you could talk to your parents about without their getting upset? Why do you think they would get disturbed at your bringing it up?

CONCLUSION

Young adult novels and medically and psychologically sound books may help open the way for a young person, teacher, friend, or parent to talk about an existing problem. They may help anorexics recognize the destructive side of their behavior and may point out to teens that that there are constructive ways for them to find and express themselves. Books have the potential to speak to teens even when their parents, teachers, and friends are pushed away or shut out. More importantly, perhaps, YA books can help parents, teachers, siblings, and friends understand the complex and confusing world that those with anorexia nervosa, bulimia, and other eating disorders live in from day to day. These books may offer a means of speaking to teens who desperately need help.

RECOMMENDED READINGS

Fiction

8.01.   LeMieux, Anne C. (1997). *Dare to be, M. E.!* New York: Avon. 226 pp. (ISBN: 0–380–97496–7). Middle School (MS).

This is a fine novel for middle school readers who have a friend who may have bulimia nervosa. The protagonists are best friends named Mary Ellen and Justine; readers have already met the pair in LeMieux's *Fruit Flies, Fish & Fortune Cookies* (1994). Mary Ellen, a middle school activist, is so disturbed by ridiculous standards that are presented in fashion magazines and even by toy manufacturers that she does a school project on the bad influence of toy makers on girls' body images. Meanwhile, Justine has just returned home after spending a year in France. While away, Justine has gained weight and now sees herself as obese. Justine is caught throwing up at a party, and Mary Ellen realizes that her friend might be bulimic. Late in the novel, LeMieux defines bulimia nervosa and uses the character of a physical education teacher to help Mary Ellen understand Justine's condition. Mary Ellen struggles with the question of whether to remain loyal to Justine by protecting her secret, or to tell the physical education teacher, or talk to Justine's mother about Justine's bulimia. Eventually, Mary Ellen talks with Justine about the condition and helps her seek professional assistance.

This novel is a light read when compared with others that focus on teen characters who have eating disorders; nevertheless, it is one of the best we have reviewed for several reasons. It does not provide prescriptions for "how to" maintain an eating disorder and demonstrates that eating disorders emerge from complex sets of problems. In Justine's case, bulimia was a reaction against the split up of her mother and father. The novel also suggests the difficult reality that even friends may not be able to help a victim of an eating disorder conquer the disease. The reality is that victims may withdraw from, and even deceive, their friends when they develop eating disorders. In addition to the focus on Justine's problem, there are many aspects of friendships and family relationships—both healthy and troubled ones—that will appeal to young adolescent readers of this novel.

8.02.   Levenkron, Steven. (1978). *The best little girl in the world.* Chicago, IL: Warner Books. 196 pp. (ISBN: 0–446–35865-7). High School (HS).

Francesca Dietrich, a high school student whom her mother describes as "too good to be true" and "so independent I don't even know she's there sometimes" (p. 14) develops anorexia nervosa. She uses dance classes as a way of exercising vigorously, then goes home to exercise for hours more before sleep. She develops what seem to be bizarre rituals, such as counting her bites and chewing to the rhythm of her tapping fingers, using the toilet without allowing any part of her body to touch it, and cleaning her teeth fastidiously so that nothing can defile them. Francesca's parents, who are preoccupied with their older daughter, notice Francesca's weight loss only when it becomes severe. The threats made by Francesca's father have no effect on Francesca, who renames herself Kessa, and redefines herself as a powerful manipulator. Francesca is "in control of the situation" while her parents and one of many therapists fight about how to treat her. Kessa is able to remain calm while her parents are "going to pieces because of her" (p. 99).

This novel is bleak and exhausting. In it, Levenkron, a therapist who wrote in 1982 that he had spent more than 7,000 hours with anorexics, does not present a tidy, pretty picture of the realities of this disturbing condition. He does, however, offer hope for Francesca and others like her. After she is hospitalized for life-threatening malnourishment, she is finally paired with a therapist who works with Francesca and the rest of the family to uncover the roots of her behaviors. The novel gives readers a glimpse into the desperate, maddening, dark world of a teen who is driven to starve herself. Through it, the message is clear: Eating disorders are about much more than food!

8.03.   Lipsyte, Robert. (1977). *One fat summer.* New York: Bantam. 150 pp. (ISBN: 0–553–24393–4). MS, HS.

This enjoyable novel, set in 1957, is the only one that we have found which features a male character who is particularly concerned with losing weight for the sake of his appearance. Bobby Marks, at 14 years old and more than 200 pounds, tells the story of the summer that he quit being a compulsive eater, lost weight, and gained self-respect. Bobby's best friend is Joanie. He explains that, "When we were alone together I felt thin, and I think she felt pretty" (p. 3). When Joanie has plastic surgery to straighten her imperfection—a large, crooked nose—Bobby feels alone as a physical misfit. He takes a job as the yardman for a wealthy man who pushes Bobby to his limits. Yet before long, Bobby notices that because of the exhausting work, his fat is being replaced by muscles. Soon he will not have to envy the high school students who wear swim trunks at the beach; he will be one of them.

This novel offers no "how to" prescriptions for compulsive over-eating; instead, it moves from the point of Bobby's habit of overeating when he feels bad about his body to a focus on Bobby's positive action. Unlike the other novels that may inadvertently encourage readers to experiment with destructive eating behaviors, this one would be safe for any reader who has grown frustrated with his or her weight. Lipsyte demonstrates, through Bobby Marks, that exercise has the power to help someone lose weight, slowly, safely, and with lasting results.

8.04.   Ruckman, Ivy. (1983). *The hunger scream.* New York: Walker. 200 pp. (ISBN: 0–802–76514–9). HS.

Lily is a 17-year-old high school student who develops anorexia nervosa. She restricts her food intake in an attempt to gain her parents' attention and admiration, and in an effort to create a perfect body that will win her the affection of Daniel, the guy next door. Although she considers giving her family some clues about her dissatisfaction with herself before the eating disorder reaches an advanced stage, Lily eventually withdraws from them. She binges whenever she feels hurt by her friends, then punishes herself with starvation for losing control. When the cheerleading coach will not allow her to try out for the senior squad because she is underweight, Lily runs away from home. She enjoys manipulating her family and secretly observing the pain she is creating for her parents, who feel helpless. Finally, Lily must be hospitalized. After many tough sessions with a young, understanding therapist, Lily begins to accept the fact that she must gain weight in order to have her life back. The therapist, Dr. Coburn, insists on meeting with the entire family, because, as she explains to Lily, "You have the symptoms, but the illness belongs to the whole family" (p. 156).

Like *The Best Little Girl in the World*, this novel is dark and difficult to read because it presents a teen in a world that is, from her perspective, almost unbearable. Lily replaces the concern of her family and friends with life-threatening self-starvation. There are, in the sections that focus on the rituals that Lily creates, some unintended hints for readers who want to find out how to sustain anorexic behaviors. It does, however, offer hope. The novel ends when Lily has gained enough weight to leave the hospital and with her entire family they partake in therapy. Lily is looking forward to her future, yet is aware that no one is ever completely cured of anorexia.

8.05.   Terris, Susan. (1987). *Nell's quilt*. New York: Sunburst. 177 pp. (ISBN: 0–590–41914–5). HS.

Set in the late 1800's, this novel presents a complex, fascinating story of 18-year-old Nell, who is torn between a strong desire to help her parents in any way she can—since they have to work grueling hours on the family's farm—and her need to rebel against her parents. Although she has dreams of moving to Boston and attending college, her parents believe that she should marry Anson Tanner, a man she does not love but one who can provide for her material needs; he is a widower with a small daughter. Nell begins to refuse to eat as a means of retaining control over at least one part of her life. She develops rituals concerning food, such as eating only white, pale things, and hiding bread that she pretends to eat. Nell is pleased when she stops menstruating because she believes that her amenorrhea is a sign that she has achieved total control over her body. As her anorexia worsens, Nell grows unable to help around the farm or to see her betrothed. Meanwhile, she devotes all of her attention to sewing an elaborate quilt; each square symbolizes one of the people who is responsible for her anguish. Her father articulates the effect of her mysterious malady on the family, " 'Do you know how you're tearing up our lives? Whatever you do to yourself, Nell, you do to us. So it's about time you stopped this demented behavior' " (p. 107).

This novel is particularly interesting from an artistic perspective. Terris uses the quilt at the center of the text, literally and figuratively. The author also depicts scenes in which Nell is teetering on the brink of insanity in a calm, matter-of-fact way; this mirrors the control that Nell felt she was able to maintain. Also, there are no quick, magic answers provided in this novel. At its close, Nell has just decided that she wants to live. Readers know that Nell has an extremely long road to travel before she recovers from the months of self-imposed starvation that she has suffered. The fact that the novel is set just before the turn of the 20th century may help some readers approach it with more objectivity than they approach books that feature contemporary adolescents in familiar settings. Readers may be able to use the temporal setting as a facade behind which they can address the issues presented within the rich text.

8.06.   Wersba, Barbara. (1987). *Fat: A love story*. New York: Dell. 156 pp. (ISBN: 0–440–20537–9). HS.

This novel, with its sequel *Beautiful Losers*, is a delightfully light-hearted read for high school students. It features narrator and protagonist Rita Formica, a compulsive overeater who lives in posh Sag Harbor, New York, with her parents. The trouble is that her family is not at all wealthy, and she is a compulsive overeater. Rita hates what she is doing to her body and her self-image but she enjoys food. She admits, "When I look back on my life, I do not see a series of events—I see a long trail of food. A long road littered with candy bars, Sara Lee Cakes, ice cream sandwiches, pizzas, jelly donuts, and my beloved gummy bears. I gaze into the far-off skies and see, not a sunset, but a cloud of cotton candy, a haze of marshmallow. I'm a very different person now—but in those days food was my god and my religion. Until I met Robert" (p. 21). Robert is the unattainable hunk who Rita follows around all summer and who is eventually swept off his feet by Rita's only female friend, 19-year-old Nicole. What Rita does not realize is that she is slowly falling in love with her quirky boss, 30-year-old Arnold Bromberg. Arnold fell for Rita the day that she applied for the job as delivery person for his cheesecake business and sees her beauty. Once she feels his respect, Rita begins to take better care of herself and control her eating. Because Rita rides a bicycle to make the cheesecake deliveries, and because she finally realizes that Robert is not for her—but that Arnold is—she grows to like herself more.

This novel is positive in the sense that the protagonist's self-esteem, once defined by her weight, is redefined by her relationship with Arnold, her independence, and her dreams for the future. Many readers, however, are likely to be disturbed by Rita's sexual activity; at 18 years of age, she moves in with 30-year-old Arnold without her parents' approval. Rita's story continues in sequels, *Beautiful Losers* (1988) and *Love Is the Crooked Thing* (1989).

8.07.   Willey, Margaret. (1983). *The bigger book of Lydia*. New York: Harper. 215 pp. (ISBN: 0–440–20537–9). HS.

Her father died when she was a child, and Lydia Bitte believes that his death was caused, indirectly, by his diminutive size. This feeling, and the fear that she, too, might be crushed by the world because of her size, gives Lydia unusual lenses through which she views the world. Michelle, the niece of a friend of Lydia's mother, moves into the Bitte house when Lydia is a 15-year-old sophomore in high school. Lydia and her mother instantly realize that Michelle is very ill; she is frail and emaciated. Further, Michelle wears bizarre clothes, has unkempt tufts of hair, chain smokes cigarettes, paints sophisticated and surrealistic art, and has been in and out of treatment centers and hospitals during her high school years. Michelle's parents are frustrated, and they hope that living with a quiet family will help their daughter. As Lydia and Michelle cautiously become friends, the reader learns that Michelle refuses to eat as a means of mourning her mother's loss of independence and individuality. Michelle has witnessed her mother, once a promising fashion designer, become an alcoholic because of self-loathing. Michelle's mother hates herself for throwing away her dreams in order to play the role of surgeon's wife.

Because she feels no pressure to eat, to participate in family activities, or even to attend school, and because she and Lydia form a bond of friendship and trust, Michelle slowly begins to recover while living with the Bittes. Her recovery is aided by weekly visits to a therapist, but readers learn very little about the nature of those visits.

Lydia and Michelle are both intriguing and unpredictable because their personalities are influenced by their unusual attachments to a parent. Lydia manifests her attachment and resulting fears by keeping a book during her childhood of small and large things; whereas, Michelle manifests her attachment to her mother by starving herself.

8.08.   Woodson, Jacqueline. (1993). *Between Madison and Palmetto*. New York: Delacorte. 128 pp. (ISBN: 0–440–41062–2). MS.

Margaret and Maizon are friends who experience various changes as they enter their teenage years; they encounter new schools, new friends, and new bodies. Margaret, who has trouble accepting her maturing body, develops bulimic behaviors. The eating disorder, however, is not the central concern of this novel as Margaret's condition is "cured" rather simply with a trip to the family physician. The doctor recommends for her to engage in daily, moderate exercise so that she will be able to handle the new weight that accompanies her new bodily features. The other important issues addressed in this novel include friendships, race relations, and estranged fathers.

Nonfiction

8.09.   Andersen, Arnold E. (1990). *Males with eating disorders*. New York: Brunner/Mazel. 274 pp. (ISBN: 0–87630–556–7). Adult (A).

This book is rare in that it deals with males who get the eating disorders that most often afflict females. It is a must read for parents and teachers who hope to understand the potential eating disorders have to disrupt lives of members of both sexes. Possible causes for eating disorders that emerge among males, along with signs and prevention and intervention strategies, are discussed.

8.10.   Hall, Lindsey. (1993). *Full lives: Women who have freed themselves from food & weight obsession*. Carlsbad, CA: Gurze Books. 271 pp. (ISBN: 0–93607–726–3). HS, A.

Employing the motif of gathering a group of friends for conversation around a dinner table, Hall allows 15 women, all of whom have struggled with an eating disorder, to tell their stories. The women who speak from around the figurative dinner table include the president of Anorexia Nervosa and Related Eating Disorders (ANRED), the founder of Eating Awareness Services and Education (EASE), the founder of the Foundation for Education on Eating Disorders (FEED), the coordinator of the State of New York's Eating Disorders Awareness Week (who is also a supervisor of the Center for the Study of Anorexia and Bulimia in New York), and the president of Eating Disorders Awareness and Prevention. The women also include a Ph.D. in counseling psychology, a Gestalt therapist, and the author of a popular autobiography of a former anorexic, *My Name Is Caroline*. Each tells how she lived through and eventually overcame her eating disorder(s).

This book will be a relief for parents and teachers who fear that there is little hope for teens who experience eating disorders. It may also show them that family members play an important supporting role for many who suffer eating disorders.

8.11.   Hesse-Biber, Sharlene. (1996). *Am I thin enough yet?: The cult of thinness and the commercialization of identity*. New York: Oxford University Press. 208 pp. (ISBN: 0–195–08241–9). A.

This book looks critically to popular media as a culprit in teaching women what they "should" look like thus leading them toward unnatural standards and health problems, including eating disorders. It is the kind of book that would have informed the character, Mary Ellen, in LeMieux's *Dare to Be, M. E.!* (reference 8.01) when she presented research to her middle school class about the damage that toy manufacturers do by selling dolls that show proportions that the great majority of human bodies cannot approximate.

8.12.   Hollis, Judi. (1985). *Fat is a family affair: A frank discussion of eating disorders and the family's involvement.* San Francisco: Harper & Row. 171 pp. (ISBN: 0–89486–263–4). HS, A.

This book offers readers support for helping family members as they work to break the patterns that sustain eating disorders. Hollis, a licensed therapist, speaks from personal experience when she writes, "With anorexia, you are saying, 'Not only don't I need YOU, I don't even need FOOD. I am so self-sufficient, invincible, invulnerable, and self-contained, I can live on air. I have overcome any "human" neediness and am completely in charge of my life' " (pp. 7–8). Although Hollis is now a successful therapist, she was a former compulsive overeater who developed and suffered with bulimia for many years.

We caution readers that, although it is valuable in presenting statistics and helping family members identify and perhaps begin to understand some of the complex feelings associated with the diseases, the book is predicated on an approach that ties the text with the Overeaters Anonymous program. We present it here, along with Sandbek's *The Deadly Diet*, as examples of "self-help" books that present a particular program as a solution.

8.13.   Levenkron, Steven. (1982). *Treating and overcoming anorexia nervosa.* New York: Charles Scribner's Sons. 224 pp. (ISBN: 0–684–17430–8). HS, A.

Levenkron is a clinical psychologist who works with patients who suffer from anorexia nervosa. He is also the author of the best selling novel, *The Best Little Girl in the World* (1978) described earlier. This nonfiction book is Levenkron's attempt to answer the most frequently asked questions from families about the disease. In his answers, he includes specific examples of how he has treated anorexics; his focus is on ways to fight the disease. Levenkron works toward this focus by presenting cases of six patients in the hope of helping readers identify and understand "what occurs between the world and the child that creates the vulnerability to anorexia nervosa" (p. xvi). The book is intended for those afflicted with the disease and those who care about someone who suffers from it. It is readable for those who are unfamiliar with medical language and provides much-needed insights into the disease.

8.14.   Sandbek, Terence J. (1993). *The deadly diet.* 2nd edition. Oakland, CA: New Harbinger. 256 pp. (ISBN: 1–879–23742–3). A.

Like Hollis' *Fat Is a Family Affair*, this book suggests a formula for battling eating disorders. Sandbek is a licensed clinical psychologist who approaches eating disorders from a cognitive-behavioral approach. He acknowledges that, "This method has no concern for *why* you have an eating disorder (what happened to you when you were a child), or how you feel about your problem. This book is concerned with teaching you *how* to learn the necessary skills needed to overcome the problem. If you still want to know why you have an eating problem, you can satisfy your curiosity AFTER you have successfully overcome the problem" (p. 3).

We list this book because it seems fairly unique in its approach to treating people with eating disorders. Parents, teachers, and other adults will want to know that there are few aspects of eating disorders on which professionals agree; this book helps make that point explicit.

8.15.   Valette, Brett. (1988). *A parent's guide to eating disorders: Prevention and treatment of anorexia nervosa and bulimia.* New York: Walker. 190 pp. (ISBN: 0–8027–1040–9). A.

Beyond the factual information about the diseases, this book demonstrates to parents that they cannot carry all of the guilt for their children's problems. It may be that, in addition to its clearly presented information, the book's assurance that they are not the only ones who have children with eating disorders will be a major benefit of this book for parents.

REFERENCES

American Psychiatric Association. (1994). *Diagnostic and statistical manual of mental disorders.* 4th edition. Washington, DC: American Psychiatric Association.

Frank, Lucy. (1995). *I am an artichoke.* New York: Bantam Doubleday.

Levenkron, Steven. (1982). Treating and overcoming anorexia nervosa. New York: Charles Scribner's Sons.

Newman, Leslea. (1994). *Fat chance.* New York: G. P. Putnam's Sons.

Pipher, Mary. (1994). *Reviving Ophelia: Saving the selves of adolescent girls.* New York: Ballantine.

Siegel, Michele, Brisman, Judith, & Weinshel, Margot. (1997). *Surviving an eating disorder.* 2nd edition. New York: Harper Perennial.

Zerbe, K. (1993). *The body betrayed: A deeper understanding of women, eating disorders, and treatment.* Washington, DC: American Psychiatric Association.

CHAPTER 9

Rights of Passage: Preparing Gay and Lesbian Youth for Their Journey into Adulthood

Patricia L. Daniel & Vicki J. McEntire

INTRODUCTION

The more we know about a topic, the more capable we are to fend off untrue statements and discount half-truths; however, conversely, the less we know about a topic, the more likely we will be prey to untrue statements and half-truths. In the past, people believed the sun revolved around the earth, the earth was flat, left-handed people were possessed by demons, slaves were inferior people, and slavery was even justified by the *Bible*. Today, in the technological and post-information age, we are living in a time when society is redefining how to treat homosexuals. Much of our society is trying to ignore the topic so that maybe it will go away. Some people are vehemently opposed to homosexuality based on their religious beliefs and fears that homosexuality will corrupt their children and all of society, while others believe that homosexuality is not at all evil and gays and lesbians should be protected by the same laws that heterosexuals enjoy.

Culture is subtly passed from generation to generation, and our American culture has taught us that homosexuality is unnatural, wrong, evil, and/or sick. Human sexuality is experienced along a continuum. At one end of the continuum are people who only have attractions and experiences with the opposite sex, and at the other end of the continuum are people who only have attractions and experiences with the same sex. Most people fall somewhere in between the two extremes, but approximately 10% of the population consider themselves to be homosexual and are having to make important decisions about how to live their lives. Today, one must consciously decide whether or not to support the efforts of gays and lesbians.

Adolescence is a time of sexual awakening. For an adolescent to realize that he or she is gay or lesbian can be the most frightening event of his or her life. Most teenagers have probably heard degrading jokes about gays and lesbians and may have witnessed some type of unsolicited harassment and hostility. Most families, churches, and school curriculum send negative messages about homosexuality or they don't say anything at all; the silence confirms the taboo. Adolescents becoming aware of their homosexual feelings and attractions fear becoming the victims of harassment, hate, and violence. These adolescents feel isolated with no one to talk to, and they often do not know where to find information to help diffuse the negative messages learned over time. One does not choose to be homosexual, but one chooses whether or not to live true to one's identity as a homosexual. That decision, whether or not to be true to oneself, has implications throughout one's entire life. Developing a positive identity is an important factor in making the journey into adulthood happily.

Many adolescents will hide their homosexuality from friends and family even when and if they admit to themselves that they are homosexuals. In effect, they decide to live a lie to those they care about the most because they do not want to risk their ridicule, anger, or rejection. One of an adolescent's greatest fears is to be seen as gay or lesbian by peers; after all, the cruelest, most despicable names that are hurled are "faggot," "dyke," "queer," and "homo." Indeed, two to three times more gay and lesbian youth actually commit suicide than their heterosexual counterparts (Krueger, 1993). Paul Gibson, the author of the Report of the Secretary's Task Force on Youth Suicide, makes it clear that this higher incidence is not an indication that homosexual youth are weak or sick or inferior. He writes, "The root of the problem of gay youth suicide is a society that discriminates against and stigmatizes homosexuals while failing to recognize that a substantial number of its youth has a gay or lesbian orientation" (Gibson, 1994, p. 16).

Schools should be a safe place for all students. Teachers can do much by not tolerating any name-calling in their classrooms, but they can do more by challenging homophobic remarks and expressing that these remarks are offensive. Teachers can order gay and lesbian literature for the library, say the words "gay" and "lesbian" in context, avoid heterosexual bias by using terms such as "significant other" rather than "girlfriend" or "boyfriend," read and become aware of the issues gays and lesbians face, and include gay/lesbian/bisexual information when studying different homosexual writers such as Herman Melville, Virginia Woolf, Willa Cather, and others.

Unks (1995) reports that the secondary curriculum ignores that homosexuals exist. Nonexistence is covertly translated to mean that homosexuals never did anything significant and is translated by homosexual youth to mean that they are not likely to make any worthwhile contribution to society since no other homosexual has ever done so. Their future looks dismal partly because they are unaware of the famous gays and lesbians throughout history and partly because they do not see gay and lesbian adult role models. Gay and lesbian youth would be better prepared for life if they could be exposed to other people like themselves who have happy and productive lives. These youth would then realize that they are not the first and only persons ever making this journey.

ORGANIZATION

We begin by presenting a simulation of a possible counseling session that could occur between Jan, a character from Nancy Garden's *Good Moon Rising*, and a therapist. In the novel, Jan has realized that she is a lesbian because of her love for Kerry. In our simulation, she explores what it means to live her life as a lesbian with the counselor. Jan sees her love for Kerry as a positive experience. Next, we include an annotated bibliography of young adult (YA) fiction, YA informational books, as well as annotated bibliographies addressing homosexuality for parents and teachers. Please note that the YA fiction selected was purposely done so to portray gays and lesbians in positive ways. No doubt the negative messages are being communicated, but young gays and lesbians ought to see themselves positively portrayed in literature, just as heterosexual youth can.

A THERAPY SESSION WITH JAN FROM NANCY GARDEN'S *GOOD MOON RISING*

Jan is assigned the role of stage manager and assistant director of the school play while the new student, Kerry, lands the leading role, much to Jan's dismay. Against many odds, Jan and Kerry become friends and then lovers. They are harassed by phone calls, large signs, and articles in the school newspaper. Jan and Kerry confront their accusers with the truth of their love for each other.

Counselor: Tell me why you are here today.

Jan: I came here because my teacher thought it would be a good idea to talk to somebody about what's been going on.

Counselor: How do you feel about being here? Do you think it's a good idea?

Jan: I guess so. There's just so much that's been happening. It's all I've been able to think about lately. I'm not getting my school work done. I have a hard time paying attention in class; I'm daydreaming a lot.

Counselor: Is there anything in particular you're thinking about?

Jan: I have a friend, Kerry. Well, she's more than a friend, and I think about her all the time. When we aren't together, I'm thinking about things I want to tell her. We were in this play together. I mean I was the assistant director but then our teacher, Ms. Nicholson, died from cancer before we opened the show. After the play I went to the cast party with Raphael so everyone would think that he was my boyfriend but he's really gay. I got so mad pretending to be something I wasn't that I wound up telling everybody there that I'm gay. I mean, they thought so even before I knew for sure. Now the whole school knows, and I know it won't be long before somebody tells my parents. I want them to know from me first, but I just don't know how to tell them.

Counselor: I can understand why you're having trouble concentrating. It sounds like there is a lot going on in your life right now. Let's look at one piece at a time so it's not so overwhelming. You said you're gay, the kids at school know, and you want to tell your parents before anyone else does. Is that right?

Jan: Right!

Counselor: Okay. Let's start with your statement that you are gay. What does that mean to you?

Jan: I'm in love with another girl, you know, like I'm supposed to be with a boy. I mean, I've never been with anyone else like I've been with Kerry—kissing and touching. Last year I spent a lot of time with Ted, this guy from school. He wanted us to be more than friends, to go "steady" even though we hadn't been "going" at all. But the times he kissed me, or tried to go further, I didn't like it. I just waited for him to stop, feeling trapped and struggling for air.

Then I met Kerry at the tryouts for *The Crucible*. She was the perfect Elizabeth, a natural talent, but had never been in a play before. As the stage manager and assistant director, I started working with Kerry individually. I started seeing more of Kerry and less of Ted. I started thinking about her at odd times in the day, writing notes to her, saving things to tell her. Then Ted asked me to go to the Junior-Senior-Get-Acquainted Dance. I'd already made plans to go see *Hamlet* with Kerry and that was more important than being with everyone else. Kerry said some people would think it was weird that I'd rather be with her than Ted, that I'd rather be with a girl than with a boy.

Counselor: Did it seem weird to you?

Jan: Not really weird, but scary. I guess that was when I first let myself say what I had been thinking, that I did want to be with Kerry like a boy and girl would. She said she'd thought about it too. After I said it, that I'd rather be with her, I couldn't stop thinking about it. Like when Ms. Nicholson fell in rehearsal, I wanted to be the one Kerry was touching so gently. I knew then that I loved her. Then we went to see *Hamlet*. Sometime during the movie we started holding hands. At first I worried someone might see us, but it felt right and not awkward like when Ted and I held hands. I didn't let go of Kerry's hand until the movie was over. When we got to the car, I didn't know what to say. Suddenly we were kissing and I wanted to touch her hair, to be even closer to her. It felt right, but I knew we'd better be careful that no one saw us because they wouldn't understand.

Counselor: Have you ever had feelings like this for another girl before?

Jan: I met a girl at summer stock—Corrin. I never touched her or anything, but now I think I must have sort of wanted to; I don't know. "I know I thought she was beautiful but I also know straight women like my mother and sister sometimes think other women are beautiful, so I guess that doesn't mean much" (p. 90).

Counselor: How do you feel about Kerry?

Jan: "She's great—funny and kind and deep and intelligent and talented and strange—not as beautiful as Corrin but pretty, especially her eyes which are very dark brown and show almost everything she feels" (p. 91). I'm really drawn to her—her intensity. I'd find myself noticing little things, like the curve of her throat. My face would get hot and I'd turn away. I like how I feel when we touch. Do you think I'm gay?

Counselor: Sexual preference is pretty complex, and it isn't determined by a few isolated sexual or emotional experiences, thoughts, or feelings. Being lesbian or gay means that a person's primary romantic, emotional, physical, and sexual attractions are with someone of the same sex. Let me ask you, do you think you're gay?

Jan: I think I'm gay, but "I don't want to be a boy even though I liked playing with boys when I was little. I just feel as if I've always been a different kind of girl. But still a girl" (p. 153). And Kerry doesn't look anything like a boy or want to be a boy either. Does one of us have to act like a boy?

Counselor: No. Your sexual identity is made up of two things: feeling and acting like a male or female and who you direct your sexual feelings and actions toward. Most of us develop an internal knowledge of our sex that is in keeping with the body we are born with. In other words, gay men see themselves as males; lesbians see themselves as females.

Jan: What causes people to be gay?

Counselor: There are several theories about why people are gay, but no one really knows for sure. Some think gay people are born that way, that the brain structure and chromosomes predetermine if someone is going to be heterosexual or homosexual. Others think people are gay because of how life's experiences—good or bad—have affected them. Some think it is a mixture of biology, sociology, and psychology, and some even believe that it is a person's choice. Ironically, no one has done research to determine why heterosexual or straight people are heterosexual.

Jan: I never thought of it that way. Why not?

Counselor: Being heterosexual is considered "normal" and normal things are usually accepted without the need for an explanation. Some people think that being gay or bisexual is considered abnormal so it must be caused by something. The truth is homosexuality, bisexuality, and heterosexuality are all simply part of human sexuality.

Jan: I don't feel abnormal. It feels more natural to be close to Kerry than it ever did with Ted. I can't imagine doing the things I do with Kerry with a boy. I haven't really dated much, but I don't really want to either now that I've found Kerry.

Counselor: You know better than anyone else what feels right for you. Do you know what a continuum is?

Jan: Is it like a line in geometry where the value changes from one end to the other?

Counselor: Yes, like that. Think about one end of the line as people who only have attractions and experiences with the opposite sex, and the other end of the line as people who only have attractions and experiences with the same sex. Most people fall somewhere in between the two extremes. Our society likes things neatly defined, but most people don't experience life like that. We are all somewhere along that continuum. Sometimes where we are on the line changes; sometimes it stays the same.

Jan: Right now I know that I'm closer to the end that feels stronger about the same sex. I think I'd be that way even if I hadn't met Kerry. It seems like no one can see any part of that line except the part they're on. I know I have to be careful about others knowing my feelings or seeing me with Kerry. I can't go parking with Kerry at the river like other couples do.

Counselor: What do you think would happen if you did?

Jan: More of the same harassment, maybe worse! The gossip column of the school newspaper had something in it about Kerry and me "flirting gaily" (p. 159). Then there were the signs, banners with three-foot high letters, saying we're gay. There was also graffiti in the bathroom and all over the walls of the school. Somebody even put a note on Kerry's aunt's shop about us! We've received hang-up calls and people have been saying stuff about us being sinners. Kent turned a kiss in the play into a French kiss and told Kerry something like, "I bet a girl never kissed you like that" (p. 129). She said she was going to bite his tongue if he did it again.

Counselor: Teenagers perform more violent acts against gays and lesbians than any other group of people. Violence against gays—or gay bashing—is a serious problem for the gay community. Sometimes law enforcement chooses to look the other way when gays are the victims. That doesn't happen everywhere, but the reality is that there are a lot of negative consequences for people who choose to live their lives as gay men or lesbians.

Jan: What do you mean by "choose"?

Counselor: A gay man or lesbian has the choice to live a life consistent with how he or she feels or to deny the feelings and live the way he or she thinks is needed in order to be accepted by family and the community. Some gays choose to not be sexual and may put their time and energy into a career or community service. Other gay men and women choose to honor and accept what feels natural and seek a fulfilling relationship with someone of the same sex.

Jan: Is that what choosing to live an alternative or gay lifestyle means?

Counselor: That's a deceptive phrase. A lifestyle is the style in which you live. Some people choose a lifestyle where earning a lot of money is really important; some people choose to work less and spend more time with family and friends. Being gay is about who you are deep down; it's part of your being. Being gay is about relationships; it's about who you feel romantic love for.

Jan: Choosing to act on being gay is scary. Raphael told me about his getting beaten up with his friend Chris at a class picnic. Both of them had to go to the hospital emergency room. They had broken bones and everything but were afraid to report it to the police because the guy who beat them up said they'd be "dead meat" (p. 212) if they did. I thought what they did to us was bad but then I think of Raphael! What do you mean by negative consequences?

Counselor: Consequences are the results of things we choose and do. They can be positive or negative. You've already told me some of the negative consequences you've experienced—the threats, the notes, being isolated or not accepted by others in your school. Can you think of any others?

Jan: Well, last Thanksgiving when Kerry went to visit her grandmother in Connecticut, I really missed her. Everybody was talking about what was going on in their lives and were happy that Anita, my sister, was close to having her baby. I wanted to tell them about Kerry, but then I remembered what Anita said before about how gay people are to be pitied. I just went to my room.

Counselor: So, another negative consequence is not feeling like you fit in with your family. Anything else?

Jan: What about us being our own family? Kerry and I have talked about living together. We've talked about having a little grey house with a garden, and a white picket fence so our dog—a golden retriever—doesn't get out. Does that sound silly to you?

Counselor: Not at all. As we get older, in adolescence usually, we start planning for our future family. For some people that means finding a mate of the same sex; for most that means finding a mate of the opposite sex. Some people dream of a house, some want an apartment, some a boat, some want pets, and some want children.

Jan: I think Kerry and I might want children someday.

Counselor: Gay people get pregnant and have children in many of the same ways heterosexual people get pregnant. A lesbian woman may be artificially inseminated or may be sexual with a male friend in order to get pregnant. The laws in some states allow gay people to adopt children. Gay men and women may also pay a surrogate mother to become pregnant and have a baby for the purpose of being adopted by one or both of the couple.

Jan: That sounds complicated, especially the stuff about the law! I guess it's not as simple as just loving Kerry and wanting to live the rest of our lives together.

Counselor: There are lots of things ahead of you. For example, you will soon be deciding on a career. Some professions won't be accepting of you if you are open about being gay—the military, for one, with its Don't-Ask-Don't-Tell rule, and teaching for another. It is often assumed that homosexual teachers "recruit" children into being gay. And worse, some people actually think gay people molest children. The fact is that most children who are molested are violated by someone in their own family, usually by someone whose primary orientation is heterosexual.

Jan: That's ridiculous, the part about molesting children! And I don't think having a gay teacher in my school would have influenced me to be gay. It would be nice to know I'd have someone to talk to who understands how hard this is.

Counselor: So, can you think of any other negative consequences?

Jan: I guess we can't really get married, like straight people can. I've heard stuff on television and we talked in a class about gays getting married in Hawaii, but it seems like everyone is arguing about if getting married in Hawaii will count if you live anywhere else.

Counselor: Many people are trying to get that changed. If you can't get legally married, many gays have commitment ceremonies that are like weddings except they don't get a legal license. That means they have to work extra hard to have rights together. If you were to get sick and couldn't make decisions for yourself, Kerry wouldn't automatically be allowed to make those decisions for you, no matter how long you had lived together. She might not even be allowed to see you if you were in a critical care part of the hospital.

Jan: But that's not fair! She would be the one who would know what I'd want, maybe even better than my parents.

Counselor: You may be right, but some hospitals and doctors might require you to have signed a legal paper naming her your health-care surrogate before you ever got sick in order to have those rights. Then there are other things like health insurance and car insurance that you might not be able to get together. Gays have to do a lot of extra work to make sure their partner has the same protections and rights that heterosexual people automatically get when they marry.

Jan: Wow! There's so much to all this!

Counselor: Deciding to live openly as a gay man or lesbian woman is difficult if you only think about the negative consequences. Let's talk about the positive consequences of being gay.

Jan: That's easy! I have Kerry. I finally feel good about myself since I'm no longer lying, trying to pretend I'm straight. But how do we meet other people like us, you know, gays?

Counselor: That's a tough one for you since you're a minor. Larger cities have community centers where teenage gays and lesbians can meet, talk, and learn from each other how to get through some of the tough times; they even have support groups. There are even churches that provide support for gays and lesbians such as the Unitarian-Universalist Church, the United Church of Christ, and traditional Friends' Meetings (Quakers). Other denominations are discussing being more open to gays and lesbians. In fact, there are Protestant Metropolitan Community Churches all over the United States whose members are mostly gay and lesbian. They plan activities and also fill the missing piece some Christian gays feel because their own church does not show them the love and acceptance Jesus taught. There's also a Catholic organization called Dignity and a Jewish one called Havurah. Religion is a pretty complex issue too, but I can give you some things to read if you want.

Jan: Are there any places like that around here?

Counselor: Let me give you a list of resources I've suggested to other gay teens. It's difficult though not impossible to find places with services for gays.

Jan: There's so much to think about, just for me. We haven't even talked about how to tell my family yet!

Counselor: The coming-out process—the knowing and accepting you're gay—is just that: a lengthy process. The first step is coming-out to yourself, thinking of yourself as a gay or lesbian for the first time. Generally, there is a period of one to two years in which thoughts, feelings, and sometimes sexual experiences are connected with a learned definition of what a lesbian woman or gay man is. You've already made it through that part.

Jan: What's next?

Counselor: The next part of the coming-out process is letting others know. You've already included Raphael and certainly Kerry in the process. And, it sounds like the school newspaper and the signs at school probably started everyone else thinking about you as gay. The kids who weren't included in the cast-party where you made the announcement have probably heard about it too. You said you wanted to tell your parents before they heard it from someone else. What makes telling them yourself important?

Jan: Well, I think they'll be hurt if they hear it from someone else, you know, that I haven't been honest with them. But then, I'm not sure they want me to be honest about this. Kerry and I watched, on television, Ellen come-out to her parents. I thought about my family when Ellen said, "You always wanted me to be honest" and her Mom said, "No dear, that was you that wanted to be open and honest. We were quite comfortable with not talking about our feelings or uncomfortable things."

Counselor: Ellen has trouble communicating about a lot of things, but she sure did okay getting the message she's gay across to her family and friends. Were there any parts of that Ellen episode you think would be helpful to you?

Jan: Well, I like how she tried to test the water by asking them what they thought about the waiter who was gay.

Counselor: Testing the waters give some general information, but there's no way to know for sure if that reaction will be the same as when you tell your family you are gay. Your family doesn't have an emotional tie to the waiter or someone you see on television. Generally, how your family reacts to you most of the time is a pretty good indicator of how they'll handle the news you're gay. Let's talk about your family. Tell me about them.

Jan: Well, my dad is an attorney. He works late a lot and spends a lot of time out of town building up his law practice. When he's home he's pretty okay, but he doesn't listen very well. Sometimes I think he doesn't really know what I'm doing.

Counselor: What about your mom?

Jan: She's great! Anita, my sister, and I always tease her that she needs to be a comedian. She says, "But I like being a housewife" (p. 5). She's supportive of whatever I'm involved in, and she really tries to help when things are rough but lets me have space when I ask for it. She says she knows me better than I think she does.

Counselor: Tell me more about Anita.

Jan: She just had a baby, Charles Dana Anthony. She had a hard time with the delivery but she's okay now. Sometimes I think she's closed minded, you know, like the comment she made that gay people are to be pitied. She does show an interest in what I'm doing, like attending plays I'm in and asking about my time at summer stock. There's too many years difference between us to be really close.

Counselor: Do you have any other family? Grandparents?

Jan: Just Hal, Anita's husband. He tries too hard to get me to like him most of the time. He's nice I guess. He and Dad seem pretty close. After all, Hal's studying for the entrance exam for law school. I don't spend much time with him when he and Anita come over so I really don't know him too well. That's it for family. No grandparents or aunts or uncles.

Counselor: Coming-out to parents, no matter who you are or how old a person is, can be difficult. There are a lot of reasons why some people wait until they are adults to tell their parents, and some gays never tell their parents. As a minor, there are some things I want you to think about first before you tell your family. Your family may be okay knowing you are gay, but the reality is that some families are not okay with having a gay child. As a minor, you are financially supported by your parents. They may kick you out of the house, hospitalize you in a psychiatric institution, or physically harm you. You know your family better than I do. Are any of these reactions possible for your family?

Jan: I've seen stories like that on television, you know, the news in bigger towns and on CNN. There was a movie on TV where the parents got really mad when they found out their son was gay. His dad beat him up and kicked him out of the house while his mom cried but did nothing to stop it. Most of that stuff is about guys. I haven't seen any movies or news stories about girls, and I really don't think my parents would do anything like that. They've never done anything to hurt me, not even when they've been super mad. I don't think they'd kick me out or not support me financially. Can parents do that to their kids?

Counselor: Not legally. Every state is required to have laws to protect children. Let's apply what you've learned in civics classes to this. The federal government through Congress set the law that parents are responsible for their child until the child's 18th birthday. States take that law and interpret or decide exactly what that means. In this case, states decide the least amount of care a parent can give the child and not break the law. Then each state sets up regulating agencies to make sure the laws are enforced. Agencies that are responsible for protecting children usually have names like Child Welfare, Child Protective Services, or the Department of Children and Families. They have workers who go out and investigate what is happening anytime someone reports that a parent is not taking care of a child or has hurt the child in some way. Depending upon what has happened to the child, the police sometimes investigate too. If the police decide the parent broke the law, the investigative reports go to the county or district attorney who decides whether or not to file criminal charges against the parent for breaking the law. The county or district attorney may also ask a judge to legally take the child out of her or his home until changes have occurred that will make it safe for the child to return home.

Jan: Nothing like that happened in this movie. This guy was 16 and the only people who helped him were his friends.

Counselor: That's what usually happens when parents kick their children out of the house for being gay; it is seldom reported to a regulating agency or law enforcement. Teens don't want to be forced to go back home where it might not be safe. They don't want to have additional restrictions on being allowed to leave home with friends. And, the closer a minor is to 18, the less likely the regulating agencies and law enforcement will step in and enforce the law for parents to be responsible for their child's care. Twenty-two states have laws against homosexual activity between consenting adults. All states have laws prohibiting sex between an adult and a minor. The law doesn't really address consensual homosexual activity between minors. But, like we talked about earlier, the law is open to interpretation. What may be enforced as criminal activity in one area or state may be ignored in another. Kissing Kerry in public is not against the law, but depending upon where you live, you could be arrested if the police thought you were soliciting her.

Jan: Solicit, as in pay her, like with prostitution?

Counselor: Solicit doesn't have to mean exchanging money for sex. The law says solicit can also mean to invite her to engage in an immoral or lewd act. The law uses the words sexual misconduct, deviate sexual intercourse, crime against nature, gross indecency, homosexual conduct, and sodomy. The law also uses the words lewdness or lewd and lascivious conduct if two people are sexual in public.

Jan: Those words sound so harsh and don't seem anything like how it is when Kerry and I are alone together. It's—it's beautiful. This is confusing, all the names and the laws being different depending upon where you live.

Counselor: It can be confusing, especially when there is other turmoil, like in deciding if you are gay and how to tell your parents. That goes back to why some teens don't report being kicked out of their house to a regulating agency or law enforcement. Many teens don't know the law and fear being arrested. With the guy in the movie, was it safer for him to be on his own with friends or to stay in the home?

Jan: In the movie, his dad didn't get over being angry until the very end. In real life, I'm not sure it would have happened that quickly. I think he was safer being with his friends.

Counselor: Getting beyond the first reaction is hard for parents, the teenager who must leave home, and the other family members who remain. Picture a huge boulder covering all the lanes of a road. The boulder represents a parent learning his or her child is gay. The parent approaches the boulder from a behavioral perspective, sending this message: "If you don't act gay or engage in gay behaviors, you're not gay. If you're not gay, you can stay with the family." The teenager approaches the boulder from a "being" perspective; the behavior is a result of who he or she is. The message sent is, "I act gay and engage in gay behaviors because I am gay." Neither side can see from the other's perspective. Some teenagers and families need time and distance to help them get beyond that first reaction; some use counseling to help them understand or accept each other's perspective.

Jan: But counseling like this is different from what you meant by parents having their child hospitalized at a psychiatric institution. Why would parents put their child in a psychiatric hospital?

Counselor: Some people consider homosexuality to be a sickness, a mental illness. It wasn't until 1974 that homosexuality was taken out of the book mental health professionals use to classify and label people's behavior when they are having difficulty coping with day-to-day life. Most mental health professionals no longer believe people should be forced to have treatment for homosexuality but some still do. Just like all states have laws to protect children, all states also have laws that say that no one, even minors, can be forced against their will to have a psychiatric examination or psychiatric treatment unless he or she is suicidal, or might hurt someone else, or is not able to take care of himself or herself because of a mental illness.

Jan: Wow! I'm glad to know there are laws like these to protect people's rights. I hadn't thought about all the things that could happen. There's just so much to think about.

Counselor: It's your decision whether or not to tell your parents and family you are gay. No one else can decide what is best for you.

Jan: I don't want to hide this from them; I want to tell them. I want them to know how important Kerry is to me. Besides, it has been spread already all over school.

Counselor: Let me ask you this, then: Have you given any thought to how you're going to tell your parents you're gay?

Jan: Well, Kerry told her parents in a letter. But they're still in Europe and won't be back for awhile.

Counselor: Do you want to write your parents a letter or tell them in person?

Jan: I want to tell them, so they both hear it at the same time. Writing a letter is really one-sided in my opinion. I want to talk to them about it, not just tell them.

Counselor: Okay, you want to tell both parents at the same time. Let's start with the basics. Where is the best place to tell them?

Jan: I want a place that's private, where we don't have to worry about other people listening. I guess that would be at home, on a weekend when Dad is home.

Counselor: Coming-out to them in a public place can make it awkward and may make it difficult to talk. What do you plan to say?

Jan: Gee, I'm not sure. I guess I need to say more than "I'm gay."

Counselor: By letting your parents know that you are telling them about your sexual orientation because you care about them and want to be closer to them, not lie and hide this important part of you from them, is usually a good start. How you share this information will have a big impact on their response too. If you are respectful and caring in how you tell them, you increase the chances they will be respectful and caring in their response. You can only do your part. Remember, you don't have any control over how they may respond.

Jan: I see what you mean.

Counselor: Let's practice this. Pretend your mom and your dad are here. What would you say?

Jan: Wow! Okay, let me think. Mom. Dad. I have something really important to talk to you about. I've thought about this a lot, and I have even gone and talked to a counselor to help me sort this out. I want you to know I love you and you are important to me. Because you're important and I don't want to lie to you or hide things from you, you need to know that I think I'm gay.

Counselor: YOU THINK YOU'RE WHAT?!?!?!?

Jan: . . . that I'm gay. And I'm really happy. I finally understand all the weird feelings I've had, why I wanted to be just friends with Ted, why I've always liked being with other girls best.

Counselor: How can you be gay? What did we do to make you be gay? Is it because your father is away from home so much; or because we let you be a tomboy when you were growing up?

Jan: No. It's nothing like that! I'm gay because I am. This is normal for me. Nobody did anything to me to make me this way. You know Kerry, from the play. She's terrific and we really care about each other. I've never been happier in my life.

Counselor: That's really good, Jan. It sounds like you are comfortable with who you are, and your parents will hear that. You've had this whole year to get this comfortable with yourself. Remember, your parents are hearing this for the first time. The news may not be a total surprise to your mom but even if she's wondered about how close you and Kerry are, hearing the words may still be hard for her. Some parents have a lot of questions right away. Others need time to think before they'll be able to give you a response. I want to give you some information to share with your parents about support groups, places they can call to talk, and information they can read when they're ready to learn more about what it means for you to be gay and for them to be parents of a lesbian.

Jan: I see what you're saying. My being comfortable with me and ready to be open about being gay is only part of the process. I can't expect them to be ready to hear it just because I'm ready to tell it.

Counselor: That's right. You and your parents will need to talk about how your living openly as a gay person will affect them. Will your dad tell people he works with? What if they find out? What will your mother say to another parent she sees at the next play or in the grocery store?

Jan: I hadn't even considered that part.

Counselor: Let's go back to where we started when you first came in. Coming-out to yourself and to others is a process. You've taken a first step on a long journey; that is, coming-out to yourself. You have discovered who you are, what you believe in, what you value, and the price you are willing to pay to be honest with yourself and others. The process will continue as you and your family change. The decision to live openly as a lesbian will influence the majority of choices you make—where to live, what career you choose, who your friends are, and what your own family will be like—as you continue the journey into adulthood.

INTERVENTIONS FOR GAY AND LESBIAN ADOLESCENTS

The learned definition of "gay" may come from libraries that carry only books with negative viewpoints. Young adults are also influenced by television, magazines, the Internet, and the collective wisdom of society at large, their parents, teachers, religious leaders, and peers. While most lesbians become aware of their sexual preference before the age of 20 and most gay men are aware of their sexual preference before the age of 15, many choose to wait until adulthood to act on their feelings.

Intervention with gay adolescents is limited because of the adolescent's status as a minor. Gay adolescents have no mobility, poor access to information, no rights in the matter of sexual preference, and they are legally and economically dependent on their parents. They are also surrounded by peers who are struggling with their own sexuality and are pressured to conform to a highly antigay world.

Attempts to discourage young gay people from the process of connecting thoughts, feelings, and sometimes sexual experiences invalidate adolescents' feelings and discourages them from accepting themselves as gay. By trying to talk adolescents out of gay feelings or get them to deny gay feelings, the helping professional is presented as someone opposed to a gay sexual preference. Most helping professionals would not do the same thing with an adolescent with concerns about heteroerotic actions.

Therapeutic interventions should help the adolescent develop a realistic approach to functioning in a nongay world by addressing current problems and developing potential solutions; include information sources that will help provide a positive, healthy, nonstereotypical picture of gay men and women; help the teen explore reasons for thinking of himself or herself as gay; and explore what it will mean to be a gay person both as an adolescent and as an adult in this society.

CONCLUSION

We can help prepare our gay and lesbian youth to make successful transitions into adulthood by providing them with opportunities to develop positive self-identities. In order to develop a positive self-image, homosexuals should be able to discuss their sexuality without fear of harassment or hostility. Gay youth should not be made to feel that they must hide or deny that part of their identity. Instead, it is time for caring adults to take the lead in making the coming-out process safe and natural for adolescents. It is important that homosexual and heterosexual youth learn of the important contributions gays and lesbians have made to society, both in the past and in the present. Gay and lesbian adults can serve as role models and reference materials should be made available. Most everyone knows someone who is gay or lesbian, and they should be better prepared to accept them for who they are rather than focusing on one part of their personhood. Education is the key, and now there is more available than ever before to help us help kids—all kids, even the gay and lesbian ones.

RECOMMENDED READINGS

Fiction

9.01.   Bauer, Marion Dane. (Ed.). (1994). *Am I blue? Coming out from the silence.* New York: HarperTrophy. 272 pp. (ISBN: 0–06–440587–7). Middle School (MS), High School (HS).

Bauer includes 16 short stories with lesbian and gay characters who encounter love, come of age, and discover the strength of their individuality. Notable YA authors, some gay and some straight, present real characters in a variety of genres. (An American Library Association [ALA] Best Book for Young Adults and an ALA Recommended Book for Reluctant Young Adult Readers)

9.02.   Block, Francesca Lia. (1989). *Weetzie bat.* New York: HarperTrophy. 88 pp. (ISBN: 0–06–447068–7). MS, HS.

Dirk engages in a fantasy where he comes out to his best friend, Weetzie Bat, and she responds positively. Dirk and Duck develop a loving relationship, and Weetzie Bat falls in love with My Secret-Agent-Lover-Man. All four of them share a house and many of life's experiences. (An ALA Best Book for Young Adults and an ALA Recommended Book for Reluctant Young Adult Readers)

9.03.   Brown, Rita Mae. (1988). *Rubyfruit jungle*. New York: Bantam. 193 pp. (ISBN: 0–553–05284–5). HS.

The protagonist, Molly Bolt, tells what it is like to grow up in the South as a lesbian. She is intelligent, spirited, humorous, quick-witted, and confused as to why everyone tries to live by tradition. Molly defies whatever does not suit her as she breaks through sexist rules in the South, a university, and in New York City. Molly lives each moment to its fullest and is an individual to be celebrated!

9.04.   Brown, Todd D. (1995). *Entries from a hot pink notebook*. New York: Washington Square Press. 306 pp. (ISBN: 0–671–89084–0). HS.

Ben Smith records his thoughts and insights in a notebook during his freshman year of high school. His dad can't keep a job or stay sober, which contributes to his parents' rocky marriage. Ben's first love is Aaron, and the two boys secretly meet each other until someone photographs them kissing and circulates the photos around school. Aaron leaves the school, and Ben is the victim of beatings. During summer camp, Ben stands up for another who is being victimized. Eventually, Ben stands up for himself, accepting that he is gay.

9.05.   Chambers, Aidan. (1983). *Dance on my grave*. New York: Harper-Trophy. 251 pp. (ISBN: 0–060–21253–5). HS.

Hal and Barry each agree to dance on the other's grave should anything ever happen between them. This is an insightful story about 16-year-old Hal's consuming love for Barry, his first sexual partner. Barry ends their relationship because commitment frightens him, but an unpleasant confrontation leaves Hal with more to deal with than just a break up.

9.06.   Donovan, Stacey. (1994). *Dive*. New York: Puffin. 240 pp. (ISBN: 0–14–037962–2). HS.

Virginia's dog is run over, her father is terminally ill, and her best friend deserts her. It is Jane who offers her understanding and real love. This quick-paced book, written with wit and honesty, has Virginia asking difficult questions that may not have answers.

9.07.   Garden, Nancy. (1982). *Annie on my mind*. New York: Farrar, Straus, & Giroux. 234 pp. (ISBN: 0–374–40414–3). HS.

Liza and Annie fall in love with each other and must reconcile their relationship to themselves, their families, their school teachers, and classmates. The focus is on Liza's introspection and acceptance of who she is and her love for Annie. (An ALA Best of the Best Books for Young Adults)

9.08.   Garden, Nancy. (1991). *Lark in the morning*. New York: Farrar, Straus, & Giroux. 228 pp. (ISBN: 0–374–34338–1). HS.

Gillian Harrison is a responsible, resourceful 17-year-old lesbian. The primary theme of this book is how Gillian helps two runaways, Lark and Jackie, by first establishing a trusting relationship with them and then by providing them with food, shelter, and transportation to their aunt's house. The secondary theme (which is a celebration because it is secondary) is the natural and respectful love between Gillian and Suzanne.

9.09.   Grima, Tony. (Ed.). (1994). *Not the only one: Lesbian and gay fiction for teens*. Boston: Alyson. 233 pp. (ISBN: 1–55583–275–X). MS, HS.

Twenty-one short stories in this collection depict the reality and the normalcy of gay and lesbian life and love. Teenagers dealing with various gay and lesbian issues, ranging from its effect on their family relationships to their own personal dealings with sexual attraction and first love, are explored. Lesbians and gay young men can likely find characters similar to themselves.

9.10.   Hautzig, Deborah. (1978). *Hey, dollface*. New York: Greenwillow. 160 pp. (ISBN: 0–688–84170–8). HS.

Val and Chloe become best friends at a private school for girls. They become aware of their intimate feelings for each other and explore the possibility of their own homosexuality or bisexuality.

9.11.   Kerr, M. E. (1994). *Deliver us from Evie*. New York: HarperCollins. 177 pp. (ISBN: 0–06–024475–5). HS.

Evie is the narrator's older sister who can fix anything mechanical on their Missouri farm. When Evie starts dating the rich banker's daughter, her family has to deal with their own prejudicial feelings and as well as face those from their small community. Told from the 16-year-old younger brother's perspective, the story is refreshingly objective as he witnesses, interprets, and gives voice to the changing relationships of each family member.

9.12.   Kerr, M. E. (1986). *Night kites*. New York: HarperTrophy. 216 pp. (ISBN: 0–06–447035–0). HS.

Erick seems to have the perfect family until he learns that his older brother Pete has AIDS, and his parents want to keep it a secret. Erick becomes involved with Nicki, who helps him stay distracted until she learns that Pete has AIDS. Erick learns first-hand the importance of others knowing and understanding the truth. He wonders how can people learn about difficult issues if everyone insists on keeping secrets? (An ALA Best of the Best Books for Young Adults)

9.13.   Ketchum, Liza. (1997). *Blue coyote*. New York: Simon & Schuster. 198 pp. (ISBN: 0–689–80790–2). HS.

Alex Beekman is searching for his best friend, Tito Perone. All he knows is that Perone's family kicked him out of their home, but no one will tell Alex why. After he finds his friend, Alex hears the truth: Perone's dad sliced his face with a kitchen knife and broke his leg as he threw him down concrete steps because of his being gay. Alex realizes that he, too, is gay. In finding his best friend, he realizes he can stop hiding from himself.

9.14.   Miller, Isabel. (1969). *Patience and Sarah*. New York: Fawcett. 192 pp. (ISBN: 0–449–21007–3). HS.

This story is based on the lives of painter Mary Ann Willson and her companion, Miss Brundidge, who lived together in the early 1800s in New York state. Their families pressure them to stay away from each other for a time, but they defy society and buy a farm so they can live together in love.

9.15.   Miller, Isabel. (1990). *Side by side*. Tallahassee, FL: Naiad Press. 235 pp. (ISBN: 0–941483–77–0). HS.

Patricia and Sharon alternately tell the stories of their lives which includes an undeniable love for each other. Their courage and integrity to live their lives honestly, acknowledging each other at their jobs and in their daily living, brings them in touch with other dedicated lesbians and gays during the rebellion at Stonewall Inn.

9.16.   Singer, Bennett L. (Ed.). (1994). *Growing up gay/growing up lesbian: A literary anthology.* New York: New Press. 317 pp. (ISBN: 1–56584–103–4). MS, HS.

This anthology contains excerpts from over 50 coming-of-age stories of gays and lesbians by many well-known authors, such as James Baldwin, Rita Mae Brown, Aaron Fricke, Radclyffe Hall, Langston Hughes, M. E. Kerr, and Audre Lorde. This anthology prompts further reading by including bibliographic information and other works including videos, magazines, and newsletters.

9.17.   Winterson, Jeanette. (1985). *Oranges are not the only fruit.* New York: Atlantic Monthly Press. 176 pp. (ISBN: 0–87113–163–3). HS.

When Jeanette is adopted by fundamental religious fanatics, she learns the ways and teachings of the church but refuses to denounce her love for Melanie. Even when the pastor and elders of the church keep her up all night in an effort to deliver her from the demons, she unashamedly and steadfastly remains true to herself. Jeanette sees no contradiction in her love for Melanie and her love for the Lord.

Nonfiction for Young Adults

9.18.   Alyson, Sasha. (Ed.). (1991). *Young, gay, and proud.* Boston: Alyson. 96 pp. (ISBN: 1–55583–001–3). MS, HS.

This practical guide for young gays and lesbians offers answers to commonly asked questions: "Am I really gay? What will my friends think if I tell them? Should I tell my parents that I'm gay? Does anyone else feel this way?" Important information regarding sexuality and health issues is included.

9.19.   Bass, Ellen & Kaufman, Kate. (1996). *Free your mind: The book for gay, lesbian, and bisexual youth—and their allies.* New York: HarperCollins. 417 pp. (ISBN: 0–06–095104–4). HS, Adult (A).

This thorough, must-have resource for gay, lesbian, and bisexual youth and their allies is written in an easy-to-read, conversational style that provides a wealth of information. Numerous topics are addressed: coming to terms with one's self, friends, lovers, family, school, spirituality, and community. Short biographical sketches of prominent gays, lesbians, and bisexuals who have existed throughout history are included as well as an excellent resource section. According to the National President of Parents and Friends of Lesbians and Gays (PFLAG), "This is the single best guide I have seen for gay youth."

9.20.   Chandler, Kurt. (1995). *Passages of pride: Lesbian and gay youth come of age.* New York: Times Books. 364 pp. (ISBN: 0–8129–2380–4). HS, A.

Chandler, a journalist, interviews six gay and lesbian youth in Minneapolis-St. Paul and documents their progress from self-realization to self-acceptance. Interviews with many leaders, both gay and straight, who are attempting to provide understanding and acceptance for gays and lesbians in our society are included. Insights are offered on a range of topics: the coming-out process, typical responses from parents after learning their child is homosexual, the need for networks and ones that are currently available. Many of the myths associated with homosexuality are dispelled by these youths' self-reflections.

9.21.   Due, Linnea. (1995). *Joining the tribe: Growing up gay and lesbian in the '90s.* New York: Doubleday. 272 pp. (ISBN: 0–385–47500–4). HS.

The author, a lesbian, interviews gay and lesbian youth and writes of the struggles they face, the violence they endure, the loneliness they feel, and the victories they achieve. These youth are fighters, leaders, and otherwise ordinary youth who are determined to be true to themselves. The subtle homophobic messages are unveiled, and the mean-spirited and painful abuse is acknowledged.

9.22.   Eichberg, Rob. (1990). *Coming out: An act of love.* New York: E. P. Dutton. 281 pp. (ISBN: 0–525–24909–5). MS, HS, A.

Coming out can be handled positively. The author has gathered many coming-out letters from gays and lesbians written to their parents as well as letters written from parents.

9.23.   Ford, Michael Thomas. (1996). *The world out there: Becoming part of the lesbian and gay community*. New York: New Press. 202 pp. (ISBN: 1–56584–234–0). HS, A.

Ford invites readers to be part of the gay and lesbian fellowship, and he has prepared an informative guide to assist a person with assuming one's responsibility in the gay community. Ford also provides reassurance that the reader is not the only gay person alive. Portraits of famous gays and lesbians as well as descriptions of gay communities in the United States and Canada are included. Ford patiently repeats that there is no wrong way to be gay, but he encourages each person to be true to herself or himself. Many top ten lists serve as quick reference guides.

9.24.   Fricke, Aaron. (1981). *Reflections of a rock lobster: A story about growing up gay*. Boston: Alyson. 116 pp. (ISBN: 0–932870–09–0). HS.

Aaron Fricke sued his high school in Rhode Island for the right to take a male date to his prom; he won. In his autobiography Fricke talks about the development of his awareness of his sexual orientation, his attempts to protect his parents, his requesting the school administration to protect him from the harassment of his classmates, his asking permission to take a male date to the prom, his enlisting the support of the National Gay Task Force, his suing his high school, and finally his taking Paul to the prom and their having a really terrific time.

9.25.   Fricke, Aaron & Fricke, Walter. (1991). *Sudden strangers: The story of a gay son and his father*. New York: St. Martin's Press. 112 pp. (ISBN: 0–312–07855–2). HS, A.

Aaron and his father, Walter, struggled to maintain a father-son relationship after Aaron's coming out. Together, they wrote this book with the hope that their story will help other parents deal with a gay or lesbian child. Their mutual respect for each other as people undergirds the strength of their relationship and success.

9.26.   Heron, Ann. (Ed.). (1986). *One teenager in ten: Testimony by gay and lesbian youth*. New York: Warner Books. 128 pp. (ISBN: 0–446–32653–4). MS, HS, A.

See next entry.

9.27.   Heron, Ann. (Ed.). (1993). *Two teenagers in twenty: Writings by gay and lesbian youth.* Boston: Alyson. 187 pp. (ISBN: 1–55583–282–2). MS, HS, A.

Forty-three gay and lesbian young adults, living all over the United States and Canada, describe what it is like to be gay or lesbian. Some of the essays describe the rejection of family members and the harassment of classmates, while other essays describe the acceptance of family and the support of friends and teachers. With courageous voices, these youth describe their individual experiences with accepting who they are in a sometimes hostile heterosexual world. Readers should note that many of the essays in the first book are included in the second book.

9.28.   Navratilova, Martina with Vecsey, George. (1985). *Martina.* New York: Alfred A. Knopf. 287 pp. (ISBN: 0–394–53640–1). HS, A.

Martina's autobiography describes the positive influences specific women have had on her life. She writes of her relationship with Rita Mae Brown who loved her without regard for how well Martina played tennis. This is an inspiring account of the tennis legend's life, up to 1985, and her determination to be the best person possible while making a positive contribution to the world.

9.29.   Penelope, Julia & Wolfe, Susan J. (Eds.). (1980). *The original coming-out stories.* Freedom, CA: Crossing Press. 308 pp. (ISBN: 0–89594–339–5). HS, A.

The authors have compiled a series of coming-out stories written by lesbians after their leaving high school. Historically, lesbians have been reconciling with sexual identity issues since before the time of their great-grandmothers.

9.30.   Pollack, Rachel & Schwartz, Cheryl. (1995). *The journey out: A guide for and about lesbian, gay, and bisexual teens.* New York: Puffin. 148 pp. (ISBN: 0–14–037254–7). MS, HS.

Written in an easy-to-read style, the authors explain terms and answer questions many lesbian, gay, and bisexual teens have about themselves. Practical advice and information on how, when, and if to come out are offered. Topics include dating, health issues, homophobia, harassment, and religion; excellent resources are given.

9.31.   Reid, John. (1973). *The best little boy in the world*. New York: Ballantine. 247 pp. (ISBN: 0–345–38176–9). HS, A.

John Reid, using a pen name to protect his parents, gives an honest
account of his coming to terms with himself while growing up gay and feeling desperate to be "the best little boy in the world." He brags about his accomplishments in the straight world: lettered in varsity sports, made the
highest grades in his class, and is now a successful IBM executive. The several updates in the afterword let readers know that he has maintained his
sense of humor throughout it all.

Nonfiction for Parents

9.32.   Bernstein, Robert A. (1995). *Straight parents/gay children: Keeping families together*. New York: Thunder Mouth. 203 pp. (ISBN:
1–56025–085–2). A.

Robert Bernstein's daughter is a lesbian. This handbook is filled
with information to support other parents of homosexual children. Myths
and stereotypes are confronted with research, statistics, and human stories. Accounts of well-known public figures and how they embraced their
loved-ones after learning they were gay or lesbian are shared. Not only
does our society and culture make coming-out difficult for gays and lesbians, it also makes accepting gay and lesbian loved ones difficult; the tone
of this book is gentle and understanding. Parents and Friends of Lesbians
and Gays (PFLAG) is specifically noted as a supportive resource in most
communities.

9.33.   Fairchild, Betty & Hayward, Nancy. (1981). *Now that you know:
What every parent should know about homosexuality*. New York:
Harvest/HBJ. 276 pp. (ISBN: 0–156–677024–1). A.

Since its first publication in 1977, this classic guide has continued
to provide helpful information and supportive resources to the parents of
homosexuals. The authors move from objective facts to the personal issues
affecting their gay and lesbian children.

9.34.   Griffin, Carolyn, Wirth, Marian, & Wirth, Arthur. (1989). *Beyond
acceptance: Parents of lesbians and gays talk about their experiences*.
New York: St. Martin's Press. 199 pp. (ISBN: 0–312–16781–4). A.

Parents of lesbian and gay youth candidly talk to other parents about their acceptance process. Honest accounts of their emotional journeys are presented.

Nonfiction for Teachers

9.35.   Harbeck, Karen. (Ed.). (1992). *Coming out of the classroom closet: Gay and lesbian students, teachers, and curricula.* New York: Haworth Press. 259 pp. (ISBN: 1–56023–013–4). A.

Reports indicate there is greater social support and legal protection than most educators are aware. This collection of 11 essays can empower gay and lesbian educators to become more visible so they can be the positive role models for their gay and lesbian students.

9.36.   Jennings, Kevin. (Ed.). (1994). *Becoming visible: A reader in gay and lesbian history for high school and college students.* Boston: Alyson. 296 pp. (ISBN: 1–55583–254–7). A.

Using both primary and secondary sources, Jennings retells 2,000 years' worth of history about the contributions and struggles of gays and lesbians. The primary sources capture the emotional investment of these people, while the secondary sources provide the social context in which they lived. Although homosexuals have been present since the beginning of time, their contributions to society have been virtually ignored. Typically, if the contribution is acknowledged, no mention of the person's sexual orientation is made. This tells more of the story.

9.37.   Jennings, Kevin. (Ed.). (1994). *One teacher in 10: Gay and lesbian educators tell their stories.* Boston: Alyson. 287 pp. (ISBN: 1–55583–263–6). A.

Thirty-five educators write about their experiences of being gays and lesbians in the classroom. Conversations between colleagues, discussions with classes, and memberships in organizations are related as these brave educators attempt to teach by example.

9.38.   Kaywell, Joan F. (1993). *Adolescents at risk: A guide to fiction and nonfiction for young adults, parents, and professionals.* Westport, CT: Greenwood Press. 269 pp. (ISBN: 0–313–29039–3). MS, HS, A.

Kaywell provides statistics, resources, and annotated bibliographies of YA fiction and nonfiction for each of the 13 chapters, ranging from alienation and identity issues to stress and suicide; two chapters are devoted to both homosexuality and AIDS.

9.39.   Remafedi, Gary. (Ed.). (1994). *Death by denial: Studies of suicide in gay and lesbian teenagers*. Boston: Alyson. 205 pp. (ISBN: 1–55583–260–1). A.

Eight research studies on gay and lesbian adolescents and the violence they are prone to confront are reported. Although 30% of adolescent suicides are committed by gays and lesbians, society does not want to acknowledge the issues that these adolescents must confront. Each of the eight studies is a wake-up call. Specifically helpful for teachers who want to make schools a safer place is the Massachusetts study, "Making schools safe for gay and lesbian youth: Breaking the silence in schools and in families." Also included is Paul Gibson's Report of the Secretary's Task Force on Youth Suicide, which is cited in most of the books in this chapter but was censored by the Bush Administration.

9.40.   Unks, Gerald. (Ed.). (1995). *The gay teen: Educational practice and theory for lesbian, gay, and bisexual adolescents*. New York: Routledge. 250 pp. (ISBN: 0–415–91095–1). A.

Seventeen essays address specific problems gay and lesbian teens face, how gay-friendly curriculum in all disciplines can be developed, how teaching strategies can be inclusive or elitist, and how to establish safe places in and out of school for homosexual teenagers. Project 10 in Los Angeles and Out Right! in Durham, NC, are described in detail. Resources include the names, addresses, and phone numbers of the contributors; thorough bibliographies at the end of each essay; and curriculum units from the Harvard Graduate School of Education Gay and Lesbian High School Curriculum and Staff Development Project.

9.41.   Whitlock, Katherine. (1989). *Bridges of respect: Creating support for lesbian and gay youth*. Philadelphia: American Friends Service Committee, 1501 Cherry Street, Philadelphia, PA, 19102. 107 pp. (ISBN: 0–910–08239–1). A.

This easy-to-read, concise guide provides comprehensive information for creating a variety of support for lesbian and gay youth. Information about legalities, organizations, and social services are provided.

9.42.   Woog, Dan. (1995). *School's out: The impact of gay and lesbian issues on America's schools*. Boston: Alyson. 383 pp. (ISBN: 1–55583–249–0). A.

As a journalist, the author interviewed almost 300 gay and lesbian students, teachers, coaches, counselors, administrators, and their heterosexual allies. Woog writes each person's story in the third person and includes enough detail to make each story complete. Books, curriculum materials, films, videotapes, organizations, schools with gay-straight alliances, school district programs, teacher organizations, and training programs are included.

DIRECTORIES

Gayellow pages. New York: Renaissance House, Box 292, Village Station, New York, NY, 10014–0292. Telephone (212) 674–0120.

This directory contains information about lesbian, gay, and bisexual organizations, resources, and businesses in the United States and Canada and is available for $10.00 from the above address.

You are not alone: National lesbian, gay, and bisexual youth organization directory. New York: Hetrick-Martin Institute, 401 West Street, New York, NY, 10014. Telephone (212) 633–8920.

National and local hotlines that serve lesbian, gay, and bisexual youth are listed in this directory. State-by-state listings of support groups for gays, addresses for pen-pal programs, and scholarship opportunities for gay and lesbian young people are also included. Write or call the Institute for a copy of the directory; a $5.00 donation is requested.

ORGANIZATIONS

American Federation of Teachers, Gay-Lesbian Caucus, 1816 Chestnut Street, Philadelphia, PA 19103.

American Library Association, Gay and Lesbian Task Force, 50 E. Huron Street, Chicago, IL 60611.

ASCD Network, Lesbian, Gay and Bisexual Issues in Education, P.O. Box 27527, Oakland, CA 94602.

Black Gay and Lesbian Leadership Forum, 3924 W. Sunset Boulevard, Los Angeles, CA 90029.

Campaign to End Homophobia, P.O. Box 819, Cambridge, MA 02139.

Federation of Parents and Friends of Lesbians and Gays (PFLAG), P.O. Box 27605, Washington, DC 20038–7605.

Gay, Lesbian, and Straight Education Network, 122 West 26th Street, #1100, New York, NY 10001.

Gay Teachers Association, Box 435 Van Brunt Station, Brooklyn, NY 11215.

National Education Association, Gay-Lesbian Caucus, P.O. Box 314, Roosevelt, NJ 08555.

National Gay and Lesbian Task Force, 1517 U Street, NW, Washington, DC 20009.

National Gay Youth Network, P.O. Box 846, San Francisco, CA 94101.

Parents and Friends of Lesbians and Gays (PFLAG), P.O. Box 27605, Washington, DC 20038.

Sexuality Information and Education Council of the United States (SIE-CUS), 130 W. 42nd Street, Suite 2500, New York, NY 10036.

CURRICULAR MATERIALS

The Harvard Graduate School of Education Gay and Lesbian High School Curriculum and Staff Development Project has the following units available by contacting Dr. Arthur Lipkin, Harvard Graduate School of Education, Longfellow Hall 210, Cambridge, MA, 02138:

- A Staff Development Manual for Anti-Homophobia Education in the Secondary Schools
- Strategies for the Teacher Using Gay- and Lesbian-Related Materials in the High School Classroom
- The Stonewall Riots and the History of Gays and Lesbians in the United States
- The History and Nature of Homosexuality (and its "Cause")
- Looking at Gay and Lesbian Literature (Packet 1)
- Reading List: Some Works of Noted Authors with Gay/Lesbian Content
- Reading List: Books about Homosexuality and Coming Out for Young Gay People

REFERENCES

Garden, Nancy. (1996). *Good moon rising*. New York: Farrar, Straus, & Giroux.
Gibson, Paul. (1994). Gay male and lesbian youth suicide. In Gary Remafedi (Ed.), *Death by denial: Studies of suicide in gay and lesbian teenagers*. Boston: Alyson.

Krueger, Mary M. (1993, March). Everyone is an exception: Assumptions to avoid in the sex education classroom. *Phi Delta Kappan, 74* (7), 569–572.
Unks, Gerald. (Ed.). (1995). *The gay teen: Educational practice and theory for lesbian, gay, and bisexual adolescents*. New York: Routledge.

AFTERWORD BY NANCY GARDEN, THE AUTHOR OF *GOOD MOON RISING*

How I long for the day when no child yells "Faggot!" or "Dyke!" to another on a school playground or in the streets, when "It's so gay" is no longer used as a put-down in school lunchrooms, and when no gay or lesbian teenager fears for his or her life or safety, or thinks seriously of suicide in the darkness of the night. Sadly, as this century draws to a close, that day has not yet arrived.

But there are signs that it is coming, and this chapter is one of them. It was not so very long ago that no educator would dream of including positive material about homosexuality in a book of this kind. Oh, sure, there might have been a chapter about homosexuality, but up until quite recently, chances are it would have said that homosexuality is an illness or evil moral weakness. There are, of course, people who still believe that and preach it, thereby contributing to the appalling suicide, runaway, and drop-out rates among gay, lesbian, bisexual, and transgendered youth, to the number of those kids who must seek medical attention for injuries suffered in gay bashings, and for the silent pain, confusion, and guilt experienced at one time or another by most of us. Thank goodness most "queer" kids (gay society is reclaiming this old pejorative) manage eventually to rise above society's prejudices and cruelty despite the backlash that, unfortunately, has grown out of their increased (and courageous and exciting!) visibility. But the journey is rarely an easy one. Thank goodness most of today's queer kids—like Jan, the character in my book *Good Moon Rising*, who is featured in this chapter—are equipped as never before to grow up to be happy, healthy, productive members of society. But again, the journey to that point is still not easy.

Patricia L. Daniel and Vicki J. McEntire, the authors of this excellent chapter, have through it contributed to making that journey easier and to moving us all toward the happy, safe day for which I long. They clearly understand what it is like to be young and gay in the United States today, and, in the fictional "therapy session" in which my character Jan is the client, they also show they are aware of the complex issues that gay kids—and gay adults—face. From coming out to thinking about marriage and children, from understanding legal matters and making career choices to finding helpful books and agencies, they've touched on most of the concerns and needs of gay kids and at the same time have provided sensible, fair, and accurate guidance to professional adults working with them. They have done this without pretentiousness or jargon and have managed to pack an enormous amount of useful information and data into both their introduction and the "therapy session" that follows. The booklist, list of organizations, and other end matter are excellent as well. I must confess to some initial trepidation at the prospect of another author's speaking for Jan, but I found the section in which she appears fascinating and surprisingly believable. My congratulations to the authors of this chapter, and to the series editor, Joan Kaywell, for a job well done!

Chapter 10

Using *Tears of a Tiger* for Psychological and Literary Analysis

Sharon M. Draper & James D. Kelly

INTRODUCTION

Capturing the attention as well as the spirit of the contemporary adolescent reader is a difficult task. Students of the 1990s have grown up with momentary video images with much sound and very little substance. Kids today are frenetic, energetic, and restless. They're channel surfers in all aspects of their lives—busy and constantly bombarded with stimuli from radio, television, and computers. Adolescents rarely take the time or even have the patience to sit quietly and read a newspaper, let alone a full length novel. If they have 15 dollars to spend, most would choose to spend it on a new compact disk rather than a book. In addition, the numbers of adolescents facing significant life difficulties are growing. Statistics for the United States show that 24 million children live in poverty, and three million are victims of crime annually (Miller, 1994). Approximately 25% of American children live in a single-parent household with usually a divorced or never-married mother (Kaywell, 1993). Thirty-seven percent of high school seniors engage in heavy drinking, and 25% of adolescents drop out of school each year (Miller, 1994).

The adolescents facing these difficult situations are often unmotivated in school and uninterested in academics. How can teachers engage their interests? And how can teachers make a difference through the use of literature? The idea of using literature as a psycho-educational tool to change behavior or attitudes is not new. Literature has been used to improve the self-concept of students with difficult family situations, self-concept problems, and abuse (Miller, 1994). In this chapter, we will explore how a particular novel can be used as both an educational enhancement to the literary development of the child as well as a psychological tool to discuss potentially dangerous social situations.

TEARS OF A TIGER BY SHARON DRAPER (162 pp.)

Synopsis

Tears of a Tiger, with favorable reviews in 1995 from both *School Library Journal* and *Booklist*, is a powerful story that deals with alienation, racism, and suicide. The first sentence of the first chapter dramatically illustrates the dangers of drinking and driving. Robert Washington, captain of the Hazelwood High School basketball team, is killed after a game in a drinking and driving crash on the highway. The four boys in the car had been drinking, and the driver, Andy Jackson, has insurmountable difficulties in adjusting to the guilt involving the death of his best friend. The story traces Andy's life from the time of the accident until his suicide a few months later. Told through fast-moving chapters which are short, compact, and unique in that each is told from a different point of view and in a different style, the reader is hurtled along with Andy to his ultimate decision to end his life. The chapters are varied in style and purpose—newspaper clippings, telephone conversations, police reports, homework assignments, even a play-by-play of a basketball game—to move the adolescent reader at a pace that demands and commands concentration without draining the attention span.

Although Andy's parents take him to a psychologist to help him deal with the trauma of Rob's death, no one is aware of the profound depth of his depression. The psychologist probes Andy's emotional barriers in an attempt to help him deal with the feelings of guilt and betrayal. As part of the research for the book, the author elicited the assistance of a noted local psychologist who specializes in problems of adolescents and young adults, specifically with cases of threatened or attempted suicide. Several areas of the text were revised to make sure that the advice given to Andy, a very troubled young man, would be equivalent to actual counsel from a trained clinician.

Psychological Commentary

Connecting Fiction with Reality

Should the issues of alienation, depression, and suicide be discussed in the literature classroom? Or should those topics be avoided because they might give credence to hidden thoughts a student might have? Should *Ro-*

meo and Juliet be discarded because the young protagonists commit suicide at the end? Swing declares boldly, "Talking about suicide won't cause anyone to commit it. In fact, discussing suicide can lessen the chance that it will happen. As more teachers accept that tenet of health professionals, they . . . have on their classroom bookshelves a rich resource for exploring the timely and painful issue of suicide" (Swing, 1990, p. 78). Singer asks, "Are we, as English educators . . . knowledgeable enough about adolescent psychology or counseling or human nature to respond in manner that is surely not damaging psychologically to our students?" (Singer, 1990, p. 73). Perhaps the danger is in NOT discussing these issues rather than avoiding them because we don't feel knowledgeable enough. We must accept the responsibility and the challenge for the kinds of writing we elicit from students, for the responses we make to students, and for the effects these responses have for students (Singer, 1990).

Suicide is the third leading cause of death among adolescents aged 15–19 years in the United States (Kaye, 1995). About five thousand young people in the United States kill themselves each year, a grim total that has tripled since 1958 (Swing, 1990). During 1988–1993, 78% of the suicide attempts were made in the residence of the attempter and 7% occurred at school. Attempts occurred more commonly during the spring months, most frequently on Mondays, and least often on Saturdays (Kaye, 1995). Among youth aged 10–17 years, 6% made a suicide attempt that resulted in death. The rate of fatal suicide attempts was three times greater for males than for females. Seventy-eight percent of attempts using firearms were fatal (Kaye, 1995).

With this said, how should the subject of suicide found in works of literature be handled in the classroom? What if a work of classic literature, such as *Macbeth* or *Romeo and Juliet*, deals with the subject? Should it be glossed over, treated as an event that only occurred in the 16th century, or compared to contemporary events of literary characters? Students are generally enthusiastic about discussing such topics and relating them to their own world. Shakespeare offers a wonderful opportunity to include the discussion of culture, social standards, and literary devices, as well as the emotional trauma of the characters portrayed. In addition, the beauty of the poetic language such as the "brief candle" and the "walking shadow" in *Macbeth* lends itself to a discussion far beyond the subject of the suicide of the queen. The depth of literary analysis found in the lines, "And all our yesterdays have lighted fools the way to dusty death," offers the opportunity for multiple levels of interpretation and discussion—like the importance of the past and the present, of light and darkness, of life and death.

The teacher in *Tears of a Tiger*, however, seems to be more concerned with the literary interpretation of the passage, rather than the possibility of the emotional impact it might have on a troubled student. She discussed the suicide of Lady Macbeth with seemingly very little awareness of the depth of Andy's problem. Had she been aware of his sensitivity to the subject, she might have understood why he ran out of the room and been able to talk to him or perhaps counsel him toward other options available to him. But the teacher who uses this text has the advantage of knowing the fictional Andy's problems and being attuned to possible concerns of the students in the class. This scene, therefore, lends itself to not only a study of Shakespeare and suicide in the classic literary tradition, but the interpretation of scenes such as these in the realities of the lives of the adolescents who read such literature.

— All right, class. We've almost finished our study of *Macbeth*. We've watched Macbeth change from a noble, trusted, dedicated soldier, willing to sacrifice his life for king and country, to a wretched, depraved, corrupt murderer who no longer has feelings of guilt or morality. It's a fascinating study of the degeneration of the human spirit.

— Ms. Blackwell, does he die at the end?

— Well, Marcus, he's just about dead inside already. He's got one little spark left—his refusal to surrender to MacDuff and the forces of good—but don't you think his death is inevitable, Marcus?

— Yeah, he deserves to die—he killed his best friend, he killed women and children, he killed the king. Yeah, I'd say my man deserves to die.

—OK, what about his wife? Does she deserve to die too? Mary Alice?

— Well, it *was* originally her idea. If it hadn't been for her, Macbeth never would have killed the king in the first place. Women have that power over men, you know. Right, Keisha?

— Right on, girl. Now you're talking!

— Ooh—You wish! You livin' in "la-la land," ladies!

—OK, Gerald, that will be enough. Keisha and Mary Alice have a right to their opinion, too, you know. But Lady Macbeth, who seemed so strong at the beginning of the play, had a rather rapid mental deterioration—remember she was walking and talking in her sleep and washing her hands uncontrollably? She finally cannot stand the pressure of the guilt, and she kills herself.

— Kills herself? What a wimp! I'm disappointed. I thought she was pretty cool for a while there.

— Sorry, Keisha. She takes the coward's way out by committing suicide and leaves Macbeth to face the end alone. But you must remember that she was a murderer. I don't think Shakespeare meant for her to be a hero. That's where we'll start today—where Macbeth learns of his wife's death. Open to page 224—Act 5, Scene 5, line 16. Anthony, would you read, please?

The Queen, my Lord, is dead.

She should have died hereafter;
There would have been a time for such a word.
To-morrow, and to-morrow, and to-morrow,
Creeps in this petty pace from day to day,
To the last syllable of recorded time;
And all our yesterdays have lighted fools
The way to dusty death. Out, out, brief candle!
Life's but a walking shadow, a poor player,
That struts and frets his hour upon the stage,
and then is heard no more. It is a tale
Told by an idiot, full of sound and fury,
Signifying nothing.

— Now let's see what Shakespeare is talking about here. What is he saying about life? B. J.?

— He says, "Life is short, and then you die. And on top of that, life don't really mean nothing anyway." But I think the only reason that he was so depressed was because he had been the cause of so much death that he couldn't find nothin' else good about livin'.

— That's a wonderful observation, B. J. See, Shakespeare isn't so bad. You're doing a great job of figuring out what's going on. Andy, what do *you* think about these lines? . . . Andy . . . where are you going? What's wrong? Someone go check on him, please. He seemed pretty upset. Keisha? Tyrone? Go out in the hall and make sure he's all right.

— OK, class. Let's go on. (*Tears of a Tiger*, pp. 95–97)

A contemporary novel such as *Tears of a Tiger* is the perfect vehicle for making the connection between the world of fiction and the world of reality in which students live. Experiencing literature in the classroom is a social activity. There is interaction, often among the readers, but always between the reader and the text—the reader and the voice of the writer (Mitchell, 1988). James Baldwin once said, "You think your pain and heartbreak are unprecedented in the history of the world, but then you read. It was books that taught me that the things that tormented me most were the very things that connected me with all the people who were alive, or who had ever been alive" (Bratina, 1984, p. 66). This text, because of the immediacy of the action and characterization, leads not only psychological insight, but to in-depth literary analysis as well.

Athletics and Alcohol

In 1990, the National Association of State Boards of Education and the American Medical Association reported that alcohol-related accidents were the leading cause of deaths among teenagers. Research has also shown a connection between the use of alcohol by adolescents and of physically risky behavior by that group, but it is not clear as to whether either action leads to the other (Caces, 1991). Other research has shown that participation in school athletics may not prevent unhealthy behavior (smoking, alcohol use, unsafe sex, weapon carrying and use) among adolescents (Skolnick, 1993). Boys who participated in competitive sports were more likely to drink alcohol as those who did not, than perhaps because athletes may be bigger risk takers than others (Skolnick, 1993).

The protagonist in this story, Andy Jackson, is deeply involved in sports. Basketball becomes both his source of redemption as well as his source of guilt. He was never quite good enough to beat his friend Rob on the court or good enough to be the team captain until after the alcohol-related accident that claimed Rob's life. It is after Rob's death that Andy is given Rob's position on the team as captain. The guilt he carries for that seemingly unearned position, as well as other factors of alienation and isolation, drives him eventually to suicide. In this scene, Andy discusses his return to the team with the psychologist who attempts to help him through his grief.

— So, how's it going, now that you're playing ball again?

— It was hard at first gettin' used to Rob's empty seat at school and going by his locker. But basketball, instead of being harder, got easier. It's like I could work out my feelings on the basketball court. The coach gave me his position—center.

— How'd you feel about that?

— I felt proud, but I also felt a little guilty because I never could have *won* that position from him. He was the best center that Hazelwood ever had.

— So why did you accept the position?

— I decided that he woulda wanted me to have it, so I worked really hard, and I really improved my game. I'm averaging seventeen points a game.

— That's good. Do you feel good or guilty when you have a good game?

— Probably a little of both. (*Tears of a Tiger*, pp. 43–44)

Suicidal Tendencies

What is often perceived as being the severest form of auto-aggression, death by suicide is actually just an attempt to escape extreme psychological pain. Suicide appears to be the only option left for people who, after trying to solve one or many of life's crises, find themselves in an untenable situation (Pahl, 1996). When examining the issue of suicidal tendencies, it is important to define what constitutes suicidal behavior, determine its prevalence, and identify psychological and biological factors that predispose one to suicide and precipitate the actual attempt. Multiple risk factors may coexist in an individual, presumably increasing his or her overall risk. The relative contribution of risk factors varies with the age and particular situation patients find themselves in prior to the attempt (Pahl, 1996). By far, the strongest predictor of suicide is the presence of psychiatric disorders. Those who attempt suicide most commonly are suffering from clinical depression (Pahl, 1996).

It is vitally important that the patient be clinically evaluated. This includes not only looking for risk factors but also assessing their relative impact. It is particularly important to determine why the patient feels suicide is the only remaining option. Inquiring about acute precipitating factors such as the loss of a loved one helps gauge whether a patient is at imminent risk. Psychiatrists agree that asking patients, both adults and teenagers, whether they feel suicidal lessens the chance that they will attempt suicide (Pahl, 1996). Candid and open discussion of suicide with students is a significant aspect of death education and helps dispel myths surrounding suicide. Educators need not fear adolescent suicide education because discussion of suicide will not make depressed students more inclined toward suicide; typically, they are emotionally relieved (Johnson, 1985).

In Andy's third visit to the psychologist, there is a deep exploration of his suicidal ideation. This should always be encouraged in this type of trauma. It should be noted that discussing this issue is NOT likely to precipitate someone to kill themselves. In fact, it can be very cathartic to talk about such feelings and relieve a tremendous amount of pressure tacked on them. Andy is almost glad to verbalize his feelings as illustrated in the following passage:

— So Andy, here we are again. Are you ready?

— You called the meetin', boss.

— How do you like all this cold weather?

— I don't. Everything is cold, and dirty, and generally depressin'.

— Do you find yourself depressed very often?

— Yeah, sometimes I don't even want to get out of bed.

— Do you feel sad?

— Not really. Just heavy, like I'm carryin' 'round Mike Tyson's punchin' bag inside of me.

— Do you ever feel like you're "out of touch" with reality?

— Well, yeah, now that you mention it. Me and Keisha went for a long walk a couple of weeks ago (I have no wheels any more—remember?). We had been talkin' 'bout Rob and the holidays and how his family must have felt.

— Have you talked to either of Rob's parents since that phone call you had from his mother on Christmas Day?

— Naw, man. I ain't got the nerve. I know they must hate me. Why would they want to talk to the person who killed their son?

— It might be worth a try, Andy. You were Rob's best friend, weren't you?

— Yeah, I guess.

— I bet they'd be glad to talk to you.

— Maybe.

— So go ahead—you were talking about the walk you took with Keisha.

— Yeah. We had stopped at a freeway overpass, and we just stood there for a minute, watchin' the cars whiz under us. Their lights were on, and they came at us like bullets, it seemed—too fast to count. I thought about the four of us the night of the accident, on that same expressway, and I noticed that the retainin' wall was really only 'bout four feet high.

— Did you remember it differently?

— Yeah. That night, it had seemed like a mountain. And the longer I stood there, the more I became like—sorta hypnotized by the slick whistlin' of the cars as they rushed beneath us. And I wanted to jump.

— Why do you think you felt like that?

— I don't know why—I just felt like I should be down there, like if I were part of that fast-movin' rush, I wouldn't *feel* anythin' anymore, and everythin' would be cool again. I think I even leaned over, really ready to join those bullet-things down below.

— So what happened then?

— Keisha grabbed my jacket and screamed at me, "Andy Jackson! Get your stupid butt away from that railing! Are you crazy?" It's like I sorta came to then, and I looked at her as if she was from another planet. I guess I was the one actin' spacey, but she just told me to take her home. By the time we got to her house, it had started to snow, and we were both breathin' normally again.

— Did she say anything else?

— No. I just looked at her, and I said, like real soft and easy—"Thanks." Then I kissed her real lightly on the lips and went home. We never mentioned it again. And nothin' like that ever happened again.

— Why did you say you felt like you should be down there with the cars? Did you feel like you wanted to die?

— Die? . . . Yeah. . . . No. . . . I don't know. Why you talkin' about dyin'?

— Have you ever thought about being dead, Andy?

— I used to. Right after the accident I wanted to be dead. I wanted it to be me that was dead instead of Rob. I wanted the hurtin' to go away.

— What about now? Do you ever think about death?

— Tell you the truth, man, I think about it all the time.

— Does that frighten you?

— Yeah, sometimes. It seems like bein' dead is the only way I'll ever feel alive again. Does that make sense?

— Sure it does, Andy. You're hurting and you can't find an escape from the pain and you're frightened because the only way out seems to be something you can't even verbalize. Am I right?

— Yeah, man. You're the first person that will even talk about death to me. People are scared of it, and nobody, not even my friends and family, wants to talk about it. It's kinda a relief to bring it out finally.

— There's nothing wrong with thinking about or talking about death, Andy. And it's normal for your thoughts to center on this subject. After all, the death of a friend is a traumatic experience in itself.

— So I ain't crazy?

— Not even a little bit.

— Suppose it's more than just thinkin' about death in general. Suppose I told you I sometimes think about killin' myself.

— I'd say I'm not surprised. Sometimes it's part of the guilt and grieving process—to consider suicide as an alternative to the pain. But the answer is *life*, Andy, not death. So then I'd tell you about other alternatives to help eliminate the pain.

— Like what?

— Like talking to Rob's parents. Like writing a letter to Rob. Like talking to other kids who might consider drinking and driving. Do you think you could handle any of those?

— Yeah, probably. Maybe. I don't really know.

— And then I'd ask you to promise me that if you got so depressed that you didn't think you could handle the situation, you'd call me before you did anything to harm yourself. Could you promise that?

— Yeah, I'd call you. But I ain't stupid, man. I might think about it, I might even threaten it, but I ain't hardly gonna kill myself. I ain't got the nerve.

— That's good. Do you feel a little better now that we've verbalized some things that you were unsure of or unwilling to talk about?

— Yeah, I do.

— Do you think if you wrote a letter to Rob, or to his parents, it would help eliminate some of the pain?

— I don't know. I never thought about it.

— Why don't you try to write one of those letters and bring it next week when you come, okay?

— Dag! Now I got homework from my shrink! I can't win.

— Yes, you can, Andy. You're a winner all the way.

— You really think so?

— I know so. You remember now—you promise to call me if you need me—any time of the day or night, okay?

— Yeah, okay.

— Peace, man.

— Later. (*Tears of a Tiger*, pp. 80–84)

EDUCATING ABOUT SUICIDE

In classrooms where education about suicide is a goal, fiction can be a powerful tool. Contemporary young adult (YA) literature can be particularly useful in starting communication. Young people can see, through the experiences of fictional characters, that they are not alone in having suicidal thoughts. In the classroom, alternatives can be explored, myths debunked, and sources of help identified (Swing, 1990).

It is well known that adolescence is a time of extremes. Teenagers die a dozen metaphorical deaths a day: over their hair, or grades, or warring with their parents, worrying over their futures, and learning how and whom to love (Farr, 1994). Most handle joy and misery and emerge safely on the other side of maturity. But experts caution that although a broken romance may trigger violence, it's rarely the only cause. Teens already standing on the edge are particularly sensitive to relationship losses (Farr, 1994). For example, when Andy's relationship with his girlfriend Keisha falters so does the delicate balance that holds his life together:

Dear Diary,

Well, it's been five months today, since me and Andy started going to-gether. October 9–March 9. It's been the roughest five months of my life, with the accident and everything. But Andy is so sweet, and so cute, and so—needing. It's like he really needs me to keep going. Sometimes it's nice, but I hate to say it, sometimes it gets on my nerves a little. Like last week he had tears in his eyes, and he said, "Sometimes it just gets to me, you know?"

I get tired of all this depressing stuff. I miss Robbie too, but Andy can't seem to get over it, and I'm the only one who knows it. He's got his parents, his teachers, even that stupid counselor at the Outpatient Psych Center fooled. They all say stuff like, "Andy sure is adjusting well," because he's smiling and cheerful. . . . But I'm the one who has to listen to him at three in the morning when he calls me up just to ask, "What do you think it feels like to be dead?" or "Do you think Rob is cold tonight—it's so cold tonight." or "If I died, would you miss me?"

I'd like to ease up on our relationship a little, but I don't know how without hurting him. . . . But it sure does seem like Rhonda and Tyrone are having more fun. (*Tears of a Tiger*, pp. 113–114)

— Sometimes you get on my nerves, Keisha.

— Me? You've got to be kidding! Do you know what I put up with from you? If I hear one more sob story from you, I think I'll puke!

— So that's the way you feel about it! I thought you cared! I though you were the only one in the world who really, really, cared!

— I *do* care, Andy. It's just that sometimes it's just too much.

— Why don't you just go to Hell!

— I believe that's what I'm getting out of. Goodbye, Andy.

— Wait a minute! You can't leave! (*Tears of a Tiger*, pp. 119–120)

Most teenage suicides remain partial mysteries, the full answers locked forever in the minds of those who take their own lives. Much has been writ-ten about suicide warning signs, but mental health experts say family mem-bers are often too close to see them, possessing a true "blind spot" to the pain of their adolescent offspring (Farr, 1994). In *Tears of a Tiger*, Andy's parents love him but are helpless to see the depth of his emotional despair. They impose their social standards on their son's life and fail to see his pain or the potential for disaster. A small mistake can have huge negative reper-cussions on a person who is depressed:

— Over here, Coach. I just have to get my shoes. I was waitin' for my dad—he said he'd be here.

— You played a terrific game tonight, Andy. I'm sure your dad was popping with pride.

— He wasn't poppin' with nothin'. He didn't come. He never comes. He always says he will, but there's always an excuse.

— What about your mom? Was she there?

— No, she doesn't like basketball—too noisy—too sweaty-somethin' like that. You know what? Rob's parents were at the game. It must have been awfully hard for them. But they *always* came to our games, even the away games. It's like they supported not just Rob, but the whole team. Seein' them up there really made us want to win tonight—it made us not want to give up. They sat there, Rob's mom holdin' back tears, and my folks didn't even bother to show up. *I* should be the one dead, not Rob. (*Tears of a Tiger*, pp. 35–36)

Andy's discussions with his father are also frustrating and unsatisfying. Many young readers will be able to see themselves in this classic conflict between parent and child:

— How have you been doing in school? Are your grades any better?

— You want some of this ham sandwich? Sure is good. Where's the mustard?

— Andrew, I asked you a question.

— Huh? Oh, grades? No problem, Dad. I'm steady pullin' 'em up. Is Monty home yet? The Teenage Warrior Space Soldier show is about to come on.

— Monty is with your mother. . . . But it's you I'm concerned about. Your report card came in today's mail.

— I'm dead meat.

— How can you possibly say your grades are improving? You failed English and chemistry, and you just barely passed history and math! You even failed gym! How can you consider yourself an athlete if you can't even pass gym?

— I lost my gym shoes.

— You what?

— I lost my shoes, and the gym teacher takes off points if you're not dressed in proper gym clothes. But I found 'em. They were in Gerald's locker.

— Forget gym. What about English and chemistry? I talked to your English teacher a couple of months ago, and it seemed for awhile there that you were improving. What happened?

— I don't know. She don't like me.

— That's a weak excuse, Andrew. She seemed genuinely concerned when she called me. That doesn't sound like someone who doesn't like you. Have you done all your assignments in her class?

— Yeah, most of 'em. . . . Well, some of 'em.

— What about tests?

— What about 'em?

— Don't play with me, boy. I'm trying to figure out what's going on here. How do you usually do on her tests?

— I guess I fail most of 'em.

— Do you study for the tests?

— Sometimes.

— How can you say you want to go to college? What college is going to take you with grades like this?

— I never said I wanted to go to college. *You* were the one who said I wanted to go to college.

— What do you mean? We've been talking about college since you were a little boy! Getting a degree—maybe even in the field of business administration.

— That's your dream, Dad, not mine.

— Well, what about basketball? Didn't you want to go to college to play ball so you could get a chance at professional basketball? You've really improved your game this year.

— How would you know? You didn't ever come to even one of my games this year! Not one!

— Well, you know how hectic my schedule is. Besides, I've seen you in the yard when you shoot hoops with your friends. I know you're good.

— Yeah, right.

— But back to the subject at hand—this absolutely reprehensible report card!

— Why you gotta always use such big words? I know my report card stinks. Why can't you just say that?

— If you had a better vocabulary, perhaps you wouldn't be failing English!

— Why don't you just get off my case?

— I'm not going to argue with you, Andrew. But I expect to see some major improvements in these last couple of months of school. Or I shall have to take some severe punitive measures.

— There you go with them big words again. What else can you do to punish me? Take away my car? It's in pieces at Joe's Auto Graveyard. Take away my driver's license? Sorry, the cops beat you to that. Stop me from seein' my best friend? He's in pieces at Spring Grove People Graveyard. I took care of that myself—I killed him—remember? So, you can't hurt me. I deal with big-time hurt every day.

— Andrew, I know the accident was very traumatic for you. But you have to get beyond it and move on. You have to be strong and show that you are bigger than the problem.

— Yeah, I know. You've told me before. Be a man. Be strong. Put this "unfortunate incident" behind you. Well, maybe I can't do that.

— So you're going to let it control your actions and ruin your life?

— No, Dad. I'm gonna get it together. You'll see. My grades for the last quarter of school will be much better—I promise.

— That's my Andrew. I know you can do it, son. I'm counting on you. Don't let me down now, okay? Do it for me.

— Okay, Dad. Whatever you say. (*Tears of a Tiger*, pp. 130–133)

LITERARY DEVICES

Different Points of View

The most immediate and obvious literary device is the use of the various voices and points of view. Chapter one is a newspaper article—written in correct journalistic style—followed by a locker room conversation, telephone calls, a police report, a prayer, and even a homework assignment—written on notebook paper and following perfect five-paragraph, persuasive-essay form. Each of these short, lively chapters is written from a different point of view and in the voice of a different character. Other chapters include a school newspaper, poetry homework assignments, a touch of Shakespeare, journal and diary entries, even a play-by-play of a basketball game. Because of a sense of reality, students identify with the characters and are drawn into the context of the story through that self-identification. Teachers can use the format of the chapters for discussion, for role-playing activities, and for modeling writing activities.

Poetry

The chapters which include poetry are perfect examples of the opportunity to discuss the literary element of the poetic devices as well as the psychological impact of the meaning of the words the character has written. For example, Andy's poem is a poem of helplessness and hopelessness. Although written in the style of a teenager completing an obligatory assignment, it shows a literary depth which mirrors the depth of Andy's pain. His use of images of darkness and light, of shadows and clouds, and the bleakness of past, present, and future, not only mirror and can be compared to the Shakespearean passage, but also shows an understanding of his own problem that Andy himself was not even consciously aware of. It is ironic that he calls it "Poem of Hope."

> It's dark where I am
> And I cannot find the light.
> There are shadows all around me
> And my heart is full of fright.
>
> Everyone is cheerful
> They never even see
> That storm clouds are forming
> Upon the peaceful sea.
>
> I cannot see the future
> And I cannot change the past
> But the present is so heavy
> I don't think I'm going to last. (*Tears of a Tiger*, p. 57)

Anyone reading this—especially his teacher and friends, should be able to see the deep psychological depression that Andy has entered. Of course, Andy fails to turn in the poem to his teacher, thus eliminating any chance of help he might have elicited from that source. This behavior shows his fear of sharing his feelings and his concern that others might perceive that he needs help—which is exactly what he needs. Keisha, of course, knows of Andy's pain, but is helpless to assist him. She writes:

> What's your problem, little man?
> Can't you deal with the basic plan?
> Your mama don't know
> And your daddy don't know
> That you got a secret
> And it's going to blow.
>
> What's your secret, little man?
> Can't you hide it under the sand?
> Your brother don't know
> And your buddy don't know
>
> That you got a problem
> And it won't let go.

What's your problem, little man?
Can't you deal with the basic plan?
Your mama don't know
And your daddy don't know
That you got a secret
And it's going to blow. (*Tears of a Tiger*, p. 61)

Motifs

Not only is poetry a good way to allow students to have a full range of discussion of this novel, but the use of symbolism through the "tears" motif is also a valid literary device that can lead to psychological understanding. The name of the basketball team is the Hazelwood Tigers, of course, but on a deeper analytical level the tiger is Andy—young, troubled, even caged, and unable to cry or express the pain he feels. He discusses this with his six-year-old brother Monty, the only person in the family that Andy feels comfortable with. But Monty is too young to be of much assistance. His knowledge of Andy's despair is marginal at best, seen and understood only through the eyes of a child:

— Actually, I like colorin' Africa pictures better than this kind of pictures—with no people in it. You know—lions and tigers and dinosaurs and stuff.

— Lions and tigers and *dinosaurs*?? That's some combination.

— Yep, and giraffes and dragons too. Hey, Andy, can I ask you somethin'?

— Sure, kid. Lay it on me.

— Do tigers cry?

— I don't know, Monty. I never thought about it, but I don't think they do. Why do you ask?

— Well, I drew a picture last week at school, and the teacher wanted to know why I put tears on my tiger. I told her he was very sad. Like you get sometime.

— You're somethin' else, little man. If you want to put tears on your tiger or dragons in your jungle, you tell your teacher that your big brother said it was just fine.

— Okay. Hey, Andy, can you take me to see that new dinosaur show at the museum?

— No, buddy, I can't—I can't drive—remember?

— Oh, did you forget how to drive?

— No, I'm not allowed to drive anymore.

— Why? Were you bad?

— Yes, Monty, I was bad. I was really, really bad. . . . Now go wash your
hands and get ready for dinner. (*Tears of a Tiger*, p. 110)

When Andy reaches the point of no return and is emotionally and psychologically drained of all hope, he once again refers to the tiger as a helpless
caged animal with no escape and no possible freedom. The tiger is the mon-
ster within and without—the tiger is the pain he can no longer incorporate.
How students react to this scene and how teachers approach it with a class is
critical. It is clear that Andy is making the wrong decision, and students
need to be led to see that. Although Andy doesn't see any further options,
they do exist. From the safety of the classroom and the reality of the present,
students can identify with the fictional Andy to discuss the choices, options,
and consequences of suicide. When students are allowed to discuss Andy's
choice, the enormity and finality of his decision is enlarged. Andy muses:

— So what do I do now? Pray? Cry? Hide under the bed from the monsters
that are inside of me? No, I'm just going to sit here and think. I'm going to
think about why I'm sittin' here on my bed, holdin' my dad's huntin' rifle,
feelin' how smooth and cool it feels. He likes to hunt—some killer instinct
left over from his ancestors who ran around in loincloths in the Congo.
Ha! What would they think if they could see him in his three-piece suit,
spear in hand, crouchin' low to stalk a tiger?

Tigers have it rough these days. Instead of roamin' the jungle, hiding
from hunters in three-piece loincloths, they are put in concrete cages with
bars of steel. Even in the modern zoos, where it looks like the tigers ought
to be happy because they are given fifteen or twenty feet of real grass, if
you look really hard, you can see tiny little electrical wires. The tiger, who
might think he's equal to all those tigers in the jungle that his mama told
him about, is quickly reminded to stay in his place. He soon learns that
he'll never get out of there. (*Tears of a Tiger*, p. 143)

The dream chapter also lends itself to valuable literary as well as psychological analysis. Andy's feelings of guilt and pain are expressed through the
dream he has of Rob. Rob asks Andy to join him, an obvious signal of
Andy's pre-suicidal thoughts. The juxtaposition of the words "live" and
"dead" throughout the scene invert normal perceptions and augment the
symbolic interpretation. Rob is cold, frightening, and embodies all of the
fears Andy has been harboring: the fear of Rob's dead body under the snow
and of Rob coming back to blame him for the accident. But just like Rob
was in life, the dream-Rob is also good-natured and ready with a smart
mouth and a good joke:

— Andy! Andy! Andy! Why are you sleepin' in that soft warm bed with the fresh blue pillowcases? I'm cold, Andy. Can I borrow a blanket?

— Who's there? Who said that?

— It's me, brother. Your main man, Roberto. And yes, I'm cold. Very cold. It's no fun bein' dead.

— I'm sorry, Rob. You know I didn't mean to hurt you.

— Understood, my man. But when're you comin' to keep me company?

— Me?

— We could play some one-on-one. You know I always could beat you.

— What you talkin' about? You want me to be dead?

— Yeah, man, with you dead, it'll be live! Wait a minute. Does that make sense?

— None of this makes sense. What do you want, Robbie?

— I want *you*, Andy. You. Ain't no black folks in the part of Heaven that I been assigned to and I'm bored.

— What?

— Computer foul-up. Since my last name is Washington, they put me in the section with George and Martha. Nice folks, but boring! . . .

— Rob, you're drivin' me crazy! None of this makes any sense. I must be dreamin'!

— Sure, you're dreamin'. . . . So when you comin'?

— I can't, Rob. Please leave me alone.

— It's all your fault, you know. All your fault. You got the beer. You drove the car. You smashed into the wall. You killed me. And now you gotta come and keep me company.

— No! I swear I didn't mean to! It was an accident! A horrible, horrible accident!

— I'm waitin' for ya, Andy. . . . I'm waiting. (*Tears of a Tiger*, pp. 89–90)

In the final chapter, Andy's younger brother Monty, now older and wiser, brings the symbolic "tears" motif to finalization. He is acutely aware of the finality and foolishness of Andy's decision and painfully, but hopefully, Monty has chosen to embrace life. At Andy's gravesite, Monty says

— It's a real pretty day today. It's warm and the sun is shinin' and everythin' smells real good. I wish you could see it. I wish you were here. I wish everything was like it used to be. Daddy says I gotta be brave and strong. I guess I can do that, but at night I get real scared and sometimes I have bad dreams. But I'm not going to cry any more, 'cause I'm tough, like a tiger, and tigers don't cry, or do they?

Mama is calling me now. She says it's time to go. I'm sure she wants me to tell you she's thinkin' about you always. I feel better now. I'm glad she let me come and talk to you. I don't know when I'll get to come again—I'm gonna start Knothole Baseball next week and I spend a lot of time learnin' how to use my computer, so you know how it is. But I'll always love you, and I'll always miss you, and I'll never forget that it's okay to put dragons in the jungle and tears on a tiger. Bye. (*Tears of a Tiger*, p. 162)

CONCLUSION

Tears of a Tiger is a work of contemporary YA literature that not only offers a fast-moving, intense story line, but also offers the opportunity for enhanced literary as well as psychological study. A teacher who chooses to utilize the tools available for study here can offer reading enjoyment to the students, literary and textual possibilities for discussion, and a sound psychological basis for in-depth analysis.

> — [Andy's] soul is probably still out there somewhere—floating in the darkness, looking for hope, hoping for forgiveness, and terribly, terribly, frightened. . . . [H]elp him find peace. (*Tears of a Tiger*, p. 160)

Perhaps teachers and all helping professionals can find more ways to help our youth find inner peace.

RECOMMENDED READINGS

For a comprehensive list of YA books that address teenage stress and suicide, readers should consult Chapter 13 of Joan Kaywell's *Adolescents At Risk: A Guide to Fiction and Nonfiction for Young Adults, Parents, and Professionals*.

REFERENCES

Attempted suicide among high school students. (1991, October 9). *Journal of the American Medical Association*, 1911.

Bratina, Sister M. Bernadette. (1984, November). YA literature—a matter of life and death. *English Journal, 73* (4), 66–67.

Caces, M. (1991, Summer). Alcohol use and physically risky behavior among adolescents. *Alcohol Health and Research World*, 228.

Draper, Sharon. (1994). *Tears of a tiger*. New York: Atheneum.

Farr, Louise. (1994, October). When young passion kills—teenage murder and suicide. *Redbook*, 108.

Fritts, Kathy. (1995, January 27). Review of *Tears of a Tiger*. *School Library Journal*.

Johnson, Wanda. (1985, February). Classroom discussion of suicide: An intervention tool for the teacher. *Contemporary Education*, 14.

Kaye, Elizabeth. (1995, August 9). Fatal and nonfatal suicide attempts among adolescents. *Journal of the American Medical Association*, 452.

Kaywell, Joan F. (1993). *Adolescents at risk: A guide to fiction and nonfiction for young adults, parents, and professionals*. Westport, CT: Greenwood Press.

Miller, Darcy. (1994, March-April). Using literature to build self-esteem in adolescents with learning and behavior problems. *The Clearing House*, 207.

Mitchell, Arlene. (1988, September). Black adolescent novels in the curriculum. *English Journal*, 77 (5), 95–97.

Monks, Merrie. (1994, November 1). Review of *Tears of a Tiger*. *Booklist*.

Pahl, Jorg J. (1996, September). The rippling effects of suicide. *USA Today*, 62.

Singer, Marti. (1990, September). Responding to intimacies and crises in students' journals. *English Journal*, 79 (5), 72–75.

Skolnick, Andrew. (1993, August 18). Students raise doubts about benefit of athletics in reducing unhealthy behavior among adolescents. *Journal of the American Medical Association*, 798.

Swing, Georgia H. (1990, September). Choosing life: Adolescent suicide in literature. *English Journal*, 79 (5), 78–82.

CHAPTER 11

Using *The TV Guidance Counselor* to Study Suicide and Its Effect on Families

Jenifer A. Nields, M.D. & Anne C. LeMieux

INTRODUCTION

This chapter will explore the manifold psychodynamics and family dynamics that enter into and result from an adolescent suicide attempt. Anne Le-Mieux's novel *The TV Guidance Counselor* will serve to exemplify and bring to life some of these issues. Other illustrations will be culled from Dr. Nields' practice as a psychiatrist and psychotherapist. The chapter aims to shed some light on a most troubling and all-too-prevalent social concern: adolescent suicide. It aims also to suggest a means—familiarity with relevant literature—that can help troubled adolescents find solace, hope, the beginnings of understanding and the knowledge that they are not alone, and that can likewise help educators to connect with the often isolated and intensely private emotional worlds of their adolescent students.

ADOLESCENT SUICIDE: STATISTICS AND RISK FACTORS

Suicide accounts for more deaths among adolescents in the United States than all natural causes combined. It is the third leading cause of death behind accidents and homicide. The rate of adolescent suicide has been steadily increasing over the past three decades from 6 per 100,000 in 1965 to 17.8 per 100,000 in 1992. The prevalence of attempted suicide is far greater than that of completed suicide. According to one study of over 11,000 high school students, 8.3% had attempted suicide during the previous 12 months, a prevalence about 466 times greater than that of completed suicides. Boys commit suicide more than four times as often as girls do, but girls attempt suicide three times as often as boys do. Gay youth commit suicide two or three times as often as their heterosexual counterparts (National Center for Health Statistics, 1994).

Among adolescents who complete suicide, at least 90% suffer from one or more psychiatric disorders, most commonly severe depression, substance abuse, conduct problems, or a combination thereof. Other predisposing factors include a disturbed family background, a physical illness, a previous suicide attempt, prior suicidality in a parent or other relative, loss of a parent by any means before the age of 13, and availability of a weapon or other means. Teen suicides sometimes occur in clusters, so-called copycat suicides, and may be more likely in a social milieu where death by suicide is relatively commonplace. A strong moral or religious taboo against suicide and a feeling of connectedness to significant others are powerful deterrents (Kaplan & Sadock, 1991).

Adolescents who attempt suicide may comprise a quite different population from those who complete suicide. Typically, they have a lower rate of psychiatric disorders, greater familial and community cohesion and support, and use methods that are less likely to result in death. This said, it is nevertheless important to note that any attempt, regardless of intent or potential for lethality, must be taken seriously. The suicide attempt typically occurs in the wake of one or more acute stressors such as a broken romance, conflicts over sexual orientation, school difficulties, arguments with parents, loss of face with peers, failure or disappointment in the context of rigid or unrealistic expectations, rejection, or bereavement. It is this healthier but far larger group of adolescents that will be the main focus of this chapter.

UNDERSTANDING AN INDIVIDUAL CASE
THROUGH LITERATURE

The TV Guidance Counselor by Anne C. LeMieux will serve as an example of the kind of literature that may be helpful in understanding adolescent suicide from a psychological viewpoint. This American Library Association (ALA) Best Book for Young Adults provides a psychologically astute and gripping account of the prelude and aftermath of an adolescent boy's suicide attempt. For the purposes of this chapter, it offers a detailed and intimate view of one suicidal adolescent's experience, elements of which can be generalized to apply to a great many others. It also provides a view that offers hope. Accordingly, it will serve to provide illustration throughout this chapter.

THE TV GUIDANCE COUNSELOR BY ANNE C. LEMIEUX (184 pp.)

Synopsis

Within the narrative structure of a double time frame, *The TV Guidance Counselor* explores both the events leading up to 16-year-old Michael Madden's impulsive and unsuccessful suicide attempt and the aftermath of the act. Italicized sections, set in the present in a psychiatric hospital, precede each chapter. These are Michael's first-person accounts of the process of his psychological and emotional reconstruction. The body of each chapter recounts, in flashback, the internal and external plot threads that converged on the bridge over the Mohegan River and propelled him to jump.

At the start of his junior year in high school, two years after his parents' ugly divorce, Michael, his displaced homemaker mother, and his six-year-old sister Amanda have just gone through a major life demotion. They've relocated from the antique colonial home where Michael grew up to a small, dilapidated rental house on a riverbank in the business district of the wealthy white-collar suburb of Eastfield, Connecticut. Michael identifies the day his life started rolling seriously downhill as the August afternoon he and his best friend and sidekick, Roderick Alister Bolton III, aka Ricky, were swimming in the river just prior to the family's move. The tone for the story is set in an encounter later that day, when Michael's marine photographer father stops by the house to say good-bye to the kids before taking off on the Royale Rum Round World Race, an international regatta set to last nearly a year. As a parting gift, he hands Michael one of his favorite cameras, an old Nikon F2, which absorbs Michael's focus immediately. The Nikon F2 quickly becomes a shield that buffers reality's impact on Michael, but the camera is also an object of conflict between Michael and his mother. For her, it is a symbol of the man who betrayed her and emotionally abandoned the family.

The free-floating hostility pursuant to the divorce exacerbates the normal tensions of adolescent-parent relationships. Michael becomes a lightning rod for his now single mother's anger, while Mrs. Madden becomes the primary target for the blame and rage Michael is unable to direct at his absent father. Sporadic communication with Mr. Madden suggests that his quest for happiness has "paid off in spades," contrasting sharply with the family's downward spiral.

Michael lands his first job at Thumm's Market, a small gourmet grocery store on the river about a block away from the new house. He is hired on the spot by Fritz Thumm, the owner. Fritz is an older, book-loving man who lives above the market with his nephew Carl. As a result of brain trauma sustained in a childhood car accident that killed his parents, Carl is slow in some respects; but in Michael's eyes, he's gifted in the area of human relations and kindness. On Michael's first day as a cashier, he meets a middle-aged and apparently autistic woman named Janey Riddley whom Fritz describes, after a T. S. Eliot poem, as a wandering and unsatisfied spirit. A regular at the market, Janey never speaks a word, looks at a soul, or buys an item; she only pores over the racks of *TV Guides* at the registers as if seeking the secret of the Rosetta Stone. Michael is fascinated by her behavior, identifying with the idea of searching intensively for something—even not knowing what it is. Michael's friend Ricky nicknames her "The TV Guidance Counselor" because of her resemblance to Mrs. Fattiben, a guidance counselor at Mohegan High.

After getting special permission to enroll in a photography course, Michael becomes increasingly obsessed with viewing the world through his lens. While at work one day, Michael snaps a picture of the TV Guidance Counselor and manages to catch a fleeting moment of her actually connecting with a stimulus from the world outside her inner world; startled by the click of the shutter, she looks directly into the camera. As the semester progresses, Michael gets romantically involved with another photography student, Melissa Ryan. Meanwhile, Ricky is upping the ego-stakes in his ongoing, long-running love-hate feud with Victoria Kaminski, the queen bee of the social hive, in a series of escalating incidents of mutual harassment.

At home, tensions are escalating: Michael abdicates active membership in the disintegrated nuclear family, Amanda acts out her own issues, and their mother flounders in trying to reestablish some semblance of stability. Mrs. Madden relies on Ricky for the support Michael is unable to give. As the financial pressures increase, the tensions between mother and son become more volatile. Because Michael cannot outwardly blame his father, he suppresses his anger at the family's worsening financial and emotional situation. He experiences his growing alienation as "coming apart at the seams," represented in a scene where he photographs the torn pieces of a picture of him which Mrs. Madden ripped up during a heated argument. As Michael distances himself from all those closest to him, his relationship with Melissa begins to unravel. At work, Carl reaches out to him periodically with shy gestures of friendship and support. While blue-fishing together one afternoon, Carl reveals that his father is "gone," too.

At school, in retaliation for a malicious offensive against him by Victoria, Ricky enlists Michael's help to get even. He gets Michael to sabotage a photo of Victoria in the school's darkroom in order to use it in a negative and lewd "publicity stunt" but Michael is caught. As a result, Michael gets kicked out of his photography class and Melissa decides to break up with him. Michael's rage gets closer to the surface, and his deliberate misinterpretation of Ricky embracing his mother causes a fist-fight between the two best friends. Ricky finally forces him to confront his father's behavior.

The next day at work is a slow Sunday, so Michael experiments with his camera, arranging still-life poses with the produce. Ricky stops by to make amends, which Michael spurns. As Janey Riddley approaches, Ricky is seized by an impulse and hides all of the *TV Guides*. Camera in hand, Michael cannot resist his own impulse to snap a picture of her confusion—which mirrors his own—but the flash sends her into a violent reaction. Janey runs screeching from the store, and collides with a parking car. Numb in the wake of the accident and not knowing the extent of Janey's injuries, Michael leaves work and wanders onto a bridge where he stands in the freezing rain until dark. Despair overtakes the numbness, and Michael throws the camera into the river; he then climbs up on the rail and "just lets go." Carl's quiet witness of all Michael's distress has prompted him to stand vigil on the dock, and only his immediate action saves Michael from drowning.

As the timeline recounting Michael's stay in the hospital and the process of his therapy converges with the events that led to the hospitalization, he returns home with his mother with the beginnings of the understanding of what has happened and how it happened. His future has opened up again, though he doesn't know in what direction he'll be going. He has achieved a restored, if tenuous, sense of connection to life. In a gesture of giving back to its owner the soul he "captured," Michael gets the earlier photograph of Janey Riddley and a *TV Guide* and slips it into the mailbox of the home where she lives with her sister. Repairs have begun on all his relationships.

The conclusion, echoing the opening paragraph, raises a question in both the character's mind and the reader's: Was he actually trying to commit suicide? Although the question is left unanswered, Michael has reached the clear realization that the consequence of his self-destructive behavior, without Carl's intervention, would have been the same, regardless of his intention.

ADOLESCENT SUICIDE FROM A PSYCHODYNAMIC AND FAMILY SYSTEMS PERSPECTIVE

Prelude to the Attempt: The Motivation Behind an Adolescent's Attempted Suicide

In the first chapter of *The TV Guidance Counselor*, the scene is aptly set for what will be elaborated and chronicled throughout the rest of the book.

The key elements of the Madden family dynamics and of Michael's emotional life that converged to result in his suicide attempt are subtly but evocatively introduced. Far from unique, these elements, or some combination thereof, characterize a great many contemplated adolescent suicides.

One of the key elements of Michael's pre-attempt experience, one that characterizes the intense angst of many adolescents, is discontinuity with a familiar past. As Michael puts it:

> There's this thing that you're part of for your whole life. It's called a family and it's a living organism. . . . [A]ll the cells fit together. Then one day, the glue that holds them in place dissolves, and the organism loses its shape. . . . What's left is this twitching, incoherent mess. Then the cells start to mutate. (pp. 1–2)

The metaphor of family life as an "organism" is particularly apt for a book on family issues. Adolescent suicidality is, at least in some instances, a result of and an influence on family dynamics. The positive view that is embodied in *The TV Guidance Counselor* is that a suicide attempt—provided that it is unsuccessful—can be an occasion for the entire family to seek help such that the "organism" is given a second chance to reconstitute itself into something coherent and viable.

The sense of discontinuity that Michael experiences is reflected in the form of his unspoken remembering prompted by his psychiatrist's questions during the opening chapter of the book. What he remembers is a series of "snapshots," as it were, of moments in his life over the past year that he does not yet know how to sequence or understand. As if through a camera lens, he sees the world discontinuously. The author's use of the motif "snap click" between images conveys this metaphor. He sees ("snap click") his father in the driveway, poised for departure; his mother ("snap click") in the family's post-divorce "shack," in front of the TV; he sees the precious picture of "me and Melissa . . . that I want to freeze," but it doesn't stay; he sees ("snap click") Mr. Dorio, the photography teacher, expelling him from class; he sees Melissa, in the parking lot, running away (pp. 4–5). He wants to shut out or wash away these images but he can't. Michael wants the pieces of his old self and of his pre-divorce family life to come back together, but they have been scattered and are floating away like the pieces of the photo of him that his mother tore up and that he threw into the river. It is only after his hospitalization—after the rage and hostility and sense of loss that had been driving apart the individuals in his family and the elements of his own inner self had been acknowledged, and after the ineffaceable pictures from the past had been pieced together and understood—that Michael and his family can begin to set up a new order and establish a new sense of coherence, one that can carry them as a viable "organism" toward the future.

The image of a camera lens conveys Michael's sense of isolation, as if there were an invisible barrier both within Michael and between Michael and the rest of the world. He becomes isolated both from his own emotions and from the people around him, prompting Melissa to leave him and resulting in his jumping into the Mohegan River, unaware of the depth and content of his inner tumult. As he silently retorts in response to Dr. Sherman's questioning, he initially feels "nothing" and is "numb." Eventually his emotions burst forth, first as rage and finally give way, at the end of the session, to tears. This session provides a microcosm of what his therapy will entail: a challenging of his defenses against feeling, a breaking of his "isolation of affect" (dysjunction of thought and feeling), and a sorting through of his memories and emotions that will eventually lead to a breaking of his isolation from others. Dr. Sherman's unobtrusive but steady presence and his ability to anticipate and tolerate the range of Michael's emotions pave the way for Michael to regain trust in himself and other people.

Another key element that the book conveys is that adolescent suicide is often unintentional. The adolescent's aim is to escape from pain, not to end one's life as demonstrated by Michael's thoughts: "I wasn't trying to kill myself the night I jumped into the Mohegan River. At least, I don't think I was" (p. 1). Nevertheless, he almost did. When a young person's world changes drastically and misery strikes for the first time, it seems the misery will last forever. Death, on the other hand, may seem unreal, romantic, and only temporary. (For a discussion of the romanticization of suicide, see the "Werther Syndrome" described below.) There may be a fantasy that others will finally understand or will at least take one's distress with the seriousness that it deserves. In Michael's case, as with many adolescents, the overwhelming need to escape from pain can obscure the danger of impulsive actions or the fact that the price, in some instances, is death.

Many of the emotions Michael was trying to escape are common to many adolescents who attempt, or contemplate, suicide. His whole family, for example, seems to have felt an unacknowledged terror, with Michael trying to distance himself from it all through his camera lens and his mother and sister trying to ward it off in idiosyncratic ways:

> Take . . . my mother. About a month after we moved from the big house where we grew up to the rented rathole on the river, she developed a very weird driving habit. All of a sudden, she refused to make left-hand turns anymore. She'd go eight blocks out of her way to get where she was going only two blocks away, all so she didn't have to make a left-hand turn.

My six-year-old sister, Amanda, has turned into a miniature bag lady. Everywhere she goes, she carries this grungy pink duffel bag crammed with her favorite stuff. I mean, everywhere—it's under her chair when she eats, next to the tub when she takes a bath, behind her pillow when she sleeps. Her teacher called Mom about some rule that kids can bring personal stuff only on show-and-tell day. Mom tried to explain to Amanda, but she refused to go to school if she couldn't tote her bag.

. . . And I'm the one who ends up in the loony bin. Figure it out if you can. I can't. (p. 2)

These are attempts at self-soothing, ineffectual efforts to maintain coherence and control in the context of a world haunted by nameless peril. This is a family in chaos with no one able to take the helm. Michael's mother tries to protect herself in dysfunctional ways and is unable to protect her children. Amanda tries to hold on to some token of safety. Rather than being able to offer genuine support to one another, the family members seek external and ineffectual sources of support. As a result, the diminished family fragments even further. A surfeit of unacknowledged feeling and unmanageable circumstance terrorizes the family and leaves its members isolated and hostile. Family life becomes chaotic and desperate, "a twitching, incoherent mess" (p. 2).

A suicide attempt may be a form of self-punishment to alleviate a conscious or unconscious feeling of guilt. The last straw precipitating Michael's jumping into the river was his having inadvertently been the cause of Janey Riddley's accident. In response to Dr. Sherman's gentle comment, "everyone's looking for something" (p. 3). Michael thinks bitterly to himself, "What if in the process of looking for your thing, you really mess up? And mess up not just yourself but somebody else, some innocent bystander?" (p. 4). Michael not only feels a peculiar connection with Janey Riddley that intensifies his reaction to her accident, but he also has a great deal of underlying guilt from other causes for which the accident seems to provide an ironic culmination. He has alienated and hurt all those closest to him—Melissa, Ricky, his mother, Amanda, and Mr. Dorio—and, like his father, he has abandoned his family and lost touch with his human connections. Ironically, the one person to whom he feels genuinely connected is Janey Riddley, a woman who seems to personify disconnectedness from the world of other human beings. Thanks to his unspoken identification with this lonely and searching woman, Michael all of a sudden feels a sense of responsibility in the aftermath of Janey's accident and sees his potential to cause genuine harm.

Adolescents at risk often feel a sense of helplessness with regard to their circumstances that may, in turn, engender both rage and despair. The rage is often diffuse, aimed at both self and others. Michael is unaware of his anger toward anyone but his mother, although he enacts it in his distancing of himself from those he has cared about. His rage suddenly bursts through when, in the first chapter, Dr. Sherman suggests that he look within himself, a suggestion that strips Michael of his tough exterior and confronts him with his helplessness and confusion. "Suddenly I feel irritated. No, I feel more than irritated, I feel really pissed. On the verge of furious" (p. 4). But then "the anger drains away as quickly as it came, leaving this numbness behind it. A deadened feeling" (p. 4).

Indeed suicidality may reflect a kind of despair that is more aptly characterized as an inner deadness such that biological death seems of little consequence. Suicide attempts often occur (as did Michael's) following the break-up of a romantic relationship when, especially from the limited perspective of adolescence, there seems to be nothing left to live for. Following such a loss, there may be a feeling as if all vitality had departed with the loved one. (See John Donne's poem "Nocturnall [sic] Upon St. Lucie's Day" for a vivid evocation of such a mind-state, p. 34.) There may also be a sense of failure, such that one's self-worth seems nullified by the rejection of a supremely valued other person. The images Michael recalls in the first chapter encapsulate his sense of both loss and failure. He tries to hold on to the picture of himself and Melissa but can't; instead, he sees Mr. Dorio kicking him out of class and the image of Melissa running away from him.

Suicidality may result when a young person's life presents a problem or conflict that seems, from his or her limited experience, insoluble. Life seems like a catch-22, from which there seems to be no way out except to "check out." The kind of therapy that can sometimes avert a suicide involves identifying the problem and opening the young person's eyes to alternatives beyond his or her present imaginings and experience. (See the case of Karen in the next section.) Along with such cognitive reworking, a successful therapy offers a benign context in which interpersonal connectedness can be rediscovered and deadened emotions can come back to life.

Furthermore, despite limited years and experience, especially in a dysfunctional family, an adolescent may feel the burden of adult conflicts and responsibilities. Following his parents' divorce, Michael is by default the man of the house, and as such the target of his mother's rage. The family dynamics are such that many of the conflicts between Michael's father and mother get played out between Michael and his mother. Michael blames his mother for the divorce and its painful aftermath. He clings to a positive view of his father, partly as a way to protect himself from his mother and from her displaced rage against her former husband and partly because he so much needs to believe in his father as a positive and affirming male role model. As Michael puts it, "talking to my [easygoing] dad [was] a good antidote to her moods" (pp. 10–11). With Michael's father's parting gift of a camera, photography becomes the symbol of Michael's positive identification and connection with his father. It is when the potential for this symbol to do harm is revealed—in the humiliating distorted photo of Victoria and in the final tragic scene involving Janey Riddley—that Michael begins to perceive the negative aspects of his identification with his father. With this revelation, he experiences the unraveling of his own precariously constructed adaptation. The positive aspects of both his outer life and his inner world turn against him. Most lethally, he comes to identify with the destructive aspects of his father.

A suicide may reflect a kind of murder of a hated part of self or of a hated or destructive other person whom one experiences as part of oneself. It may reflect an attempt to kill off, or, as Michael says, to "drown" or "wash away" the offending part (p. 5). In another sense, a suicide may be a form of punishment or a seeking of redemption. In trying to "wash away" the pictures, Michael sought to cleanse himself of the ugly evidence of his sins, the sins themselves, and the murderer in himself—identified with his murderer-father—the man who killed Michael's former life. Michael's alienating behavior kills his relationship with Melissa and, as Michael fears, might have caused the death of Janey Riddley. The image of father-as-murderer is offered, like so many others, in the first chapter of the book: "My mother was standing there looking grim as a homicide detective, eyeballing my father like he was the number-one suspect. It was ugly" (p. 12). Therapy would involve coming to grips with these "sins," shrinking them to life-size and seeing them in the context of the complex web of human interactions and emotions that engendered them.

Suicidality may develop in a relatively healthy adolescent when he or she faces a developmental impasse that, from an adult's perspective, seems clearly transient. Adolescents typically see things in categorical terms. This is part of what goes into their passionate rebellions and their idealism. There may seem to be only two options: a right way and a wrong way, the way of the past and the way of the future, radical independence from parents or total dependency. A clinical example of Karen in the section that follows exemplifies such an impasse and the therapy that helped her past it.

PSYCHOTHERAPY FOR AN ADOLESCENT WHO HAS ATTEMPTED SUICIDE

The beginning of the first chapter of *The TV Guidance Counselor* consists of a therapy session with Dr. Sherman during Michael's hospitalization following the attempt. A great deal goes on in that session, but most of it, as with many adolescents, is unspoken. It goes on in Michael's head and is signaled by his actions. Indeed, the chapter begins with Michael's unspoken thoughts within the session: "I wasn't trying to kill myself the night I jumped into the Mohegan River. At least, I don't think I was" (p. 1). Nobody knows what prompted that particular thought, but Dr. Sherman keeps asking him questions—"How did you feel after the divorce?"—that Michael doesn't want to contemplate, let alone answer. The questions "Doc" asks prompt a train of unwilling associations that we, as the fortunate readers, are privy to. These associations are peppered with Michael's smart-ass and hostile unspoken retorts against "Doc" but then proceed to his own spontaneous remembering. Dr. Sherman allows Michael his space, but challenges Michael's nonverbal cues by accurately imputing the unconscious anger that is manifest in Michael's white-knuckled fist or the wistful searching that seems implicit in Michael's gazing out the window, avoiding the session and the memories that are crowding in on him there. It is when Dr. Sherman comments that the answers can't be found "out there" and exhorts Michael to look within himself for the answers that Michael suddenly feels the full force of his anger, shouting back, "Why would I want to look within myself? There's nothing in there!" (p. 4). Suddenly, Michael's anger gives way to numbness—"a deadened feeling"—and then the key moments of the past months appear in his mind as a series of snapshots. When he can bear it no longer, Michael squeezes his eyes shut with the thought, "I wish I could squeeze my brain until I squeezed all the pictures right out of it" (p. 5). Dr. Sherman again responds with a question, "If you weren't trying to kill yourself, Michael, what were you trying to do?" (p. 5).

Michael's response is again unspoken, but it seems Dr. Sherman has at last broken through to him:

> I was trying to get away from—
> I was trying to drown out—no, not drown—
> I was trying to wash—wash away—
>   the pictures—the pain
>   what happened
>   everything
> Dr. Sherman watches me with this kindness I can't stand. He pushes a
> box of kleenex across the desk. I can't believe I'm crying. (p. 5)

This first session of the book establishes the trajectory that the rest of Michael's therapy during his hospitalization will follow. Through Dr. Sherman's perceptive probing and despite Michael's resistance, Michael begins to develop an awareness of his own inner world. Albeit unwillingly, Michael is touched and affected by Dr. Sherman's attempts to establish contact. Eventually, through the persistent exploration of present feelings and past events in the context of a benign relationship, Michael begins to regain a sense of coherence and is able, once again, to connect with other people. In his symbolic gesture toward Janey Riddley near the end of the book, when he delivers to her house a *TV Guide* with a copy of the photograph he had taken of her pasted inside, Michael means both to give her what she has been looking for and at last to restore to her her soul which he had "captured" in the photograph. The gesture carries the suggestion that Michael also has found something he was looking for that he had lost and that he has, perhaps, with Dr. Sherman's help, regained his soul.

The prognosis for a troubled adolescent may depend a lot on how the family responds. (See the clinical examples of Karen, Phoebe, and Simon below as examples of different family responses.) Unfortunately, as in Michael's case, it is often only after an attempt is made that the family and patient alike are able to admit there is trouble and accept help. Treatment for the adolescent involves several components: helping the adolescent discover and identify his or her feelings, especially those identified earlier; establishing a safe place in which to air them (unlike the family where one may be "treading on eggshells" and where others' guilt and fears may preclude safe self-expression); and helping the patient to find alternatives to the narrow and unlivable world view that precipitated the attempt. Therapy involves helping him or her find new solutions and new sources of support. It should lead to a resumption of the ability to feel, to function effectively, and to connect with others. Some clinical examples of other suicidal adolescents, including an overview of their psychotherapy, are offered here in order to further elucidate the therapeutic process.

To Go or Not to Go

Case Description of Karen

Karen, a 17-year-old girl who had never been away from home for any substantial length of time, became suicidal for the first time during her senior year in high school. She had obtained a full scholarship to a very competitive Ivy League school across the country from where her parents lived. Her older sister had not gone away to college but, instead, had remained at home until she married. Her father was very invested in Karen's success, but she was terrified of going to school so far away. That fall, Karen developed intractable crying spells whenever she went away even for an overnight.

Perceiving the depth of her distress and in response to the suicidal thoughts that she expressed, her parents immediately sought treatment for her.

Karen's Psychotherapy

The work of the therapy that ensued—fortunately there was no actual attempt—focused on the no-win situation that Karen had set up in her mind. Karen believed that either she would go away and risk intractable despair and loneliness or she would stay at home and never, at any forseeable future time, be able to separate from her parents. The alternatives seemed unbearable to her: She would either be forever terrified and lonely or be forever stuck. The work of the therapy involved modulating these polarized views. It seemed, furthermore, that her own emotions were unbearable, unacceptable, and humiliating. After several sessions in which a great many tears were shed, it became clear to her that such emotions could come and go and that she could endure and grow in the process. As a result, she became able to consider her options in clearer light. Several were discussed: She could leave home stepwise; she could defer for a year; she could start out at a state school and transfer if she later chose to and were able; she could visit the school—knowing she didn't *have* to go there—talk with other students about their experience and perhaps learn that they, too, had been anxious at the start. What had seemed like an impasse, in which the very possibility of a future had become unimaginable, became more manageable as we negotiated it in halting, precarious, and stepwise fashion. The bouts of suicidality became attenuated and, following a last minute panic and reversal, Karen made a relatively confident choice to go away to school.

Mirror, Mirror on the Wall

Case Description of Phoebe

Phoebe, an attractive 15-year-old high school sophomore, had been a child model. She nevertheless remained intensely insecure about her appearance. When occasionally she developed a minor blemish on her face, barely noticeable to anyone but herself, she would be too ashamed to go to school. She would make up an excuse or feign an illness. Her mother, intensely appearance-conscious herself, was privy to Phoebe's problem and colluded with it, thus reinforcing Phoebe's conviction that she was indeed not fit to be seen. Phoebe kept her preoccupation secret from everyone but her parents who on the one hand were themselves prone to criticize her appearance or her dress, and on the other hand berated her for being so obsessed and dysfunctional. Phoebe's parents had divorced when she was 12 years old. Her father had begun to "stray" around the time Phoebe began to lose her delicate, little-girl beauty and became for a time a rather gangly preadolescent. Her mother involved Phoebe in her desperate attempts to keep her husband. On one occasion, she forced Phoebe to stay up until her father came home after an unexplained evening out and implore him—for Phoebe's sake—never to leave again. He ceased his womanizing briefly but then it resumed. Phoebe's mother would say, "You have to get him to stay. You are my only hope. You are such a pretty child. He might come back because of you." Phoebe's father eventually found a younger woman with whom he developed a serious relationship, and he left for good.

It was around this time that Phoebe's obsession began. She began to miss more and more time from school, social events, and family gatherings. Near the beginning of her sophomore year, she began dating a high school senior named Paul, a football player who was considered a "catch," but in whose presence she became increasingly insecure, fearing that she would not be able to "hold onto him." She would cancel dates at the last minute if her appearance wasn't "perfect" and, ashamed of her preoccupation, would not tell him the reason. Although Paul very much enjoyed her company and was proud to be seen with her, her cancellation the evening of his senior prom proved to be the last straw. He told her over the phone that she was a "sick person" and that he couldn't tolerate her "moodiness" anymore. Phoebe was able to see, ironically, that she had caused exactly what she had most dreaded. While her mother was herself out on a date, Phoebe raided the medicine cabinet and took a near-fatal overdose of one of her mother's medications. She was hospitalized briefly for detoxification and then referred to me for treatment.

Phoebe's Psychotherapy

My work with Phoebe involved elucidation of the exaggerated valuing of appearance in her family, the superficiality of the relationships, and the conviction—passed on to her by her mother—that a woman's worth consists in being able to hold on to a man. Phoebe also began to see the many ways she had been put in the middle and "used" by her parents, either as a pawn in their own battles or to bolster, by means of her attractiveness, their own fragile self-confidence.

The work with Phoebe's parents involved helping them see the role they had played in Phoebe's difficulties and helping them take more responsibility for their own disagreements as well as those involving Phoebe. The suicide attempt brought to their attention the need, despite their animosity toward each other, to be co-responsible for their daughter. Phoebe's parents were extremely resistant to change, and indeed, once the immediate aftermath of the suicide attempt had passed, they reverted to their old ways of being and relating. Nevertheless, they continued to support Phoebe's treatment. Eventually, when her parents tried at times to "put her in the middle," Phoebe herself became increasingly able to refuse this position. Phoebe also began to seek out a different, less appearance-conscious group of friends. After reading a book on body dysmorphic disorder, *The Broken Mirror* by Katherine Phillips, she realized that she was not alone in her exaggerated preoccupation. Not only did her preoccupation have a name, but it also had a treatment. She began to actively work on overcoming her disorder, both through therapy and with medication.

Not Wanted

Case Description of Simon

Simon was a 19-ycar-old youth who had grown up in a very strict, evangelical family. His father was a tough man, an immigrant from a European country who had made his way, through hard work and discipline, to a relatively comfortable livelihood. Simon, in contrast to his father and three older brothers, was, like his mother, a dreamer. His father accorded no value to Simon's intellectual giftedness and imagination but berated him for his bookishness and lack of physical toughness. Prone to violent anger, his father believed in physical punishment that, in Simon's case, was tantamount to abuse. Simon had the sense that he had been "not wanted" in the first place, in particular by his father. His brothers had also been hit, but being by nature as well as age tougher and stronger than Simon, were better able to avoid the appearance of being "lazy" which occasioned their father's contempt.

From an early age and increasingly during adolescence, Simon found himself in conflict with regard to his sexual orientation, a conflict that he soon began to enact. He sought out very sweet and submissive girls with whom he developed chaste, tender, and fairy-tale-like relationships in which they would dream of marriage, a beautiful wedding, and beautiful children. At the same time, to his own dismay and confusion, he found himself compelled to engage in high-risk, unprotected sex with older men. Intensely ashamed of his predilection, he would seek out male prostitutes toward whom he would develop obsessional attachments. Given the risk of HIV infection, Simon's activities constituted a kind of suicidal behavior. The sex with older men was a way of seeking closeness with and proving his desirability to a father-figure while at the same time seeking punishment (via HIV infection) for his unacceptable homosexual desires. Deeply conflicted, he was, in the same act, rebelling and seeking punishment for his rebellion. Alternately, he spun out, with his fiancée, dreams of the gentle, loving home and family indicative of the perfect childhood he had never had. In his rebellious, "dark" mode, Simon engaged in what was, by his family's standards, the most shameful behavior imaginable. In his "fairy-tale" mode, Simon sought to engender his family's pride in him. His family knew nothing of his "dark" practices, but an aunt to whom he had been quite close noted that he had mood-swings. This aunt thought he might be "manic-depressive" and encouraged him to seek therapy, which she was willing to subsidize herself.

Simon's Psychotherapy

When Simon came to treatment, he presented himself as a polite, scrupulously well-put-together young man. He was engaged to be married and prided himself on always having been able to "cope." He acknowledged a feeling of having been "not wanted" and then, increasingly, to despair and confusion. If not for the shame it would bring on his family, Simon would end his life. Gradually, the nature of his confusion and the activities that constituted his "dark side" came to light. He alluded to these practices at first obliquely and always with excruciating shame and self-loathing. Eventually the link between these episodes and specific instances of having been devalued or hurt by his family became clearer, as did the link between the most risky of his sexual encounters and his rage at his father. It became obvious how unremittingly he was living his life in reaction to his family, alternately seeking revenge against them and desperately seeking their approval.

Faced with sorting out what he wanted for himself, Simon was confused and at a loss. Was his attraction to men based purely on self-punishment, or would embracing a gay identity (unimaginable to him at the time) eventually bring peace? Was his desire for marriage to a woman based on a fantasy of an ideal life that he could never imagine himself capable of sustaining because it wasn't what he genuinely wanted? Or did he simply see himself as doomed to failure and degradation, the "black sheep" of the family unable, therefore, to sustain a positive dream of success and happiness in marriage and family life?

At the time of this writing, the answers to these questions remain unclear. But as the toxic origins of his behaviors have been elucidated, the more dangerous ones have begun to abate. He has begun to verbalize, not just to enact, his despair and confusion. Having dropped out of high school shortly before graduation and taking on a menial but physically demanding job in a further manifestation of his self-destructive and ambivalent entanglement with his father's expectations of him, he has now returned to school with the hope of going away to college. The prospect of living a life for him-self—rather than in reaction to his family—has become a genuine possibil-ity. The thought of living out his own dreams—rather than succeeding or failing at living out his parents'—has become (barely) imaginable to Si-mon. In some sense, his future hinges on whether and how he can learn to value his own life despite having been "not wanted" by his parents.

THE AFTERMATH: HOW A SUICIDE ATTEMPT AFFECTS THE FAMILY AND POTENTIAL HEALING EFFECTS

In the denouement of *The TV Guidance Counselor*, Michael returns to a home and family that are far less chaotic than those he left when he entered the hospital. He and his mother converse somewhat anxiously in the car on the way home, but with greater honesty and clarity than ever before. The "rathole" where they live "seems like home for the first time." His mother has enrolled in a course in preparation for getting herself a job. The "organ-ism" is beginning to reconstitute itself.

With regard to the cases described above, Karen's parents ("To Go or Not to Go") were well aware of her distress and quickly sought treatment. They had been and remained supportive of her and of the decisions she made. Thus a therapy that accomplished the relatively simple task of elu-cidating her developmental impasse and helping her envision her future in a more flexible way was sufficient to restore her sense of hope and confidence.

Phoebe's suicide attempt ("Mirror, Mirror on the Wall") was the occa-sion of her parents finally coming to attention and seeing the need for and supporting her treatment. Up until then, they had minimized and berated her for her difficulties and saw psychotherapy as "a waste of time and money." While they continued to support her treatment following the attempt, they remained caught up in their own insecurities, still too fragile to want to ex-plore any role they might have played in the development of Phoebe's diffi-culties or any possibilities for healing or change in themselves. Theirs was, nevertheless, a "good enough" response to enable Phoebe's recovery.

For Simon ("Not Wanted"), the future remains less clear. His treatment will, no doubt, have to proceed without his parents' emotional or financial support. Fortunately, he is at an age when greater independence from his par-ents is possible, and the question is how and whether he will be able to take advantage of this. His aunt seems to be the one consistently positive and supportive figure in his family. Through her presence and her financial support, she may have saved his life. It will be important, though, for Simon to find in the wider world, one or more positive and supportive male role models: men with whom he can identify, whom he can healthily aspire to be like, and who can affirm him for who he is. Perhaps he will find such an affinity with one of his teachers, presuming he is able to live out his dream of going to college away from his parents. Perhaps his love of literature will ultimately provide a positive connection with a teacher/father figure rather than, as with his own father, engendering alienation and contempt.

PSYCHOTHERAPY FOR FAMILY MEMBERS FOLLOWING THE ATTEMPT

The TV Guidance Counselor does not indicate how Michael's mother may have been involved in Michael's treatment and whether or not she received treatment herself during his hospitalization. It is clear that she was, in the main, supportive of his treatment and also that she has ongoing difficulties of her own. She appears to be coping better by the end of the book than she was at the beginning. Her hostility toward Michael and toward his father appears to have abated some, but she remains diffusely anxious as evidenced by her ongoing inability to make left-hand turns. Treatment might help her to deal more capably with her own emotions, find better ways to meet her own needs, and be more responsive to the needs of her children. It will be important for her to be alert to her daughter Amanda's reactions to Michael's hospitalization and to find age-appropriate ways to explain to her what has happened. The importance of talking openly about a suicide attempt in the family is illustrated by the case below.

Speaking the Unspeakable

Case Description of Margaret

When Margaret was 15, her older sister Jane, a freshman in college, had attempted suicide. Their parents, in an effort to "protect" the younger sister, never spoke about it in her presence. Nonetheless, Margaret would hear her mother talking in worried and hushed tones on the phone and behind closed doors, emerging red-eyed but determined to keep up appearances as best she could. During her senior year in high school, Margaret became listless and at times suicidally depressed. She sought treatment without her parents' knowledge, imploring the therapist not to speak with them. As their financial support was needed, she eventually gave consent for them to be contacted. At first irate at having been "left out" of their daughter's choice to seek treatment and informed only after it was in process, they eventually realized how deeply such secretiveness was ingrained in their family's life. Margaret was "leaving them out" and trying to "protect" them from the trouble she felt in herself much as they had tried to protect her from her sister's trouble. Clearly the result, in each case, was a sense of anxiety and bewilderment, not of safety and protection. The parents came to realize their mistake in not talking to Margaret about her sister's suicide attempt, the gravity and fearfulness of which she could not help but sense even though it was unmentioned. Indeed, the secrecy made it all the more fearful. Additionally, Margaret knew nothing of the details of her sister's recovery. Margaret's world was pervaded by an unidentified sense of danger, unmentioned, unmentionable, never addressed and hence unremitting.

Margaret's Psychotherapy

The treatment that ensued was brief but extensive, involving both individual work with Margaret and several sessions with a separate therapist that included all four family members. The goal of the family work was to facilitate communication within the family and to offer a way to approach difficult issues more openly and effectively. All four family members were, as it turned out, highly motivated, and the treatment proceeded quickly and fruitfully. As a result of this work, the mother went on to seek treatment for herself. An intergenerational pattern of "secrecy" and shame with regard to emotional life thus came to light, and alternatives to it were sought and found both among the family members and within the family as a whole.

PREVENTION AND THE BROADER COMMUNITY: WHAT CAN FAMILY MEMBERS, TEACHERS, COUNSELORS, AND FRIENDS DO TO AVERT AN ATTEMPT?

Predicting or preventing suicide attempts poses a significant challenge. Especially since suicidality often occurs in the context of emotional isolation, those around a troubled adolescent may be unaware of the depth and nature of his or her distress. Even when signs of distress are obvious, it may be difficult to find an effective way to intervene. Known risk factors such as substance abuse, suicide in the family, suicide of a friend, and/or psychiatric illness may alert caring adults to the possibility of suicidality and the need for treatment. At the same time, however, there are many more adolescents who fall into any one of these categories who do not ever attempt suicide than who do. Among adolescents who confide in someone, that someone is most often a friend, a parent, a teacher, or a school counselor. An atmosphere in the home, school, and community that places a positive value on seeking help for emotional difficulties and that is receptive to expressions of emotional experience is likely to facilitate an adolescent's seeking the help he or she needs.

Teachers, especially English language arts teachers, may serve a crucial function in promoting self-awareness among their students and in enhancing communication skills. Literature provides access to the broader world beyond the adolescent's immediate experience. It may offer a kind of solace and companionship unavailable in a young person's family and peer group. It may demonstrate to a youth that someone else has had feelings similar to his or her own, and that there are ways to put such feelings into words. For Michael Madden, Fritz Thumm's borrowed characterization of Janey Riddley as a wandering and unsatisfied spirit was one that resonated with Michael's own experience of himself and sowed the seeds for his identification with this wandering, searching woman. Fritz's ability to find solace and peace through literature, despite having lived through harsh circumstances, provides a welcome and stark contrast to the emotional chaos and self-absorption in Michael's own family. A similar peacefulness and other-directed awareness in Fritz's nephew, Carl, enables Carl to perceive Michael's distress, keep watch over him, and eventually save his life.

While school-based education about the availability of help may be beneficial, not all attempts to facilitate dialogue about teen suicide have been successful. Several studies suggest that education about suicide may actually increase suicidal behavior, so it behooves educators to be thoughtful and cautious in their approach to this topic. Educational exposure to the idea of suicide as a means, albeit maladaptive, to escape a crisis or deal with distress may lead adolescents to consider suicide as an option. One study showed that there was an increase in adolescent suicide after exposure to television programs whose main theme was the suicide of a teenager. Other studies have failed to replicate such findings. Disturbed adolescents may identify with a peer who has died by suicide, causing clusters of suicides among young people who know one another or who go to the same school. Similarly, young people may identify with and imitate a celebrity or otherwise highly publicized suicide. This phenomenon is known as the Werther Syndrome, after the protagonist in Goethe's novel, *The Sorrows of Young Werther*, who kills himself. The novel was banned following its publication 200 years ago because of a rash of suicides by young men who had read it, some of whom had dressed like young Werther or left the book open to the passage describing his death when they killed themselves. Accordingly, literature on this topic must be chosen with care and sensitivity to the various reactions it might engender in adolescent readers. Books such as *The TV Guidance Counselor* that emphasize recovery, that portray with sensitivity and in detail both the protagonist's despair and his emergence from it, and that show how adolescents and families can develop and grow, may be the wisest choice.

All-in-all, the best approach to suicide detection and prevention involves a combination of elements. On a community level, the most promising are school- or community-based programs that do not in any way glamorize suicide or inadvertantly teach its methods but rather combine the provision of information about the availability and potential benefits of help along with systematic screening to identify adolescents at risk. Parents and teachers should be urged to take suicide threats seriously, and peers should be advised to tell a responsible adult even if they have been asked not to. Failure to do so will ultimately be experienced as lack of concern and could result in needless tragedy. Literature relevant to the emotional and developmental concerns of adolescents, chosen and taught with sensitivity and care, may be very beneficial as well. For any individual, however, what is most important is that there *be someone*—be it a friend, relative, teacher, mentor, therapist, or clergy—who is able to relate empathically to the adolescent's troubled inner world and can refer them to help if necessary.

COMPLETED SUICIDE

This is a whole different issue, beyond the scope of this chapter but important to mention. Unfortunately, whether or not a suicide attempt was made out of a genuine wish to end one's life, it may result in death. As Michael realizes by the end of the book, such might have been his own fate had it not been for the sensitivity and vigilance of the "slow" but benevolent and perceptive Carl. Completed suicide in a family is a risk factor for future suicides. Reactions among family members of suicide victims include survivor guilt, reunion fantasies, fear, rage, and bereavement, all of which can lead to suicide. The process of healing for a family after the completed suicide of one of its members is infinitely more difficult and complicated than that following an unsuccessful attempt. One mother's process of healing following the suicide of her adolescent son is chronicled in Sue Chance's book *Stronger than Death*.

THE FUTURE: CRISIS AND OPPORTUNITY

The Chinese character which denotes "crisis" also denotes "opportunity." A suicide attempt signals a crisis. In the best of scenarios, treatment can turn that crisis into an opportunity to develop genuinely new patterns of relating within a family and new adaptations within an individual. It is vitally important, whenever possible, for the actual attempt to be averted and, as in the case of Karen ("To Go or Not to Go"), treatment begun before the crisis yields to the attempt. Unfortunately, both purposeful and inadvertent deaths occur all too frequently.

Nevertheless, with luck, perseverance, and understanding, life goes on in all its richness of potential. In Michael's words that mark the end of the book: "So I was walking and thinking these thoughts, and all of a sudden I stopped and looked over my shoulder. I'd walked all the way across the bridge."

RECOMMENDED READINGS

A Cautionary Note

All books chronicling completed suicide must be chosen with sensitivity and care for the viewpoint and vulnerabilities of their projected readership. Some of the books presented here may serve as cautionary tales, others as beacons of clarity for the stormy seas of adolescent experience. Teachers recommending these books should be alert to potentially harmful identifications with characters as exemplified by the "Werther Syndrome" described earlier in reaction to *The Sorrows of Young Werther*.

With this caveat in mind, the books listed here may provide a means by which troubling experiences can be articulated, managed and understood, and may facilitate vitally important dialogues between students and teachers or teenagers and their parents.

Fiction

Other ALA Best of the Best Books for Young Adults

11.01. Bennett, James. (1990). *I can hear the mourning dove*. Boston: Houghton Mifflin. 197 pp. (ISBN: 0–395–53623–5). High School (HS).

Grace attempts to kill herself after her father suddenly dies; and, as a consequence, she spends most of her junior year in a mental institution. A psychologist, teacher, and friend try to help Grace rebuild her life, but it is a juvenile delinquent who actually gets through to her.

11.02. Crutcher, Chris. (1989). *Chinese handcuffs*. New York: Greenwillow Books. 202 pp. (ISBN: 0–588–08345–5). HS.

This powerful survival story relates the processing of 16-year-old Dillon Hemingway's grief and confusion, and records the process of his recovery in the wake of the violent suicide of his older brother Preston, who'd previously lost both of his legs in a senseless motorcycle accident, a suicide that Dillon witnessed and couldn't prevent. Against a middle class Washington backdrop, the book examines a complex group of dynamic, interlocking, family and friend relationships, with Dillon at their center. Among these are his friendship with an incestuously sexually abused high school basketball star, Jennifer Lawless, his sibling relationship with Preston—which he voices in a series of cathartic letters to his dead brother that examine both causes and impact of the handgun suicide—and his ongoing ties to his deceased brother's girlfriend. The book addresses a gamut of tough issues, among them, suicide and suicidal feelings, psychological trauma survival, and survivor guilt as well as grief, incest, broken families and step-families, teen motherhood, drug abuse, parental negligence, and the capacity for cruelty, violence, and evil which is part of the human condition. In the end, Dillon is able to act effectively at a crucial moment and prevent Jennifer from "escaping back into the universe by [her] own hand," the words he uses to characterize his brother's death.

Many teen readers may identify with the powerless sense of being trapped in an inescapable situation, the metaphorical Chinese handcuffs, events impacting their lives, but ones over which they seemingly have little or no control, situations in which the harder one tries to get free, the tighter the hold becomes.

The mature subject matter, handled sensitively but without pulling punches, is balanced by a pervasive sense of the possibility of redemption through recognition of the truth, and through making responsible choices. And Dillon, through athletic endeavors as a triathalete, through creative potential evidenced in his acute self- and other-scrutinizing writing, and through an earnest search for integrity in his relationships, ultimately achieves that redemption by the end of the book. Also clearly demonstrated is the value of support and assistance from responsible, caring adults wherever they may be found, in therapy, among teachers and coaches, as well as parents and relatives, while instances wherein the adults and child protective services system fail are addressed as well.

The present tense of immediacy in many of the passages, and the first-person intimacy of Dillon's letters—which provide a window into the psychic workings, the emotional conflicts, and the choice making process of a highly intelligent, wounded young man—make for compelling reading. Crutcher's realistic and in-depth characterization invites strong reader identification. Highly recommended for its sensitive and responsible approach to all the difficult issues addressed.

11.03.   Guest, Judith. (1976). *Ordinary people*. New York: Ballantine. 245 pp. (ISBN: 0–345–30734–8). HS.

The death in a sailing accident of a beloved older son leaves the remaining Jarrett family members reeling with grief, and 18-year-old Conrad, stricken by survivor guilt, attempts suicide in the aftermath of the event. Told in an intimate third-person style, from the points of view of Conrad and both of his parents, the story recounts the family members' struggles to process their grief and reintegrate, not only their individual personalities, but the trauma-shattered family unit as well. The plot unfolds through the lenses of the characters' emotional reactions to the events. As the emotions themselves are processed and brought into focus, the beginnings of a tenuous balance are restored.

Serious depression, psychiatric treatment, panic attacks, the fine line which defines "sanity," the processing of grief, and the remolding of identity in the wake of a breakdown are all dealt with in this deeply moving story of ordinary people attempting to bear unbearable tragedy. It also addresses self-image, and the "box" of other people's expectations in which one can become confined.

For adolescent readers mature enough and with the empathic perspective to comprehend the adult points of view as well as accept adult failings, the book offers a vision of the enormous effort required at times in life to achieve psychological and emotional balance. The novel ends on a hopeful note that balance can be accomplished. The scenes between Conrad and his psychiatrist are especially well drawn, showing moments in therapy during which real and useful insights are achieved.

11.04.   Peck, Richard. (1986). *Remembering the good times*. New York: Dell Laurel-Leaf. 181 pp. (ISBN: 0–440–97339–2). HS.

With both the resistance to and acceptance of change as its core theme, the story follows Buck Mendenhall and his two close friends, Kate Lucas and Trav Kirby, from the 8th grade through their sophomore years in high school. Peck examines the dynamics of a three-way friendship against a backdrop of very diversified social strata. In school, this falls out as the Slos, the Subs, and the Spaces; and, in the Slocum Township, the locals fall out as the new influx of corporate offspring and the Generation X fringe culture. The small Midwestern town also undergoes change, as its rural character is increasingly encroached on and eroded by the "progress" of development. Through Buck's voice, identity issues are explored as he watches his close friend Trav, a wealthy and brilliant teenage son of "perfect" parents, feel the pressure of perfectionism himself so deeply that he is "quietly out of control." Trav moves through a "cry for help" episode of shoplifting toward deeper despair which ultimately ends in his suicide. Issues of divorce, geographic separation from one parent, random violence, sexual harassment, revenge, and taking justice into one's own hands are also touched upon.

The interactions and details of Trav's home life occur largely "off screen," and thus the development of his problems lack a full context. The adolescent characters, however, are richly drawn and several adult characters, with loving integrity, demonstrate that adult support is both available and sometimes necessary. The author's insight into the workings of adolescent minds is acute, and readers from age 11 up will be drawn into the intimate first-person account of platonic love and loss.

The novel makes an important point—that suicide is permanent, while problems are often temporary—during a support session set at the high school after Trav's suicide. For readers to see the irrevocable consequences of a despairing impulse may drive home the finality of the act. Also brought out is the necessity for expressing grief, which doesn't bring the deceased back but does bring the survivors "back." In the end, the book, more than providing answers, provokes fruitful questioning about how to cope with pressures from without as well as from within.

11.05.   Pfeffer, Susan Beth. (1990). *About David*. New York: Dell Laurel-Leaf. 176 pp. (ISBN: 0–440–90022–0). HS.

Lynn is emotionally distraught after learning that her close friend, David, killed his parents and himself. She struggles to understand why David did such a heinous thing and what his actions say of her. Lynn records her thoughts in diary form, letting readers see the process she goes through to figure out why it happened and her part in the tragedy.

11.06.   Sachs, Marilyn. (1988). *The fat girl*. New York: Dell Laurel-Leaf. 176 pp. (ISBN: 0–440–92468–5). Middle School (MS), HS.

Tables turn on Jeff when he learns that Ellen, a girl he has been unmercifully teasing about her weight, is suicidal. Jeff realizes—in time—his contributions to her dwindling self-esteem. They become friends and teach each other a lot about the good things and bad things about life and living.

Other Titles

11.07. Eyerly, Jennette. (1978). *See Dave run*. New York: J.B. Lippincott. 126 pp. (ISBN: 0–397–31819–7). HS.

The life of a 15-year-old runaway is sketched through a series of succinct first-person chronicles by both close and passing friends, mother, step-father, and father, various law enforcement officials, medical professionals, and people with whom Dave Hendry briefly connects along his travels. Dave leaves a middle-class suburban family situation which ranges from neglectful to actively abusive, aiming vaguely toward Colorado, where he thinks he may find his accident-handicapped musician father, with whom he has long since lost contact.

The impressions of the various narrators often create a sense of a "missing person" or lost child as well as a sense of journey. Several issues are addressed: child abuse and neglect; alcoholism within a family; drug use (marijuana); joblessness and homelessness; economic and physical survival; prostitution; homosexual child molestation; venereal disease (note: since the book was written before the knowledge of the AIDS epidemic spread, the absence of any mention of AIDS comes across as out-of-date); imprisonment; and finally, teen suicide. In the final chronicle, as an ineffective legal and social services system and a malignantly dysfunctional family fail the boy, he hangs himself in a jail cell.

Although the story is accessible for ages 11 and up, younger readers may miss some of the more sinister aspects of some situations; the author handles them with subtlety. The realistic framework, including newspaper columns and police procedures, serves to enhance the impact of the events recounted. The book successfully de-glamorizes any notion a youngster might entertain about the "freedom of the open road" for an adolescent without adequate resources. Even the sporadic assistance of various "friendly strangers" along the way cannot prevent Dave's journey from disintegrating into a downward slide into the quiet despair that leads him to take his life.

Readers might be asked to consider alternatives to Dave's choices which might have led to a different outcome. It would be especially useful to point out that Dave did not seek help from competent, caring adults—the parents of friends, teachers, or other relatives.

Nonfiction

11.08. Hermes, Patricia. (1987). *A time to listen: Preventing youth suicide*. San Diego: Harcourt, Brace, & Jovanovich. 132 pp. (ISBN: 0–15–288196–4). MS, HS.

Written by an acclaimed author of children's fiction, this book is a compilation of carefully edited interviews with young people who've attempted suicide and survived, of friends and family members of suicide victims, and professional therapists, along with valuable commentary and analysis. Both succinct and accessible, it is a valuable addition to the literature, covering such topics as warning signs, possible causes and family patterns that may predispose a young person to suicidal feelings, options for friends and families coping with crisis. The book could be a departure point for serious discussions on suicide prevention, either therapeutically or educationally, even at the middle grade level. Especially emphasized is the need for communication, for talking and for listening, and for bridging the sense of isolation that suicidal people feel, with specific guidelines for when professional support and intervention may be warranted.

11.09.   Sparks, Dr. Beatrice. (Ed.). (1989). *Jay's journal*. New York: Pocket Books. 192 pp. (ISBN: 0–812–90801–5). HS.

This is an edited account of a true story based on a teenager who actually kept a journal in which he chronicled his own loss of self to outside forces. Jay tells of his downward spiral into drug abuse, crime, and Satanism, and his suicide note alludes to the extreme despair and isolation that he felt. Readers are exposed to many of the warning signs of Jay's impending suicide, possibly teaching them the signs to look for in other troubled youths.

REFERENCES

Chance, Sue. (1992). *Stronger than death*. New York: Norton Press.
Donne, John. (1994). Nocturnall [*sic*] upon St. Lucie's Day. In *The Complete Poetry and Selected Prose of John Donne*. New York: Modern Library Association.
Goethe. (1988). *The sorrows of young Werther*. New York: Suhrkamp Publishers.
Kaplan, Harold I. & Sadock, Benjamin J. (1991). *Synopsis of psychiatry*, 6th Edition. Baltimore, MD: Williams & Wilkins.
LeMieux, A. C. (1993). *The TV guidance counselor*. New York: Avon.
Patrick, Susan. (1994). *Prevalence and correlates of suicidal behavior in high school students*. Thesis from Central Connecticut State University. (System #34289230).
Phillips, Katherine. (1996). *The broken mirror*. New York: Oxford University Press.

CHAPTER 12

A Therapeutic Reader's Response to Michael Dorris's *A Yellow Raft in Blue Water*

Joan F. Kaywell & Sara Anderson Powell

INTRODUCTION

A common retort of parents to their children during the 1950s was, "You didn't come with a manual." Today, parents can benefit from active parenting classes as well as various research-driven manuals on how to raise their children. It is common knowledge that family dynamics are cyclical in nature. In other words, abused kids tend to become abusers themselves because they do not know any other way to parent unless they have sought some type of intervention. The familial cycle perpetuates until an individual makes a conscious choice to learn a new way of parenting. This final chapter presents the stories of three generations of women—Rayona, the daughter; Christine, Rayona's mother; and Aunt Ida, the family's matriarch—and attempts to illustrate the power of reader response theory in helping a "patient" see how one family's dysfunction is passed from one generation to the next.

Ten actual reader responses to this contemporary award-winning novel are offered for discussion. For the purposes of this chapter and because of the problems associated with confidentiality, I agreed to play the part of the "patient." Dr. Sara Powell, a clinical psychologist, provides responses to her "patient's" writing and sometimes a dialogue ensues. Dr. Powell identifies potential issues for Rayona, the teenage protagonist in *A Yellow Raft in Blue Water*, as she seeks her independence. As you read, consider the potential benefit of having a troubled teenager, particularly one with marginal literacy skills, think and write from a novel before venting in a therapist's office. Our goal is to show how it is possible to help disturbed adolescents improve their literacy skills while addressing their emotional concerns. Through the use of young adult books, therapists will have more available treatment options.

A SYNOPSIS OF *A YELLOW RAFT IN BLUE WATER* BY MICHAEL DORRIS (372 pp.)

Michael Dorris's *A Yellow Raft in Blue Water* is written in three distinct sections, each representing a particular character's viewpoint. Readers first meet Rayona, then her mother Christine, and finally Aunt Ida.

Rayona (pp. 3–137)

This section begins with Rayona visiting her mother Christine in the hospital. Although it is not directly stated, readers are led to believe that Christine is often in the hospital as a result, perhaps, of her poor relationship with Rayona's father Elgin. When Elgin arrives, not to visit but to return Christine's car, Christine flies off the handle and accuses Elgin—in front of Rayona—of having numerous affairs. Christine escapes from the hospital with the intention of driving to the spot where Elgin proposed to her and where Rayona was conceived because "it's the one place your father will understand" (p. 12). The possibility exists that Christine is contemplating suicide, but Rayona gets in the car and refuses to get out. Christine comes up with a new plan; she will take Rayona to the Indian reservation where Aunt Ida lives. On the way out of town, they stop by a video store where they rent two tapes (even though they do not own a VCR), go to their apartment where they throw their belongings into four garbage bags, and get some Percocet from a neighbor. Christine abandons Rayona at Aunt Ida's where Rayona learns more about her family origins.

Christine (pp. 141–293)

Christine's section begins during her adolescence when she identifies herself as "the bastard daughter of a woman who wouldn't even admit she was my mother and the fat sister of the prettiest boy that ever lived" (p. 141). She and her younger brother, Lee, were raised on an Indian reservation by their mother, a woman they were made to call Aunt Ida. After preparing for the Last Judgment Day only to learn that the missionaries had lied about it, Christine becomes a wild, party girl. Despite Christine's numerous boyfriends and joyrides, Lee remains her favorite person in the world. Aunt Ida also dotes on him and doesn't have a whole lot of respect for Christine.

When Lee develops a deep relationship with a half-breed named Dayton, Christine decides to separate them by convincing her brother to join the service after he graduates from high school.

"By the time you realize that your life isn't headed the way you expected you're too busy to look over your shoulder to see what went wrong. That's what happened to [Christine]" (p. 220). In a short time span, Christine learns that Lee was killed in Vietnam, she meets and marries a strapping black man named Elgin, and has her adulterous husband's baby. Christine hopes that Rayona will warm Aunt Ida's heart, but Aunt Ida remains as cold as ever to her. Hospitals become a significant part of Christine's life. First Christine meets a friend of Aunt Ida's named Clara, who dies, and then she herself is told in the hospital that she "had burned [her]self out and probably wouldn't live another six months" (p. 234). The rest of the section retells the events that occurred in Rayona's section but from Christine's perspective.

Ida (pp. 297–372)

Aunt Ida opens her section with a revealing statement, "I never grew up, but I got old" (p. 297). At 57 years of age, she recalls her own adolescence. Readers learn about the secrets that never should have been kept, why she always insisted that Rayona and Lee call her Aunt Ida instead of mother, the reason behind her strained relationship with Christine, and why Lee was her favorite. Aunt Ida's story comes full circle until the final Judgment Day that Christine spoke about in her section. Readers are privy to Aunt Ida's point of view of that key day.

A READER RESPONSE DISCUSSION BETWEEN "PATIENT" AND THERAPIST

"Patient's" Reader Response #1

I started reminiscing about my own mother starting on page eight where Rayona comments about hearing noises not otherwise heard while her mother was in the hospital. My mother was frequently in the hospital when I was little. My parents were separated and eventually got a divorce when I was thirteen. At those times, when Mother was hospitalized, I would be sent to another family to stay until she recovered. Beginning around 16 years of age, I was left alone in a two-story house that I found to be very creepy. I can remember being scared stiff, especially at night, but still not wanting to have to go elsewhere. I'm sure, now that I'm thinking about it, there must have been a subconscious worry about my mother but then again it was an event of life that I had grown accustomed to.

Therapist's Response to #1

It sounds as if your world was kind of unpredictable as a child—that you couldn't rely on any one grown-up to be "there" for you. I wonder if you learned to rely on yourself more than most kids have to do? Staying alone at age 16 understandably taxed your resources. With no one there for comfort and reassurance, it's easy to see how a young girl could struggle with worries of bad things happening. I wonder what helped you get through that time?

"Patient's" Response to Therapist's Response

You've posed two questions to me: one about independence and another about what helped me get through my teenage years. About independence—I would have to say that "Independent (with a capital I)" would have to be my middle name. Two of my infamous lines of growing up were, "I can do it by myself!" and "LEAVE ME ALONE!!!!!!!" Because of my parents' divorce, I vowed to never be dependent on anybody for my financial needs. I learned that books—homework included—provided both a healthy escape and a safe haven from my parents. I also had enough sense to realize that education was a possible ticket to financial independence. My mother was extremely talented but did not have the same options as my father because he had a college degree and she did not. She was a product of the times that placed more emphasis on the education of men rather than women. My poor mother paid dearly for that societal norm.

Secondly, I believe I got through that time period because of a horse my mother bought for me. Because of their divorce, both of my parents were emotionally unavailable. In retrospect, I know now that I became clinically depressed, but no one noticed or seemed to care (or so I thought). I contemplated suicide on more than one occasion, but the fact that my horse, Kitty Kox, needed me to take care of her always got in the way of my following through with my thoughts. I still believe to this day that my being responsible for another living thing saved my life. Sometimes I think that my mother might have been more aware of my emotional state than I believed at the time. She probably just didn't know what to do to help me because she was so consumed with trying to help herself.

Therapist's Response to "Patient"

It is often the case that divorcing parents become so emotionally entangled with each other that they are emotionally unavailable for their children.

Kids will think that their problems don't even come close to the magnitude of their parents' problems and will stuff their feelings as a result. Depression is just one of the possible manifestations of a person with blocked emotions. Sudden outbursts of anger and suicidal thoughts are two others.

"Patient's" Reader Response #2

Farther down on page eight, there's a belief system expressed about being guaranteed the Last Rites if a person attends nine First Friday masses in a row. My mother used to tell a great story concerning her own guarantee of the Last Rites, but I never could remember what the Catholic ritual was that she said she did to guarantee it. The story goes something like this:

Even though my mother was told not to have more children because it could threaten her life, my father convinced her to try again so he could have the girl he always wanted; I was that girl. I struggled for my life, but Mom supposedly died as a result of my childbirth. Mom said that while she was "dead" she walked down a dirt road toward *the Light*. At the end of the path was Jesus Christ hanging on the cross. She said she walked right up to Him and pointed her forefinger in his face saying, "You promised! You promised that if I did . . . (perhaps nine First Fridays) that you would guarantee me having the Last Rites before I died. Well, I didn't get them, and I have five children up there who need me, and . . ." With that, Jesus looked down at her and said, "You're right. You're absolutely right" and took a deep breath and blew down at her. At that moment she woke up. While wheeling my mother to the morgue, you can imagine the nurse's surprise when my mother opened her eyes and said, "My feet are cold. Would you mind rubbing them?" When the nurse complied, Mom thanked her and then said, "You have a nice smile. I shall have to paint it in a portrait someday." There is an epilogue to the story if you ever want to hear it.

Therapist's Response to #2

This is an incredible story of your mother's struggle to bring you into the world and your own very early struggle to stay. It is also a powerful story of your mother's bold assertiveness with God and God's response to it. Of course, I'd love to hear the epilogue.

"Patient's" Response to Therapist's Response

The epilogue involves my brother, Jerry, during a time when he was studying to be a Catholic priest. After visiting me over Spring Break one year and upon his returning to the seminary on Easter Sunday, he was greeted by a barrage of his peers who insisted that he meet this new brother right away. While driving to Florida from New York City, the new seminarian impulsively went an hour out of his way to visit his grandparents. He wanted to ask them for a particular painting of the Blessed Virgin Mary that he loved as a child, to hang in his room at the seminary. He also remembered being told that the artist lived in Florida, and he thought it would be nice to try and find her to let her know how much her work meant to him. When he showed the painting to my brother, Jerry couldn't believe his eyes. My mother's signature was on the portrait! As it turns out, this new seminarian's mom was the same woman who was with my mother when she came back to life. It was her smiling face that Mother used as the face of the Blessed Mother. In Jerry's words, "It's a little more than a coincidence and a little less than a miracle" that this young man from New York City should decide to become a priest and study at the same seminary at the same time as the son of a mother who . . . and drive an hour out of his way on impulse for a painting that. . . . Bizarre, isn't it?

Therapist's Response to "Patient"

Yes, mystical stories are fascinating. Thanks for sharing that wonderful story with me.

"Patient's" Reader Response #3

I drifted off in thought after reading the following passage: "I'm over my limit with Mom. I can't keep pace with her. Ever since I can remember I've been caught up in her ups and downs and all it leads to is this: me sitting in a dented car with a mother convinced she's about to drive herself off a cliff in a public park, just to spite my father, whom she just told she never needed anyway" (p. 15).

Mom and Dad used to battle about money all of the time. My mother came from wealth and my father came from poverty—so it goes. The only way Mother could get him to spend money, she would say, was to be sick. My father used to call her a legalized drug addict. I think it's possible that Rayona's mother "needed" the Percocet because of her traumatic relationship with Elgin. Because I was the youngest child, I was left home alone with her and this was during the volatile period surrounding their divorce. There were times that she forgot that she had taken her medication, and I'd be put in a position to prevent her from overdosing.

After saving her life for the umpteenth time, I was once told by a doctor in the hospital's emergency room that I ought to be a proud little girl for saving my mother's life again; I was only thirteen. He explained that she had an adrenal insufficiency and couldn't handle stress, so I could not go through the normal phase of teenage rebellion. If Mother asked me to do something, I needed to do it without talking back. To cause conflict, he said, could kill her. At that point, I became the "perfect child." I still remember the pressure of thinking that I could kill my own mother if I blew up over something. Living with her, however, was like never knowing when the other shoe would drop. I know it was the drugs that contributed to her mood swings, but all of us kids figured that she did them to spite my father—a man who could stir her emotions like lava in a volcano.

Therapist's Response to #3

This is more evidence of how life and existing in it was a continual struggle in your early years. How dare that doctor burden you so profoundly. He was certainly myopic or shortsighted. I hope you now give yourself permission to "talk back." Wouldn't it be great if you could talk back to that doctor? What would you say? You must have built up a huge "storage capacity" for your mother's anger or found a way to have it run off you somehow. How did you manage to cope with her volatility?

"Patient's" Response to Therapist's Response

Your first comment gave me an insight about myself. I am one who certainly doesn't hold back when it comes to saying my mind. In fact, when I "talk back" I have to be careful that I don't bulldoze a person with my strong feelings on a given issue. Surprisingly, I would have only a few words for that doctor. I would tell him that his reckless advice might (or might not have) helped to extend my mother's life, but his words seriously harmed me. His ignorance was cruel!

I coped with my mother's volatility by "shutting down." I could be completely emotionless during rough periods because I had to be. You said earlier that blocked emotions could lead to depression. Well, I was depressed. I tried my best to escape into my schoolwork, as I explained earlier, and spent a lot of time with my horse. I also had a dog that gave me much comfort.

"Patient's" Reader Response #4

On page 106, Rayona finally spills her guts to Evelyn and lets the truth flood out about her messed up family and her envy of Ellen and her "perfect" family. Because of the aforementioned incident where I felt I had to be the perfect daughter, I made a pact with myself that I would never burden anyone with my problems. Mom frequently told me stuff about Dad, and I really never liked hearing any of it. She always wanted to be my friend rather than my mother. In many ways, I was more of a mother to her during that time period than the other way around—just like Rayona.

I was popular at school, one of the "intellectuals" who was known as a class clown. I remember a friend of mine asking me why I was always so sad even when I got good grades and lived in a nice house. One evening we played a waiting game on some stairs at my house. She said she would wait all night until I told her why I was always so sad; she could see right past my clowning around. Mom was in the hospital, and I had been left alone in that big house until my friend came over. I remember I broke down at about three in the morning and finally told her my life story. I cried and cried in her arms and felt so relieved to finally be able to get it all off of my chest "and the world didn't come to an end."

Therapist's Response to #4

Clearly, you were more of a mother to your mom than she was to you during that time of your life. It sounds like your experiences with your mom may have compelled you to find more satisfaction in relationships and achievement in your high school community. Thank God for your friend's wisdom and perseverance! Speaking the truth—telling *your* story—was such a powerful correction for what the idiotic doctor told you.

"Patient's" Reader Response #5

On page 114, Rayona wonders whether or not her mother has bothered to search for her, has made up with Aunt Ida, or if anyone is even worried about her now that Rayona has "disappeared."

This part reminds me when I ran away from home three days after graduating—with honors—from high school. I dropped off of the face of the earth for 2½ years without contacting either of my parents. Mother told me years later that she knew where I was all along because she hired a private investigator to keep her apprised of my whereabouts. Mom and Dad were too caught up in their own mess of life to complicate things further by dragging me back home. I probably wouldn't have stayed anyway.

Therapist's Response to #5

But I'm sure you must have wondered, like Rayona, if they cared. It makes perfect sense that you would have chosen a world in which you could be yourself over your family's, where your needs were secondary to the demands of your ill mother and your father (about whom you haven't really said much). What a striking contrast your post high school life had with before! How did you feel when your mom told you that she had kept up with your whereabouts?

"Patient's" Response to Therapist's Response

At the time I didn't believe her, but now I think she probably really did hire someone to find me. She really did care about me.

"Patient's" Reader Response #6

The best line of the book so far is the one said by Rayona while riding a horse in a rodeo: "On Babe, I would have burned out my circuits rather than choose safety. Up there, my only worry was gravity" (120).

Therapist's Response to #6

Rayona came alive on Babe, didn't she?

"Patient's" Response to Therapist's Response

I used to sing the song "You've Got a Friend" by Carol King to my horse when I'd ride her. I felt one with her many times. I saved her from a miserable life when I bought her from people who regularly beat her with wooden boards. It was cathartic being able to just worry about gravity for awhile.

"Patient's" Reader Response #7

On pages 160–161, Christine is having a fight with Aunt Ida over her brother Lee. It is then that Christine notices that there are pictures of him in every corner of the house, but there's nothing of her anywhere to be found.

The "chosen one" in my family, as it were, was my brother Jerry. Jerry was my mother's favorite and we all knew it. Looking back as an adult, I can hardly blame her. He was—and still is—a virtuoso on the piano with the personality to go with his talent; he could—and still can--charm anyone. To meet my brother is to love him, and the following story will illustrate his kindness and sensitivity—even at the age of five.

Because there were five kids in the family, Mother would get her alone time by getting up at four in the morning to have her coffee in the quiet. Jerry had gotten up in the middle of the night to go to the bathroom and saw her in the kitchen all by herself. Afterwards, he made it a point to get up and join her every morning for coffee so she wouldn't have to be alone. To Mom's credit, she let him. Perhaps that started their unique closeness, but I think it was just Jerry. You'd have to meet him to understand. He's the most holy person I've ever met and was even that way before becoming a priest.

None of us kids really had any problems about his and Mom's relationship as we all were inordinately close siblings. Jerry and I, for example, have a spiritual bond that I have difficulty explaining except that I can actually feel when I need to call him. In any case, the way the rest of us figured it, his being the chosen one kept Mother at bay. We felt sorry for him more than anything else. Things got really bad as we got older, and each of us left home as soon as we each found a way. Jerry joined a seminary in Pennsylvania and Mother followed. When he left the seminary and moved to California, Mother followed. In fact, at the time of her unfortunate death, she was living literally next door to him in an apartment building.

Therapist's Response to #7

Your brother sounds like a wonderful man, and I would like to know him. But it also sounds as though he took on the early burden of a mother who needed someone to care for her. I can't help wondering, though, if you were able to avoid the natural comparisons and competitions that siblings have. I wonder if you ever questioned whether you had as much value as Jerry did, since he won the "prize" of being your mother's chosen child.

"Patient's" Response to Therapist's Response

As far as I know, none of us had trouble with competitions or comparisons. None of us wanted to be Mother's "chosen one" and he really didn't either. All of us kids made a pact when I was five years old. My oldest brother John was the initiator of what was basically this: Since our parents were so messed up, we would form our own self-governance as kids. I was forbidden to tell on my brothers for any of their infractions, and I was to go to John if there were any problems. We grew interdependent with each other, and I would say I am extremely close with my siblings even to this day.

"Patient's" Reader Response #8

On page 173, Christine recounts her job as an airline black box maker. You may find this hard to believe, but the worst job I ever had in my life was working at an airline food carrier factory. I was 18, had run away from home, and was working the racetrack circuit. I needed money to supplement my racetrack income, and the only job I could find at the time was working the graveyard shift at this factory. Because I would be so tired, I would work really hard to keep myself awake. The other employees used to get on my case when the supervisor would leave, saying my pace was making everybody else look bad. I explained that I'd fall asleep otherwise, but they insisted that I slow myself down or just nap periodically. I wound up slowing myself down to protect my hands. They used to get bloody from squeezing rivets closed. I remember being amazed at a couple who were married and had worked there for 20-something years. I couldn't believe that people could actually do that as their life's work. I left after 2½ months when I got burned from doing a job I had no business doing. I walked out and didn't even get my last paycheck.

Therapist's Response to #8

Wow! That sounds pretty grueling! The difference between the pace and drive you had and the couple who'd been there 20 years is the 20 years, I'd guess. If you had to do something as repetitive and lackluster, maybe you'd want to go into a trance at a slower pace and enjoy some reverie and peace. After all, your paycheck and your future would be no different whether you'd burn up the place or take your time. James Taylor had a song about millwork. "Millwork ain't easy, millwork ain't hard. Millwork ain't nothing but an awful boring job. I'm looking for a daydream to take me through the morning to take me to my coffee break where I can have a sandwich. Then it's me and my machine for the rest of the morning for the rest of the afternoon. For the rest of my life. . . ."

"Patient's" Response to Therapist's Response

I cannot imagine doing something like that for the rest of my life and wonder what the circumstances are that enable those who do that kind of work to continue.

"Patient's" Reader Response #9

On page 232, Christine describes the relationship Rayona had with her father. Elgin "would call her on the phone and make grand promises . . . and then he'd forget."

I wish I could forget the story I'm about to tell, but it's why I never make a promise I won't keep unless an act of God prevents me from keeping it. As you know, my mother and father had a bitter divorce. I was 13 and the last of the five children to be at home through all of it. Remember, all of my siblings left home as soon as they were able. I lived alone with my mother in a huge two-story Palm Beach house around the corner from the Kennedy estate. My parents' biggest fights always revolved around money. Mom used to get sick all of the time, and Dad couldn't stand spending money on "quacky" doctors; he believed my mother was a hypochondriac.

Besides academics, my main enjoyment in life during that time period was riding horses. The man who owned the stables where I used to ride passed away, and his son was selling all of the livestock. "My horse," Star, was going to be sold, and I pleaded with each of my parents to buy her for me. I may have only been 13 but I wasn't stupid. After all, we did live in Palm Beach. Even a friend of mine who lived in an apartment with only her mother was able to purchase "her horse." My mother said it was up to my father because she didn't have the money, and he always said we couldn't afford one. I was often the go-between when they had financial matters to work out.

My 14th birthday is a day I'll never forget. Mom was in the hospital—again—and I was sick with the flu. Mom was the one who handled birthdays, but my father must have felt extremely sorry for me that day as I didn't have a single present to open. He gave me a birthday card with this written inside: "Star is yours. All I have to do is work out the details." I flew out of bed, ran down the stairs jumping and screaming and hugging and thanking and squeezing him saying he was "the king of dads!" For two weeks, I asked him repeatedly when we were going to get Star, but every time he would tell me that there were more details to work out. During typing class one Monday at school, a quasi-friend of mine told me that her parents bought her a horse over the weekend named Star. At lunch, I called the owner who confirmed Star's sale and learned that my father never made the first phone call to him. I immediately confronted my father about it when I got home. He told me that he thought the horse thing was a phase that I would grow out of. He never had any intention of buying that horse. He had given me that card because I was sick on my birthday, and he wanted me to feel better. It took many years for me to get over that betrayal.

Therapist's Response to #9

Parents who divorce should not use their kids as messengers or, to use your words, "go-betweens." I'm sure that it took you a long time to trust your father again. The divorce had already broken some of your trust, and this particular instance just confirmed for you that you couldn't depend on either of your parents. It's no wonder that you're such an accomplished person, having learned to rely on yourself so early on in life.

"Patient's" Reader Response #10

On page 233, Christine describes how she wanted to raise Rayona in ways that were better than the way Aunt Ida raised her. Christine describes it this way: "I wasn't ashamed to let [Rayona] see me cry or to let her know I cared about her. I never lost my interest in her life. I never expected her to be perfect. I never wished she was anybody else but who she was." I know exactly what Christine is talking about here.

I have a great relationship with my son. I am deeply interested in who he is and what he likes to do. I have exposed him to a variety of activities so he can choose what he likes and dislikes; we do many of them together. I think it's important for me to love him for who he is rather than who I think he should be. By contrast, I'm sad to say that my father never knew me; he only knew my vita. It was only after receiving my doctorate that he told me that he was proud of me. Before then, I was "overeducating [my]self right out of a husband" or "teachers are a dime a dozen so why don't [I] become a dental hygienist so [I] can make a decent salary." I have since learned a lot about why my father and I had the type of relationship—or lack of one—that we had. He was the product of his own family system and did not have much of a relationship with his own father. Fortunately, I was able to take some "active parenting" classes and make decisive changes in how I interact with my son. I believe that most—if not all—people can benefit from such classes. Now that these parenting classes are as developed as they are, I wish people were required to get a parents' license. I believe the world would be a much better place if that were true.

Therapist's Response to #10

I have seen how you interact with your son, and I can tell that you two have a beautiful relationship. It is obvious that you love him, and he is lucky that you appreciate his uniqueness the way that you do.

One of the ironies of today's society is that parents are not required to take any type of parenting classes unless they are getting a divorce. Many times a judge will mandate a divorcing couple to attend such a class. Unfortunately, that is when the divorce is already in motion. The purpose is for parents to learn how to spare their children from some of the negative effects of the divorce rather than for them to learn how to keep their relationships healthy, something they needed to learn from the start.

CONCLUSION

The cyclical nature of family dysfunction is aptly captured in the last line of the book where Aunt Ida is braiding her hair. Aunt Ida metaphorically speaks of a person's inability to "identify the rhythm of three strands, the whispers of coming and going, of twisting and tying and blending, of catching and of letting go, of braiding" (p. 372). For this matriarch, the old adage that "hindsight is 20–20" is fitting. Chances are good that if she could do things over, she would definitely do so but that's impossible. Each of the women are inextricably linked and bound to each other and their respective histories. Rayona has a chance to break the "twisting and tying and blending" and experience the benefit of "letting go" of her past if she is willing to learn about her family origins and address some of her issues.

Potential Issues for Rayona as She Becomes Independent

Because of her mother's alcoholism, Rayona had to become precociously independent as a child. She learned early how to buy things at the store on her own, for example, when her mother was involved with a man at the apartment. She learned to adjust to one school after another, to gain what knowledge she could in each, and to tolerate the good intentions of helping professionals who discovered her intelligence and her "situation" with her mother. Rayona needed to learn early to assess her mother's condition and determine whether she could relax and relate to her in a "normal" way or whether her mother was under the influence of alcohol or depression. She needed to keep her guard up and watch what she said. Rayona knew that her mother was not the kind of mother that she could trust to take care of her needs, but she did know that her mother loved her and that mornings were often a time when she could receive a modicum of nurturing. Rayona's relationship with her father, on the other hand, was much less supportive: "I have tried all kinds of things on Dad too, before I became no fool: tears, good grades, writing letters, getting him presents. At first every one of them seemed to do the trick. He'd smile or send me a postcard or promise to call tomorrow and then weeks would pass" (p. 9). One can assume that he has his own story, but readers are not given that information.

Rayona is a teenager who has had to put her attention outside of herself most of her life. That is to say, she could not afford to experience life from her own senses and needs. Rather, Rayona had to watch what those in charge of her security were doing and respond to what their senses and needs were at any given moment (even if they seemed unpredictable and illogical at times). Consequently, Rayona's biggest challenge as an adult will be to know what her own feelings are, to trust that these feelings will tell her what she needs, and then to learn to express her needs in a productive manner. Rayona's pathway to this form of mental health can begin with her experience at the rodeo. Even though Rayona is injured, she has no choice but to listen to her mother explain why the Last Judgment Day had such a profound impact on her emotional development.

Significant Insights the "Patient" Gleaned from the Reader Responses

About Rayona

Rayona wished she could have the picturesque family that Ellen has, but I suspect Ellen's life isn't all that grand either. After all, Ellen ripped her parents' letter in two and threw it on the ground. Just because Ellen's parents bought her a fancy car doesn't mean she feels their love. Everyone has problems, and it's better to work towards your own dreams than spend time wishing that things were different. At a very young age I learned to take total responsibility for my life.

About Myself

It sounds like I have it in for my mother the way I've spoken about her. Actually it took a long time before my mother and I reconciled our relationship. It occurred while she was on her deathbed after a car accident that eventually took her life. Since she was intubated and couldn't say anything, I had a captive audience. I exhausted everything I could think of that I ever wanted to tell her; I even told her about my plans for a child. One morning—I'll never forget it as long as I live—she looked at me and pointed her forefinger at me and mouthed, "I love you. You know that." I have grown much in understanding, admiring, and respecting my mother now that I am an adult. She was a courageous woman who was born way ahead of her time and was married to a traditional, overbearing man caught up in the privileges of the 1950's man.

Therapist's Response to "Patient's" Insights

Actually, I hadn't experienced you as "having it in" for her. It seemed that you had come to accept her and your description was honest but not overly blaming or resentful.

I'm so glad that you got the opportunity to "hear" what you needed to in the end. Do you think you might write about your mother and her struggles? It sounds as though it would be a powerful story and might demonstrate the cyclical nature of things.

"Patient's" Response to Therapist's Response

My mother was definitely a remarkable woman who was way before her time. In the 1950's, she established the first black dancing school (taught by a white woman) which she held in our back yard. The neighbors were none too thrilled, but she stood up for their rights. She designed a shoe worn by gymnasts, was partly responsible for the infusion of ballet in competitive gymnastics, and coached Olympians. She wrote and produced a couple of records on ballet and edited a dancing magazine. She, herself, was a fairly talented artist and a wonderful dancer. My mother figured out how to take an older brother and me to Europe by arranging tours and serving as a tour guide. Through her tour efforts, I even made my debut in Vienna, Austria, when I was 15 or 16; there was no way my father ever would have paid for such a trip. My mom was adept in figuring out how to make things happen.

I also know that she, too, was given away to be raised by "Mother Dear" when she was growing up. It is my understanding that Mother Dear was strict and verbally abusive. The movie *Mommie Dearest*, starring Faye Dunaway playing Joan Crawford, struck a chord for both my mother and me. I know that the relationship I had with Mama Jennye, her real mother, caused her great conflict. She was jealous of our relationship and guilty that she felt that way at the same time. It is my belief that Grandma Jennye tried to make up for her own lack of parenting Mom through me. When Grandma Jennye died, Mom and I had a big fight over Grandma's wishes. I knew Grandma, in my opinion, better than my mother—her daughter. My father offered some wisdom at that time and encouraged me to back off and let Mother have her place as Mama Jennye's daughter; I was, after all, the granddaughter.

After the burial, Mom shared the only pleasant memory she had of her father with me. Apparently, he took her for an ice-cream sundae at a soda shop one day. It was just the two of them and it was pleasant. She encouraged me to try my best to make pleasant memories with my own father. I hated my father for most of my teenage years and used to doodle very sadistic pictures and sayings about him while I was in school. He had his own issues that I did not learn about until adulthood. I wish teenagers could be spared from the pain of their inability to understand some things.

Therapist's Response to "Patient"

Sometimes experience is the only teacher. Your mother sounds as if she also had to rely on herself for most of her life. Can you see now how she passed that on to you? It's similar to how Christine has contributed to Rayona's need to fend for herself. Perhaps your mom's independence contributed to the conflict your parents experienced during the 1950's when women were typically very dependent on their husbands. Often grandparents do better the second time around as they gain maturity and wisdom with age. It is a shame that this country treats the elderly the way they do; it's a virtually untapped resource for today's youth.

My grandmother was a tremendously positive influence for me. Her growing-up story is also fascinating and explains why she had the relationship she did with my mother and why she felt compelled to give my mother away to be raised by someone else. I'll not go into it here. Just know that I'd have to write a novel like this one in order to make it all clear for an outside reader. I'm glad that my grandmother tried to make up for her failings through me, and I can see how "the rhythm of three strands" (p. 372) of women in my family have contributed to the person I have become.

A FINAL CAUTION

By no means are we suggesting that teachers try to do this kind of reader response activity with their students. As Ted Hipple says, "We are English teachers, not guidance counselors!" Students who have problems beyond typical adolescent angst would be better served by a licensed psychologist or psychiatrist. Because teachers often have trouble teaching students with heavy emotional baggage, we hope that therapists can see some value in using literacy enhancement activities in their treatments. We also hope that teachers and parents have been able to glean some significant insights about the emotional conflicts some of our youth experience. Finally, we hope that this chapter will serve as a point of departure for discussions on how we can best help troubled teenagers.

REFERENCE

Koontz, David & O'Neill, Terence. (1981). *Mommie dearest*. Paramount Pictures.

Author Index

Numbers are recommended reading citation numbers, not page numbers.

FICTION

Adler, C. S., 4.01, 4.02
Ames, Mildred, 7.01
Angell, Judie, 7.02
Arrick, Fran, 2.01, 4.03, 5.01
Avi, 2.02

Bauer, Marion Dane, 9.01
Beatty, Patricia, 7.22
Bennett, Cherie, 3.01
Bennett, James, 11.01
Bennett, Jay, 5.02
Birdseye, Tom, 4.04
Block, Francesca Lia, 5.03, 9.02
Blume, Judy, 2.03, 3.02, 3.03
Boyd, Candy, 2.04
Bridgers, Sue Ellen, 2.05, 3.04
Brooks, Bruce, 2.06, 2.07, 4.05
Brooks, Martha, 2.08
Brown, Rita Mae, 9.03
Brown, Todd D., 9.04
Bunting, Eve, 3.05, 4.06, 5.04
Butterworth, William, 5.05

Calvert, Patricia, 7.03
Cannon, A. E., 2.09
Cardillo, Joe, 3.06
Carter, Alden R., 2.10, 2.11, 4.07
Caseley, Judith, 2.12
Chambers, Aidan, 9.05
Childress, Alice, 7.04
Christopher, Matt, 7.23
Clark, Clara, 2.13
Cleary, Beverly, 3.08
Cleaver, Vera, 7.05
Cohen, Miriam, 7.06
Con, Pam, 2.14
Conley, Jane Leslie, 2.15, 4.08
Cormier, Robert, 2.16, 3.09, 5.06,
    5.07, 5.08
Creech, Sharon, 3.10
Cresswell, Helen, 7.07
Crutcher, Chris, 5.09, 11.02

Daly, Niki, 4.09
Deaver, Julie, 2.17, 4.10
de Jenkins, Lyll, 2.18

NONFICTION

Title Index

Numbers are recommended reading citation numbers, not page numbers.

FICTION

NONFICTION

About the Editor and Contributors

JOAN F. KAYWELL is an Associate Professor of English Education at the University of South Florida where she has won Teaching Awards in 1991, 1994, and 1996. She is passionate about assisting preservice and practicing teachers in discovering ways to improve literacy. She donates her time extensively to the National Council of Teachers of English (NCTE) and its Florida affiliate (FCTE), and holds these offices: She is a Past-President of FCTE, the 1999 President of ALAN, the former Adolescent Literature Column Editor for *English Journal*, and a reviewer for *The New Advocate*. She is published in several journals, regularly reviews young adult novels for *The ALAN Review*, and has four textbooks: *Adolescent Literature as a Complement to the Classics, Volumes One, Two, & Three* (1993, 1995, 1997) and *Adolescents At Risk: A Guide to Fiction and Nonfiction for Young Adults, Parents, and Professionals* (1993, Greenwood Press).

CYNTHIA ANN BOWMAN is Assistant Professor of Secondary Education at Florida State University in Tallahassee, Florida, where she teaches middle school and secondary methods courses and multicultural education. She is committed to creating learning opportunities for at-risk adolescents and is involved in providing preservice teachers opportunities to work in urban settings. As a recipient of the 1991 James Britton Award for Inquiry in English Language Arts, she was invited to serve as a delegate at the International Federation of Teachers of English Conference that convened in New York City in 1995. She presents regularly at National Council of Teachers of

English (NCTE) Conferences and has been actively involved in state affiliates and local literacy organizations. She is published in *NCTE Ideas Plus*, *The Virginia English Bulletin*, *The Ohio Journal of English Language Arts*, and Nancy McCracken and Bruce Appleby's *Gender Issues in the Teaching of English* (1992).

PAMELA SISSI CARROLL is an Associate Professor and Coordinator of English Education at Florida State University in Tallahassee, Florida. She is the winner of two recent university teaching awards, and she is particularly interested in studying how adolescents respond to literature. Sissi Carroll has chapters in volumes 1, 2, & 3 of *Adolescent Literature as a Complement to the Classics* (1993, 1995, 1997) and in *Writers for Young Adults*. She also has published articles in *English Journal*, *The ALAN Review*, and *Middle School Journal*, and serves as the editor for *The ALAN Review*. She is on the Executive Board of ALAN and SIGNAL (branches that concentrate on young adult literature of the National Council of Teachers of English and the International Reading Association, respectively). She is on the Board of Directors for the Florida Council of Teachers of English (FCTE) and serves as Co-Chair, with Dr. Gail Gregg, of FCTE's Commission on Multicultural Education that was recognized by NCTE in two recent years.

MAE Z. CLEVELAND uses her psychology background in her work as a nutrition counselor at the Student Health Center of Florida State University. She currently works with a team of health-care professionals, helping college students recognize and deal with the physical and emotional problems associated with eating disorders. Her research interests include the growing incidence of young girls and members of social organizations, such as sororities, who use extreme dieting measures to remain thin. As an avid runner herself, she is particularly concerned with the increasing number of female athletes whom she treats for eating disorders.

PAM B. COLE, a former secondary English teacher at Whitewood High School in Virginia, earned her Ph.D. in Curriculum and Instruction from the Virginia Polytechnic Institute and State University. She is currently an Assistant Professor of English Education at Kennesaw State University in Georgia, where she teaches both undergraduate and graduate classes in English Education. She is actively involved with the National Council of Teachers of English (NCTE) and its Georgia affiliate (GCTE). Pam Cole is the current editor of *Teen Lit Connection* and serves on the Elections Committee for ALAN. She directs an annual Children's Literature Conference, conducts young adult literature workshops throughout the state of Georgia, and has published in several journals and textbooks on the topic of young adult literature, including chapters in volumes 2 and 3 of *Adolescent Literature as a Complement to the Classics* (1995, 1997).

CHRIS CRUTCHER is a former teacher and director of a K–12 alternative school in Oakland, California. He is a certified mental health counselor and child mental health specialist who has worked for 13 years at the Spokane Community Mental Health Center in the area of child abuse and neglect, working with family members of all ages. He currently does that same work in private practice and is the chairperson for the original Spokane Child Protection Team, a group of voluntary professionals who advise Child Protection Service workers on high-risk cases. Chris Crutcher is also the author of six young adult novels and a book of short stories (*Athletic Shorts*, 1991)—all designated as ALA Best Books for the year of their publication—as well as an adult suspense novel. His award-winning novels include *Ironman* (1995), *Staying Fat for Sarah Byrnes* (1993), *Chinese Handcuffs* (1991), *Stotan!* (1990), *The Crazy Horse Electric Game* (1987), and *Running Loose* (1983).

PATRICIA L. DANIEL earned her Ph.D. in Language Arts Education from the University of Oklahoma in 1991. Having taught middle school students for 12 years in Oklahoma, she is currently teaching English language arts methods and young adult literature courses at the University of South Florida in Tampa, Florida, and is serving as the university liaison at a nearby professional development school. She is an active member of the National Council of Teachers of English (NCTE) and is published in *English Journal*, *Language Arts*, and *Equity and Excellence in Education*. Her areas of interest include young adult literature and educational reform. Pat Daniel has chapters in volumes 2 and 3 of *Adolescent Literature as a Complement to the Classics* (1995, 1997).

SHARON M. DRAPER was honored by President Clinton as the 1997 National Teacher of the Year. She is a professional educator, as well as a popular writer. She is the published author of *Tears of a Tiger* (1994), *Forged by Fire* (1997), *Ziggy and the Black Dinosaurs* (1994), *Ziggy and the Black Dinosaurs: Lost in the Tunnel of Time* (1995), *Ziggy and the Black Dinosaurs: Shadows of Caesar's Creek* (1997), *Let the Circle Be Unbroken* (poetry), and *Buttered Bones* (poetry). Sharon Draper currently lives in Cincinnati, Ohio, where she has spent more than 25 years teaching junior high and high school students how to appreciate the beauty of literature and how to com-municate their ideas effectively. She travels extensively, and is an accom-plished public speaker, discussing issues of educational and literary significance to both national as well as international audiences.

BONNIE O. ERICSON, a former high school English teacher, is a Profes-sor of Secondary English and Reading Education at California State Uni-versity, Northridge, where she supervises student teachers and teaches credential and Master's Degree courses in English Methods, Content Area Literacy, and Technology for English Classrooms. She is active in the Na-tional Council of Teachers of English (NCTE) and the California Associa-tion of Teachers of English (CATE) and is currently serving on NCTE's Secondary Section Steering Committee as the liaison with NCTE's Council on English Education (CEE). Bonnie Ericson has chapters in volumes 1, 2, and 3 of *Adolescent Literature as a Complement to the Classics* (1993, 1995, 1997), is published in *The ALAN Review* and *California English*, and has edited the "Resources and Reviews" column for *English Journal* for the past four years. Her research and teaching interests include multicultural literature, adolescent literature, and teacher education.

JENNIFER FIKE received her M.Ed. in Rehabilitation Counseling and Reading Specialization from Kent State University and has worked as a classroom teacher, transitional coordinator, adult basic literacy instructor, and student teaching supervisor in the university setting. She is currently completing her Ph.D., is employed as a Crisis Intervention Specialist with the Kevin Coleman Center, and is an instructor at the Kent State University Trumbull Campus. Her research in the areas of metacognition, traumatic brain injury rehabilitation, and foster care has been presented at local, state, and national conferences. Jennifer Fike is published in *School Psychology International*, *Language Experience Forum*, and the *Yearbook of the Col-lege Reading Association*.

ROGER D. HERRING is a Professor of Counselor Education at the Univer-sity of Arkansas at Little Rock, where he teaches and supervises school counselors. He has served as an Administrative Assistant at Littlefield Jun-ior/Senior High School in Lumberton, North Carolina, and has taught in junior and senior high schools in Pembroke, North Carolina. His primary areas of research are multicultural and cross-cultural issues, especially con-cerning Native American Indian and multiethnic youth.

JEFFREY S. KAPLAN is an Assistant Professor of Educational Foundations at the University of Central Florida in Orlando and Area Education Coordinator for the UCF Daytona Beach Campus. He is the recipient of the State of Florida Teaching Incentive Program Award (1996–1997). His research interests include the development of innovative teaching strategies to improve literacy and teaching thinking across the curriculum. He is an active member of the National Council of Teachers of English (NCTE), the Florida Council of Teachers of English (FCTE), and the Florida Staff Development Association. He currently chairs FCTE's Commission on Mediacy and serves on the Self-Study for Teacher Education Committee of the American Education Research Association (AERA). Jeff Kaplan is published in several journals and is a contributor in two textbooks: *Adolescent Literature as a Complement to the Classics, Volume Three* (1997) and *Teaching Multicultural Literature* (1997).

JAMES D. KELLY is a clinical psychologist in private practice in Cincinnati, Ohio. He received his Ph.D. in Psychology from the Union Institute in Cincinnati in 1987. His practice consists of working with adolescents, children, and families facing a myriad of behavioral, emotional, and adjustment issues. He also serves as a consultant to a number of social service agencies that serve families and children.

ANNE C. LeMIEUX is the author of two young adult novels, *The TV Guidance Counselor* (1993), an ALA Best Book for Young Adults, and *Do Angels Sing the Blues?* (1995), a Parents' Choice Silver Medal winner, as well as several other books for middle grade and younger readers. She received her B.A. in writing with a minor in illustration from Simmons College in Boston, and now lives in Southport, Connecticut, with her family.

WILLIAM A. LONG, JR. is a Professor of Pediatric and Adolescent Medicine at the University of Mississippi in Jackson, Mississippi. He has written numerous articles on his theory of personalities in adolescents.

VICKI J. McENTIRE earned her Master of Social Work at Our Lady of the Lake University in San Antonio, Texas, in 1994, and is currently the Clinical Manager of Acute Care Services at the Harbor Behavioral Health Care Institute in New Port Richey, Florida. She has 14 years of social work experience in mental health and substance abuse crisis intervention, assessment, and treatment. Her areas of interest include client advocacy and broadening the scope of mental health and substance abuse services to include the person within his or her environment.

DIANA MITCHELL, a middle and high school English teacher for 29 years, is an avid reader of young adult literature. She has held many professional offices: She is a Past-President of ALAN, President of the Michigan Council of Teachers of English (MCTE), a Board of Director for NCTE's Conference for English Education (CEE), and Co-Director of the Red Cedar Writing Project at Michigan State University. She is published in several journals, is co-editor of the *Language Arts Journal of Michigan*, serves as an Editorial Review Board Member for *The New Advocate*, is a frequent reviewer for *The ALAN Review*, and is the Teaching Ideas Column Editor for *English Journal*. Publications include *Explorations in the Teaching of English* co-authored with Steve Tchudi; a chapter in *Adolescent Literature as a Complement to the Classics, Volume One* edited by Joan Kaywell; an essay in *Writers for Young Adults* edited by Ted Hipple; and a chapter in *United in Diversity* edited by Jean Brown and Elaine Stephens.

ELIZABETH M. MYERS has recently completed her Master of Science Degree in English Education at Florida State University and is a teacher of high school English. As a dancer for most of her life, Elizabeth suffered first with anorexia, then bulimia, and watched her athletic sister struggle with anorexia. She knows first-hand the impact the disorders have, not only on the person who has them, but on the entire family. She is eager to tell her story because she believes that, through her story, parents and teachers may better understand the emotional agony that accompanies the disorders. She hopes, too, that females with the disorders might listen to her—someone who has been there and done that!

AUGUSTUS Y. NAPIER, a former member of the psychiatry faculty at the University of Wisconsin-Madison, is currently Director of The Family Workshop, a treatment and training institute in Atlanta, Georgia. He is a frequent consultant and workshop leader in family therapy and is active in both The American Family Therapy Association and The American Association of Marriage and Family Therapy; he has served on the Commission of Accreditation for Marriage and Family Therapy Education. Augustus Napier has numerous publications including *The Fragile Bond* (1988) and *The Family Crucible*, a book he co-authored with Carl Whitaker, M.D. He also serves as an advisory editor of two publications: *Contemporary Family*

Therapy and *The Journal of Divorce*. He enjoys working with his wife, Margaret, who is also a family therapist and educator.

JENIFER A. NIELDS, M.D. is an Assistant Clinical Professor of Psychiatry at Yale University and a psychiatrist in private practice in Fairfield, Connecticut. She is a graduate of Harvard College where she majored in English and of the Columbia College of Physicians and Surgeons. She did her residency training at Yale where she continues as a psychotherapy supervisor and teacher. She has published articles on psychotherapy and other aspects of psychiatry in *The Psychoanalytic Study of the Child*, *The American Journal of Psychiatry*, *The Journal of Clinical Psychiatry*, *The Lancet*, and *The Psychiatric Quarterly*. A former classical musician, she has served as a consultant to fiction writers regarding the psychodynamics, family dynamics, and psychopathology of their characters and has a particular interest in psychoanalysis and the arts.

SARA ANDERSON POWELL is a clinical psychologist in private practice in Tampa, Florida, for the past ten years. Prior to receiving her Doctorate in Psychology, she was a classroom teacher with Bachelor's and Master's Degrees in Special Education, focusing on the needs of educable-mentally retarded, learning disabled, and emotionally disturbed adolescents. She received an award from the American Psychological Association in 1985 for her paper on interventions for students under stress.

BARBARA L. STANFORD earned her Ph.D. in Secondary Education from the University of Colorado and is Coordinator of the Secondary Education Program at the University of Arkansas at Little Rock, where she teaches English language arts methods and adolescent literature courses. Barbara Stanford is author or co-editor of 13 books on global and multicultural literature and conflict management. She has directed a statewide project in teaching conflict management in the schools, and her most recent book—tentatively titled *Charting Change* (in press)—examines processes of school change, including those stimulated by gangs.

SHARI TARVER-BEHRING is Assistant Professor and School Counseling Coordinator in the Department of Educational Psychology and Counseling at California State University, Northridge. She earned a Master of Science Degree in Clinical Psychology from Marquette University in 1981, and a Ph.D. in Educational Psychology with a specialization in school psychology from the University of Wisconsin, Madison, in 1986.

She is a credentialed school psychologist and school counselor and a licensed psychologist in the state of California. She has extensive clinical and teaching experience in the area of child and adolescent psychology. Shari Tarver-Behring has also published and made numerous presentations in the areas of school consultation with diverse youth, the school counselor's role in full inclusion, school interventions for at-risk youth, and gender identity development.

PAT ZIPPER MSW, CSW, ACSW, BCD is a clinical social worker who has been in private practice for 20 years. In addition, she has worked in an emergency psychiatric facility for children, as a mental health consultant for an inpatient substance abuse unit, and as a co-owner of an outpatient psychiatric clinic. She continues to work with clients with concerns involving alcoholism, including alcoholics, their families, and adult children of alcoholics. She also works with clients with problems related to anxiety, depression, and concerns about sexual orientation. Her practice also includes adults who were sexually abused as children as well as clients who are dealing with chronic and terminal illnesses.